NOSTALGIA

Nostalgia is a topic that most lay people are familiar with, but, until recently, few social scientists understood. Once viewed as a disease, nostalgia is now considered to be an important psychological resource. It involves revisiting personally cherished memories that involve close others. When people engage in nostalgia, they experience a boost in positive psychological states such as positive mood, feelings of social connectedness, self-esteem, self-continuity, and perceptions of meaning in life. Since nostalgia promotes these positive states, when people experience negative states (such as loneliness or meaninglessness), they use nostalgia to regulate distress.

This book explains in detail what nostalgia is, how views of it have changed over time, and how it has been studied by social scientists. It explores issues like how common nostalgia is and whether people differ in their tendency to be nostalgic. It looks at the triggers and inspiration for nostalgia, and the emotional states that are associated with it. Finally, the psychological, social, and behavioral effects of engaging in nostalgia are discussed.

This volume provides the most comprehensive overview to date of the social scientific research into the complex and intriguing phenomenon of nostalgia. It will be of interest to a range of students and researchers in psychology and beyond, and its accessible writing style and engaging anecdotes will also be appreciated by a wider, non-academic audience.

Clay Routledge is a leading expert in the psychology of nostalgia and experimental existential psychology. He has published over 80 scientific papers. Dr. Routledge's work is regularly featured in the media and he writes the popular blog More Than Mortal for *Psychology Today*.

ESSAYS IN SOCIAL PSYCHOLOGY
Series Editors
Monica Biernat, Kansas University
Miles Hewstone, University of Oxford

Essays in Social Psychology is designed to meet the need for rapid publication of brief volumes in social psychology. Primary topics will include social cognition, interpersonal relationships, group processes, and intergroup relations, as well as applied issues. Furthermore, the series seeks to define social psychology in its broadest sense, encompassing all topics either informed by, or informing, the study of individual behavior and thought in social situations. Each volume in the series will make a conceptual contribution to the topic by reviewing and synthesizing the existing research literature, by advancing theory in the area, or by some combination of these missions. The principal aim is that authors will provide an overview of their own highly successful research program in an area. It is also expected that volumes will, to some extent, include an assessment of current knowledge and identification of possible future trends in research. Each book will be a self-contained unit supplying the advanced reader with a well-structured review of the work described and evaluated.

Published titles

Complex Interpersonal Conflict Behaviour
Van der Vliert

Self-Theories
Their Role in Motivation, Personality, and Development
Dweck

The Uncertain Mind
Individual Differences in Facing the Unknown
Sorrentino & Roney

Reducing Intergroup Bias
Gaertner & Dovidio

Cooperation in Groups
Procedural Justice, Social Identity, and Behavioral Engagement
Tyler & Blader

The Psychology of Closed Mindedness
Kruglanski

Self-Insight
Dunning

Standards and Expectancies
Biernat

When Groups Meet
The Dynamics of Intergroup Contact
Pettigrew & Tropp

Nostalgia
A Psychological Perspective
Routledge

Forthcoming titles

Motivated Cognition in Relationships
Murray & Holmes

Conceptual Metaphor in Social Psychology
Landau

For continually updated information about published and forthcoming titles in the Essays in Social Psychology series, please visit: https://www.routledge.com/psychology/series/SE0533.

NOSTALGIA

A Psychological Resource

By Clay Routledge
North Dakota State University

NEW YORK AND LONDON

First published 2016
by Routledge
711 Third Avenue, New York, NY 10017

and by Routledge
2 Park Square, Millon Park, Abingdon, Oxon OX14 4RN

Routledge is an imprint of the Taylor & Francis Group, an informa business

© 2016 Taylor & Francis

The right of Clay Routledge to be identified as author of this work has been asserted by him in accordance with sections 77 and 78 of the Copyright, Designs and Patents Act 1988.

All rights reserved. No part of this book may be reprinted or reproduced or utilised in any form or by any electronic, mechanical, or other means, now known or hereafter invented, including photocopying and recording, or in any information storage or retrieval system, without permission in writing from the publishers.

Trademark notice: Product or corporate names may be trademarks or registered trademarks, and are used only for identification and explanation without intent to infringe.

Library of Congress Cataloging-in-Publication Data
Routledge, Clay.
Nostalgia : a psychological resource / by Clay Routledge North Dakota State University.
pages cm
Includes bibliographical references and index.
1. Nostalgia. I. Title.
BF575.N6R68 2016
155.9–dc23
2015014585

ISBN: 978-1-84872-516-4 (hbk)
ISBN: 978-1-84872-517-1 (pbk)
ISBN: 978-1-31566-931-1 (ebk)

Typeset in Bembo
by Cenveo Publisher Services

CONTENTS

Acknowledgements   viii

Introduction   1

1 From the Past to the Present: A History of Nostalgia   3

2 How We Perceive and Experience Nostalgia   8

3 What Makes People Nostalgic?   25

4 The Affective Consequences of Nostalgia   43

5 The Social Functions of Nostalgia   51

6 The Self-Related Functions of Nostalgia   69

7 The Existential Functions of Nostalgia   84

8 Individual Differences and Nostalgia   100

9 The Future of the Past: Emerging Research on Nostalgia   116

References   127
Index   144

ACKNOWLEDGEMENTS

I would like to thank David Malone for his assistance completing the list of references. I would also like to thank my wife, Jenny Routledge, for everything else.

INTRODUCTION

I did not initially set out to study nostalgia. Early on as a graduate student I was very much interested in researching how the ability to think temporally affects people. My main interest, however, was on how thoughts about the future influence present attitudes and behaviors. I was specifically interested in the consequences associated with the knowledge of future mortality. As humans, we are able to contemplate a future without us in it. And this awareness of death, as I will discuss in detail in Chapter 7, is distressing and leads to a number of attitudes and behaviors focused on finding and protecting perceptions of enduring meaning. So I guess I was always fascinated by the idea of mental time travel, but I was fixated on how people travel forward, not backward, in time. So how did I get in the nostalgia game?

Well, a couple of things happened. First, my PhD advisor, Dr Jamie Arndt, was just starting to explore nostalgia as a potential means to counter anxieties about death. The basic idea was that when people think about their future demise they may gain some comfort from reflecting on the past. That is, perhaps people can counter the existential threats associated with the future by revisiting a meaningful past. By nostalgically reflecting on personally treasured past life experiences, people can reassure themselves that they have lived meaningful lives. Second, Jamie was also invited by another scholar to contribute a chapter to a book on the psychology of time. The idea was that he would write about how temporal consciousness can both be existentially threatening and contribute to efforts to cope with existential threat. He asked me, as his PhD student, if I was interested in taking the lead on this chapter. I jumped at it. And that is when I first really started to think deeply about nostalgia.

When I was working on the chapter, I was reviewing the many ways that people mitigate the threat of death-awareness. Many of these coping strategies involve present attitudes and behaviors. However, people's ability to mentally time travel is not restricted to the future. We can also reflect on our pasts. And, as my advisor was starting to find with his newly established research program on nostalgia, people might purposefully turn to the past to cope with fears about the future. But this program of research on nostalgia in our lab was in a very early stage. We had yet to write up any data for publication. So I started reading and thinking more about nostalgia. What exactly is nostalgia? I had my own lay conception of nostalgia. But was it correct? And how common is nostalgia? What makes people nostalgic? What are the psychological effects of nostalgia? I wanted to know everything I could about nostalgia so I could begin to understand precisely how it may help people cope with existential fears.

That is when I realized that very little empirical work had been conducted on nostalgia in psychology. This was back in the early 2000s. As I will discuss in the first chapter of this book, many scholars had chimed in on the topic of nostalgia. However, with the exception of some research in the areas of marketing and consumer psychology, the science was scant. Most of the scholarship was theoretical or anecdotal. And there was no programmatic experimental work on the topic. Moreover, I was surprised to find out that for much of its history, nostalgia was considered a psychological vulnerability or illness. As someone prone to nostalgia, I had assumed that there would be a fair amount of research on this topic. And I assumed that this research would indicate that nostalgia is a very positive emotional experience. What I was reading was not squaring with my own experiences with nostalgia. Was I weird? Plenty of people would say yes to that question, but I assumed that this was not the result of me having a unique type of nostalgia. More critically, though the work in our lab was in an early stage, our preliminary results supported the idea that nostalgia has positive psychological effects. I knew then that much work was required. Nostalgia needed to be studied more systematically and empirically.

I was not the only person thinking this. Across the pond at the University of Southampton, UK, social psychologists Constantine Sedikides and Tim Wildschut were also launching a program of research on nostalgia. Social psychology is a small world so pretty soon we discovered each other and joined forces. Our goal was to embark on a comprehensive investigation of the psychology of nostalgia, to answer the questions that I assumed had already been answered when I conducted my first literature search on nostalgia while writing the chapter on temporal consciousness. It's been a little more than ten years since we started and we have learned a lot. This book is an attempt to review this work and the amazing work that is being done by others who have also launched programs of research on nostalgia in recent years. This area of research is still young. And there is much yet to learn. So this book is also an attempt to push the field forward. It is an exciting time to be studying nostalgia.

1
FROM THE PAST TO THE PRESENT
A History of Nostalgia

I recently had a very poignant experience. My wife and I attended a high school orientation with our daughter who had just started her freshman year. Of course, prior to this event I was fully aware of the fact that my daughter was about to begin her first year of high school. But to be honest, I had not put a whole lot of thought into the matter. Kids go to school and each year we take part in these back to school nights. It was old hat by this time. But this night I was sitting in the large auditorium of her high school and looked up at the screen of the presentation that was about to begin and saw the words "Class of 2017". Then it hit me full force. My daughter is growing up and will be leaving our home before I know it. Where has the time gone? How could she already be starting her final years of secondary education? The room was spinning and I am sure I was noticeably uncomfortable.

In this moment of distress, my mind retreated to the past. It was just yesterday that we brought our sweet little baby girl home from the hospital. It was just yesterday that, after much anticipation, she took her first steps, said her first interpretable words, and started her first day of kindergarten. I savored these memories. In this moment of anticipated loss, I turned to nostalgia. And it provided some needed relief. It stabilized me. My daughter will soon be leaving the nest to start her own adult life in college and beyond. But my wife and I will always have these memories. And we can always return to them.

The Origins of Nostalgia as a Medical Disease

My anecdote about a recent experience of nostalgia is by no means unique. When the present or future seems overwhelming, we often look to the past nostalgically to right the ship (an idea I will consider in detail later in this book).

In other words, distress, sadness, and loss often instigate nostalgia. But this idea of nostalgia being a response to psychologically negative experiences is a rather new observation, at least in the scholarly world.

The term nostalgia was coined in 1688 by the Swiss medical student Johaness Hofer (1688/1934). In his medical dissertation, Hofer described cases of an illness that bore similarities to afflictions observed in other countries: Schweizerkrankheit in Germany, *mal du pays* in France, and *malatia del pais* in Spain (McCann, 1941). Hofer was, however, the first to explicitly define this condition as an illness and crafted the word nostalgia from two sounds: *nostos* (return to the native land) and *algos* (pain). Nostalgia, then, as originally construed, is the pain caused by the desire to return to the one's native land. Hofer conceptualized nostalgia as a medical disease afflicting Swiss soldiers and mercenaries who had travelled from their Alpine homes to the plains of Europe to wage war. Symptoms of this disease included constant thinking about home, sadness, anxiety, irregular heartbeat, insomnia, loss of thirst, disordered eating, physical weakness, and fever (McCann, 1941; Sedikides *et al.*, 2015a). In other words, nostalgia was believed to be causing a significant amount of psychological and physical distress. Ultimately, Hofer viewed nostalgia as a neurological ailment. He specifically proposed that nostalgia is a "cerebral disease" (Hofer, 1688/1934, p. 387) resulting from "the quite continuous vibrations of animal spirits through those fibers of the middle brain in which impressed traces of ideas of the Fatherland still cling" (ibid., p. 384).

Other physicians of the time accepted Hofer's conceptualization of nostalgia as a disease. However, they offered divergent views on its etiology. For example, J.J. Scheuchzer (1732), a fellow physician, advanced the position that nostalgia was caused by "a sharp differential in atmospheric pressure causing excessive body pressurization, which in turn drove blood from the heart to the brain, thereby producing the observed affliction of sentiment" (cited in Davis, 1979, p. 2). Scheuchzer (1732) believed his account helped explain why nostalgia was afflicting Swiss soldiers who were fighting wars in regions with a much lower altitude than their homeland. Based on the assertion that nostalgia was a Swiss disease, other physicians of the time proposed that it was caused by the never ceasing clanging of cowbells in the Alps, which would cause trauma to the eardrum and brain (Davis, 1979). Regardless of the particular explanation, nostalgia was viewed as a neurological or medical illness well into the nineteenth century.

And despite early assertions that it was an ailment burdened largely by the Swiss, reports of nostalgia diagnoses were not confined to one particular nationality. For instance, nostalgia was observed among British soldiers (Jackson, 1986) as well as French soldiers fighting in the Revolutionary and Napoleonic armies (O'Sullivan, 2012). This nostalgia disease also reached beyond Europe. Indeed, during the American Civil War, Union physicians reported thousands of cases of nostalgia among Union soldiers (Matt, 2007). Some scholars even asserted that nostalgia was not exclusive to humans. Kline (1898), for instance, argued that nostalgia is experienced by dogs, cats, horses, and cows. I am trying really hard right now to imagine a nostalgic cow. Nope, can't do it.

Nostalgia appeared to be a widely experienced illness, but an illness nonetheless, and one that seemed to be associated with separation from home. However, this view of nostalgia as a medical disease would eventually start to face some challenges. Physicians seeking to identify a bodily location of nostalgia were unsuccessful (Boym, 2001) and there was no evidence that people diagnosed with nostalgia were suffering from any actual bodily disease (Rutledge, 1977). In addition, Charles Darwin argued that nostalgia was, in fact, a feeling that could be rather pleasant (Sedikides et al., 2015b). When describing people's recollections on the past, Darwin (1896, chapter VIII, p. 216) wrote: "The feelings which are called tender are difficult to analyse; they seem to be compounded of affection, joy, and especially of sympathy. These feelings are in themselves of a pleasurable nature, excepting when pity is too deep, or horror is aroused, as in hearing of a tortured man or animal."

Nostalgia and the Rise of Psychology

Medical scholars eventually abandoned the study of nostalgia. However, as the field of psychology grew in the early twentieth century, nostalgia again became a topic of scholarly interest. For psychologists from the psychoanalytic tradition, nostalgia was similar to depression and represented an "acute yearning for a union with the preoedipal mother, a saddening farewell to childhood, a defense against mourning, or a longing for a past forever lost" (Kaplan, 1987, p. 466). Nostalgia was now construed as an unpleasant state associated with difficulties of individuation or separation (Neumann, 1949/1971; Peters, 1985) or even a subconscious yearning to return to one's fetal state (Fodor, 1950). Psychologists were thus continuing the tradition of viewing nostalgia as an ailment. They did not believe that nostalgia was necessarily a disease of the body. Instead, it was a disorder of the mind.

However, during this time, scholars started to distinguish nostalgia from the concept of homesickness. When nostalgia was originally considered as a medical disease, the focus was on a yearning for home. This focus made sense, because much of the medical interest in the topic revolved around soldiers who were far from and longing for home. With a new emphasis on a general longing for aspects of one's past (e.g., childhood) as opposed to a specific longing for one's home or homeland, during the twentieth century, views on nostalgia started to change. McCann (1941), for instance, recognized that just as people can long for home, they could also long for a wide range of objects or people. Indeed, psychoanalysts tended to believe that people could be nostalgic for any object that symbolized aspects of their past that they missed (Peters, 1985). The study of homesickness would continue with its focus on the specific longing for home and, more specifically, the distress associated with young people's transitions away from the home environment (Hendrickson, Rosen, & Aune, 2010; Kerns, Brumariu, &

Abraham, 2008; Thurber & Walton, 2007). But by the late twentieth century, for most scholars, nostalgia was no longer a concept equated with homesickness.

This broader view on what people could be nostalgic for was accompanied by a deeper consideration of what emotional states relate to nostalgia. Psychologists began to view nostalgia as a bittersweet emotion (Castelnuovo-Tedesco, 1980; Kaplan, 1987; Werman, 1977). Nostalgia was not simply an unpleasant emotional state akin to depression. It was also a pleasurable feeling. That is, scholars began to appreciate that nostalgia involves pleasant memories of the past. Thus, reflecting on or idealizing past experiences and states can generate positive feelings in the present. However, because one cannot return to the past, nostalgia also includes a sense of loss and longing. Furthermore, the memory itself may involve experiences that had both negative and positive elements. When this broader consideration of nostalgia as pleasure mixed with pain began to emerge, the view of nostalgia as a mental illness started to lose ground.

Scholars were beginning to see the upside of nostalgia. If nostalgia was an experience that could generate positive affective states, then perhaps it had psychological value. For example, Davis (1979) offered a positive take on nostalgia from a sociological perspective. He proposed that nostalgia helped people cope with major life changes or experiences of discontinuity by "encouraging an appreciative stance toward former selves; excluding unpleasant memories; reinterpreting 'marginal, fugitive, and eccentric facets of earlier selves' in a positive light; and establishing benchmarks of one's biography" (pp. 35–36). Clinical psychologists were also beginning to consider the possible therapeutic benefits of nostalgia. For example, Mills and Coleman (1994) asserted that nostalgic reminiscence helps restore a sense of identity among older adults suffering from dementia. Hertz (1990) proposed that nostalgia may serve as a resource to help people cope with trauma. In general, by the end of the twentieth century, psychologists were beginning to embrace a more positive and functional view of nostalgia (Batcho, 1995, 1998). However, social scientists had yet to empirically explore nostalgia in a rigorous and systematic manner. For instance, even though experimental social psychology was thriving by the later part of the twentieth century, social psychologists had not tested the effects of experimentally manipulated nostalgia. Though nostalgia's reputation was changing, much work was needed to determine whether the psychological consequences of nostalgia are generally negative or positive.

Nostalgia in the Age of Marketing

In the late 1980s, nostalgia became a topic of empirical interest in the field of marketing. Researchers in this area discovered that throughout life people feel attached to or display preferences for the products they consumed in their late teens and early twenties. For instance, people display an enduring preference for movie stars that were popular (Holbrook & Schindler, 1994) and films that they watched (Holbrook & Schindler, 1996) in their youth. Similarly, people like music that was popular in their teens and early twenties more than they like music that was popular before their teenage years or after their early twenties (Holbrook & Schindler, 1989). And males, but not females, exhibit a similar pattern of attachment to automobile models from their youth (Schindler & Holbrook, 2003). Studies such as these, which I discuss in more detail in Chapter 3, began to shed light on the potential power of nostalgia.

When it comes to aesthetic preferences and media consumption, nostalgia may influence consumer choice. Not surprisingly then, companies frequently employ nostalgia when marketing products (Havlena & Holak, 1991) and many films and television programs are created with the intent of capitalizing on nostalgia for past decades (Brown, Kozinets, & Sherry, 2003). And research suggests that such nostalgia-based strategies work. For example, Pascal, Sprott, & Muehling (2002) found that advertisements that induced nostalgia increased positive attitudes towards a brand and intention to purchase that brand. Similarly, Muehling & Pascal (2012) found that using nostalgia to advertise a product increased how much attention people paid to the ad as well as how favorably they viewed the ad and the brand being advertised.

In all, research focused on consumer preferences and responses to marketing campaigns and advertisements indicates that nostalgia influences attitudes and behaviors. And though this area of research continues to evolve by exploring variables that may moderate and mediate the effects of nostalgia-based marketing on consumer attitudes and purchases (e.g., Muehling, Sprott, & Sultan, 2014), it does not answer critical questions about the psychology of nostalgia. Of course, marketing researchers are most interested in determining whether or not nostalgia-based advertisements and products influence consumer behavior. Psychologists are needed to better understand how nostalgia affects mental states. However, until recently, nostalgia was not a topic of interest among empirical psychologists.

Toward a New Psychology of Nostalgia

The research from the field of marketing suggests that nostalgia is a feeling that people enjoy. If nostalgia was an unpleasant state, as originally believed, people would not be motivated to consume products that remind them of the past. People want to mentally time travel to the past. Nostalgia is a desired state. The concept of nostalgia has had an interesting journey from the late 1600s when it was treated as a medical illness, to the late 1900s when it was treated as tool to sell consumer products. A critical turning point for this construct was when scholars began to differentiate it from the more unpleasant state of homesickness and also recognize that people's longing for the past may reflect both positive and negative feelings that may serve psychological functions. But it was not until the beginning of the twenty-first century that nostalgia would captivate the interest of experimental psychologists. Over the next eight chapters I describe this exciting new era of psychological scholarship on nostalgia.

2
HOW WE PERCEIVE AND EXPERIENCE NOSTALGIA

I regularly receive emails and phone calls from reporters, science writers, and radio show producers who want to interview me about my research on nostalgia. When I first started conducting research in this area, I never would have guessed that it would be such a news-worthy topic. But people seem quite fascinated by nostalgia. Having done this research for over a decade, I now see why. Nostalgia is a phenomenon that is very relevant to people's lives. Lay people understand and identify with nostalgia. And, as I will discuss in this chapter, it is a prominent experience in their day-to-day lives. As a result, people are naturally interested in learning about the science of nostalgia.

As discussed in Chapter 1, nostalgia was historically viewed as a neurological disease or mental illness. And though over time these labels lost their relevance as scholars and the general public alike began to perceive nostalgia as a normal and even pleasant activity, it was not until researchers started to systematically study the content of nostalgic memories that this past-oriented emotional experience could be truly rebranded. In the present chapter, I consider the research on the content of nostalgia. When people are nostalgic, what are they thinking about? Though people have their own unique constellation of life experiences that define their personal story, are there themes that typify nostalgic memories? If there are common themes underlying nostalgia, then we may be able to begin to piece together a picture of how revisiting these memories, affects people.

But before discussing how people experience nostalgia, first, it is important to consider how people conceptualize nostalgia. Content analyses of nostalgic memories involve asking people to bring to mind experiences from their past that generate feelings of nostalgia. In other words, the content of people's nostalgic memories will be tied to their conceptions of what it means to be nostalgic. Thus, it is critical to understand lay conceptions of nostalgia.

How Do People Conceptualize Nostalgia?

In Chapter 1, I provided an historical account of nostalgia. However, these were the views of scholars and medical or mental health practitioners throughout history. They do not reflect the more general understanding of nostalgia. How do lay people conceptualize nostalgia? Are they sympathetic to the views of scholars past, perceiving nostalgia as some form of illness or mental vulnerability? Might they have a more positive view of nostalgia and perceive it as a healthy activity? Or perhaps there is no lay consensus on how nostalgia should be conceptualized. That is, maybe people do not possess any clear sense of what nostalgia is or hold any firm views as to how it should be perceived. Or maybe different people have clear but opposing views. Some may believe nostalgia is a pleasant experience, whereas others may find it to be unpleasant.

Hepper, Ritchie, Sedikides, and Wildschut (2012) conducted a series of studies to answer this question regarding lay conceptions of nostalgia. They specifically set out to establish whether or not there is a general consensus on what features characterize nostalgia. They began their examination of this issue with a study that involved having research participants generate a pool of prototypical features of nostalgia. Specifically, in a free-listing format, Hepper and colleagues instructed participants to spend five minutes listing all of the characteristics and features that describe and distinguish nostalgia. The goal of this initial study was to generate a list of words or phrases that people believe characterize the experience of nostalgia and to organize these characteristics into a list of distinct categories that could be utilized in subsequent studies to determine the centrality of different features to the nostalgia construct.

On average, each participant generated about eight features of nostalgia in the free-listing task. Subsequently, the researchers grouped participant responses into distinct categories. For example, exemplars such as "past", "old times", and "days gone by" were put into the category of "the past". Likewise, exemplars such as "emotions", "feelings", and "sentimental" were placed in the category of "feeling". This coding process resulted in the formation of 35 distinct categories which appeared to broadly capture more general themes related to memory, different affective states, relationships, and the self. The three most frequently utilized themes were "memory/memories", "the past", and "happiness". The theme of "social relationships" also appeared frequently in participants' lists.

It is also worth noting that this study utilized participants from two different countries: the UK and the US. Thus, the researchers examined whether or not there were meaningful differences in the categories generated by these different samples. Out of the 35 categories generated, only three differed significantly between the two groups. Participants from the UK were more likely to list features in the categories of "memories" or "fond memories", whereas participants from the US were more likely to list features in the category of "homesickness". Overall, however, people from each nation listed features from these categories to a similar extent. This finding is consistent with other research indicating that nostalgia serves similar functions across cultures and age groups (see Routledge, Wildschut, Sedikides, & Juhl, 2013; Sedikides et al., 2015b), a topic I will discuss in detail in later chapters.

As noted, the goal of this initial study was to generate a list of words or phrases that people believe characterize the experience of nostalgia and to organize this list into distinct categories. In a second study, the researchers endeavored to examine the centrality of these categories to how people conceptualize nostalgia. To assess this, the researchers provided this category list to a different sample of participants and asked them to rate how central each of these categories is to the concept of nostalgia. Specifically, participants indicated the extent to which each of the 35 categories was related to their own personal view of nostalgia (1 = *not at all related*, 8 = *extremely related*). Is there a consensus on how people view the features and characteristics that represent nostalgia?

The results from this study suggest that there is indeed a consensus. Participants' ratings were highly reliable: people by and large agreed on how related each category was to nostalgia. In addition, centrality ratings in this study were generally consistent with frequency of categories in Study 1. That is, the characteristics of nostalgia that were frequently listed by participants in the first study were typically rated as highly central to the concept of nostalgia by participants in the second study. Evidence that different people have a similar view of nostalgia was beginning to emerge.

To further examine the centrality of different categories of features to the concept of nostalgia, Hepper and colleagues used a median split technique to create two category groups. Categories that were above the median in rated centrality in Study 2 were classified as central features. Categories that were below the median in rated centrality in Study 2 were classified as peripheral features. In reality, the centrality of categories to the concept of nostalgia is best described as being on a continuum. And this is how these categories were considered in Study 2. That is, participants did not divide categories into central and peripheral groups. Instead, they rated the centrality of categories on a continuous scale. However, the researchers used the median split method of deriving two groups from a continuous variable in order to fashion central and peripheral nostalgia manipulations that could be utilized in subsequent studies. Examples of categories that fell into the central group included "memory/memories", "the past", "remembering", "rose-tinted memory", "childhood/youth" and "longing/yearning". Examples of categories that fell into the peripheral group included "comfort/warmth", "homesickness", "ageing/old people", "wishing/desire", "change", and "regret". For the complete list of central and peripheral nostalgia features, see Hepper et al. (2012).

Having created a demarcation between central and peripheral features of nostalgia, Hepper and colleagues sought to further ensure that the characteristics determined to be central to the concept of nostalgia do in fact best represent the concept of nostalgia. Therefore, in one study (Study 3 of the package), the researchers presented sets of central and peripheral nostalgia features to participants. Specifically, nine central and eight to nine peripheral features were displayed one at a time on a computer screen for four seconds. Each feature was embedded in a statement connecting it to nostalgia. For example, a participant may see the statement: "Nostalgia is about childhood" (a central feature) or "Nostalgia is about regret" (a peripheral feature). Subsequently, participants were given a surprise recall task in which they were given three minutes to list all the features of nostalgia that they had just seen. After this free-recall task, participants were given a list of all 35 features and instructed to circle the features that they had seen earlier in the study. These different memory tasks thus allowed the researchers to assess the recall as well as the correct and false recognition of central and peripheral nostalgia features.

The results supported the notion that the features previously determined to be central to the construct of nostalgia are in fact prototypical characteristics of nostalgia. First, in the free-recall task, participants listed significantly more central than peripheral features of nostalgia. In other words, it was easier for participants to recall nostalgia's central features (e.g., "Nostalgia is about childhood") than it was for them to recall nostalgia's peripheral features (e.g., "Nostalgia is about regret"). For the recognition task, participants similarly correctly recognized both central and peripheral features that they had previously seen. That is, if they had in fact seen the word, they were fairly successful at being able to recognize it in a list of words regardless of which group that word came from. However, participants falsely recognized more central than peripheral features. In other words, when participants were presented with a list of central and peripheral features that included both features that they were and were not previously exposed to, they were more likely to incorrectly remember having seen central features.

These findings lend support to the proposal that there is consensus on the prototypical features of nostalgia. It is easier for people to recall nostalgia's central features. Further, people are more likely to incorrectly recognize nostalgia's central features, suggesting that these features in particular are associated with the construct of nostalgia in the memory system.

In their next study (Study 4), Hepper and colleagues further tested the idea of a lay nostalgia prototype by assessing the speed at which people classify central and peripheral features as characteristic of nostalgia. Specifically, participants were presented with a series of words one at a time on a computer screen and asked to indicate by clicking a YES or NO button on the computer screen whether or not each word was a characteristic of nostalgia. Participants were presented with central, peripheral, and neutral words in randomized order. Responses and response times were recorded.

The results provided further support for the proposal of a lay consensus on the conceptualization of nostalgia. First, further verifying the distinction previously established between central and peripheral nostalgia features, central features were more frequently classified as characteristic of nostalgia than peripheral features: participants were more likely to click the YES button when the word on the screen was taken from the central features list than when it was taken from the peripheral features list. In addition, peripheral features were more frequently classified as characteristic of nostalgia than neutral words. Furthermore, participants were quicker to categorize central features as characteristic of nostalgia than peripheral features. In other words, participants could very rapidly, without much deliberation, conclude that features from the central category group were representative of nostalgia. Also, participants were quicker to categorize peripheral features as characteristic of nostalgia than neutral words. Therefore, though peripheral features may have required more deliberation than central features, they were still more swiftly classified than control words.

In sum, people are more likely to classify central features as representative of the construct of nostalgia than peripheral features, and are quicker to do so. And they are also more likely to categorize and faster at categorizing peripheral features than neutral words. These findings further corroborate the proposal that there is a shared understanding of the experience of nostalgia.

Hepper and colleagues then decided to examine the lay conception of nostalgia by testing whether or not the presence of central and peripheral features of nostalgia in autobiographical narratives convey a sense of nostalgia to readers of these narratives, even when the word nostalgia is never used (Study 5). If central features are diagnostic of the experience of nostalgia, then when people read about someone's memories, the presence of central features should prompt the reader to believe that these memories are nostalgic ones. The researchers wrote a number of vignettes and embedded central or peripheral features of nostalgia in them. They also wrote control vignettes that contained neither central nor peripheral features. Importantly, the word nostalgia was not used in any of these vignettes. Participants then read the vignettes in randomized order and rated the extent to which different feelings were expressed in the narratives. Critically, one of the feelings participants rated was nostalgia. If nostalgia has a common lay conception and this conception distinguishes it from other constructs, then people should be able to identify nostalgia by the presence of its central features.

In support of the notion that central features of nostalgia make people more likely to perceive someone's autobiographical memory as a nostalgic one, participants rated the vignettes that contained central features of nostalgia as more nostalgic than the vignettes that contained either peripheral or no features of nostalgia. I particularly like this study because it taps into how humans often learn about and understand the world – through stories (Shank & Abelson, 1995). The poet Muriel Rukeyser once said, "The universe is made up of stories, not atoms" (Rukeyser, 1968). Of course, the universe is made up of atoms, but it is through storytelling that people have come to understand this fact. And when people read stories about other people's memories, they know nostalgia when they see it.

In their next study (Study 6), Hepper and colleagues asked participants to write about one of their own autobiographical memories. Some of the participants were asked to write about a nostalgic memory and some were asked to write about an ordinary memory. Then, participants were presented with the full list of 35 central and peripheral features of nostalgia and asked to rate the extent to which their memory reflected each feature.

Further supporting the lay conception of what features are central to the experience of nostalgia, participants in the nostalgia writing condition rated central features as more associated with their memory than participants in the ordinary autobiographical memory condition. The two conditions, however, did not differ on the ratings of peripheral features. In other words, when people are reflecting on their own life experiences, nostalgic memories are likely to contain the features that were previously determined by an independent group of people to be central to that concept.

In the final study (Study 7), Hepper and colleagues tested the potential for central traits to be used as a nostalgia induction. Experimental research on nostalgia typically induces nostalgia by explicitly asking participants to reflect on a nostalgic memory (see Routledge et al., 2013). And often, these instructions are accompanied by a dictionary definition of nostalgia. Having established evidence for the centrality of specific features to the experience of nostalgia, Hepper and colleagues wanted to determine if these features could be used to induce nostalgia to the same extent as the more explicit induction. That is, can nostalgia be successfully manipulated without actually using the word nostalgia in the experimental induction?

To test this possibility, Hepper and colleagues presented some participants with a list of central features and some with a list of peripheral features and then instructed participants to bring to mind a past event that was characterized by at least five of these features. Participants were also instructed to circle the features from the list that were relevant to their memory. There were two additional conditions. Some participants were given the more explicit and commonly used nostalgia induction in which they were instructed to "bring to mind a nostalgic event in your life. Specifically, try to think of a past event that makes you feel most nostalgic" (Wildschut, Sedikides, Arndt, & Routledge, 2006). Finally, the remaining participants were in a control condition and instructed to "bring to mind an ordinary event in your life. Specifically, try to think of a past event that is ordinary". In these latter two conditions, participants then spent a few minutes writing about the event they brought to mind. Subsequently, all participants completed a face valid measure of state nostalgia, e.g., "Right now I am feeling quite nostalgic" (Wildschut et al., 2006).

The results demonstrated that the central features induction induced nostalgia to similar levels as the explicit nostalgia induction. That is, these two distinct nostalgia conditions did not differ significantly in levels of induced state nostalgia, but both conditions produced levels of nostalgia significantly higher than the peripheral features induction and the ordinary event control condition. The peripheral features and ordinary event conditions did not differ significantly. In short, having people think about a memory that contains the established central features of nostalgia induces feelings of nostalgia without using the word nostalgia in the induction. And it does so as well as a more direct induction that explicitly instructs people to bring to mind a nostalgic memory.

In all, this series of studies by Hepper et al. (2012) paints a picture of how lay people view nostalgia. There is a common understanding of the characteristics and features that reflect the experience of nostalgia. Though people may have some unique perspectives on nostalgia, they tend to concur on its central elements. They are also able to quickly, with little conscious contemplation, identify the central characteristics of nostalgia. And when they see these elements represented in the memories of others, they agree that these memories are nostalgic in nature. Further, when they reflect on their own experiences of nostalgia, they identify these central characteristics as reflective of their experiences. Finally, bringing to mind life events that contain these central features generates nostalgia.

The research by Hepper et al. (2012) offers compelling evidence that people in the US and the UK generally agree in how they conceptualize nostalgia. However, is this the case cross-culturally? That is, do people all over the world have similar views on nostalgia? Hepper et al. (2014) conducted a study to address this question. In this study, over 1,700 students from universities in 18 different countries were presented with the list of the 35 prototypical features of nostalgia identified by Hepper et al. (2012) and asked to rate how closely each feature was related to their own view of nostalgia. Participants were then asked to write down any words or phrases that they believed described nostalgia but were not listed as one of the features. It is worth noting that these 18 countries broadly represented different regions and cultures of the world. They included Australia, Cameroon, Chile, China, Ethiopia, Germany, Greece, India, Ireland, Israel, Japan, Netherlands, Poland, Romania, Turkey, Uganda, the UK, and the US.

The results from this cross-cultural study provided evidence for the universality of lay conceptions of nostalgia. Across the 18 different countries, there was strong agreement on which features are more or less prototypical of nostalgia. People all over the world tend to agree on what is at the core of the nostalgic experience. In addition, when participants were given the opportunity to list additional features of nostalgia not already covered in the list they were given, nearly 80 percent of participants did not list anything, suggesting that they found the list adequate in its representation of the concept of nostalgia. Trained coders examined the words or phrases that were provided and determined that only about 6 percent did not fit well into one of the existing 35 categories. And these unclassifiable words or phrases came from a range of countries, but no single word or phrase was provided by more than two participants. In short, the 35 features identified by Hepper et al. (2012) appeared to describe the concept of nostalgia adequately and consistently across cultures. Nostalgia is a universally understand concept.

In sum, lay people are in agreement. They view nostalgia as a past-oriented experience focused on fond memories, often associated with childhood and youth.

Lay people also view nostalgia as social in nature, focused on close relationships. And they associate nostalgia more with positive feelings such as happiness than negative feelings. That is, lay people conceptualize nostalgia as meaningful memories viewed through rose-tinted glasses. Finally, lay people associate nostalgia with a sense of longing, loss, and even a desire to return to the past. It is worth noting, however, that most of the participants (though not all) in the research by Hepper et al. (2012, 2014) were young adults. Thus, more work is needed to consider possible age cohort differences in how nostalgia is conceptualized. However, as discussed, Hepper et al. (2014) found remarkable similarities in how people around the globe view nostalgia.

How Do People Experience Nostalgia?

Research on lay conceptions of nostalgia provides compelling evidence that there is a general consensus among people on what nostalgia is and its central characteristics. Now I turn to the issue of how people experience nostalgia. Studying the content of nostalgic memories is useful for a number of reasons. First, in addition to developing an understanding of how people conceptualize nostalgia, it is also important to understand how people actually experience it. When people engage in nostalgia, what are they thinking about? Are there particular types of life experiences or themes that tend to be featured in people's nostalgia? What about the emotional profile of nostalgic memories? Are nostalgic memories emotionally-rich? If so, what kinds of emotions are reflected in these memories? Second, in order to begin to understand the psychological and social consequences of nostalgia (topics addressed in subsequent chapters), it is critical to detail the types of cognitions and emotions that are prevalent in nostalgic memories. That is, to know what nostalgia does for people we have to first understand what it is and how it is experienced. Finally, understanding the content of nostalgia is important for establishing how this experience is similar to and distinct from other modes of temporal thought or self-reflective exercises.

One of the first attempts to analyze the experience of nostalgia was made by researchers in the field of marketing (Holak & Havlena, 1992). Prior to this research, most of the scholarly consideration of the content of nostalgic memories relied on individual case studies. Therefore, little was known about how nostalgia is commonly experienced. Holak and Havlena solicited nostalgia essays from a diverse group of American adult participants. Participants were specifically tasked with writing about three distinct experiences of nostalgia related to objects, events, and people respectively. The researchers then summarized the themes that were commonly featured in these narratives.

This qualitative analysis of nostalgia suggested that the most prominent theme of nostalgia is relationships. Whether people were writing about objects, events, or people, relationships were often prominently featured in the memory. Family, for example, was a very common focus of narratives. Nostalgia is often about those most dear to us. And this extends beyond family as the researchers also discovered that friends and old classmates were also regularly discussed.

Even when people wrote about objects of nostalgia they also regularly focused on relationships. For example, photographs are a common object of nostalgia and often feature close ones, e.g., children, parents, grandparents, spouses. Think about the photos you have taken. How often is it that you take a photo that does not include people in it? For those of us who are not professional landscape photographers, it is probably relatively rare for our photos to not be of people. In general, objects of nostalgia are often reminders of people.

And the events that people are nostalgic about also tend to be interpersonal in nature. Holidays, family vacations, trips with friends, weddings, religious ceremonies, and class reunions are the kinds of events people tend to be nostalgic about. In short, this qualitative analysis of the content of nostalgic memories suggests that nostalgia is about relationships and personally treasured objects or life experiences that remind us of or connect us to close ones.

Though the research by Holak and Havlena paved the way for a more systematic approach to the study of nostalgia, quantitative data was still lacking. Within the field of marketing, researchers were finding that a general disposition to nostalgia predicts preferences for consumer products from the past (e.g., Holbrook & Schindler, 1994). But few psychologists had yet to study nostalgia empirically. Marketing researchers and consumer psychologists were discovering that nostalgia plays an important role in peoples' lives as consumers, but psychologists were not studying the intrapsychic features of nostalgia or the psychological effects of engaging in nostalgia. Nostalgia appeared to be an experience shared by many, but one scientists knew very little about. Therefore, my colleagues and I launched a program of research to systematically study the psychology of nostalgia.

To begin to investigate the content of nostalgia, my colleagues and I asked participants to think about an experience that made them nostalgic and to detail this experience (Wildschut, Sedikides, Arndt, & Routledge, 2006). Specifically, we recruited undergraduate students from a large university in England and instructed them to think about a past experience that they were nostalgic about and to spend a few minutes writing about this experience and how it made them feel. Participants were provided with paper and allotted several minutes to bring to mind and detail their experience of nostalgia.

Subsequently, we trained research assistants to content code these nostalgic narratives. There is a long tradition of narrative content coding in psychology. The idea is to take qualitive text information and transform it into quantitative or numeric data. This allows researchers to employ statistical tools to describe the content of the information. My colleagues and I wanted to determine the prevalence of specific themes across different people's nostalgic memories and thus needed to classify and measure the frequency of distinct themes in nostalgia narratives. Therefore, we established a coding scheme – rules on how to determine if a theme is present or not – and tasked our coders with evaluating the narratives.

This content analysis revealed that there are indeed core themes that typify nostalgic memories. First, the most common objects of nostalgia were people. When individuals engage in nostalgia they typically think about close ones such as family members, romantic partners, and friends. This finding echoes the work by Holak and Havlena (1992). Momentous or personally cherished life events came in second as the most common nostalgia theme. These events included weddings, family reunions, vacations or any other experience that participants described as a personally meaningful. Of course, many of the life events that people cherish are highly social in nature. Thus, for many people, nostalgia is about revisiting personally valued experiences shared with close ones.

In addition, the self was prominently featured in nostalgic narratives. It was rarely the case that the self occupied a minor or observer role. It was also very rare for the self to be the sole actor. Nostalgic memories tend to involve others but the self is typically the protagonist.

Concerning the emotional content of nostalgia, though nostalgic narratives contained some negative affect, positive affect was more prominent. In this way, nostalgia appears to be a bittersweet emotion, but more sweet than bitter. Furthermore, most of the narratives followed a redemptive sequence in which negative events or feelings gave way to an emotionally positive conclusion. In other words, though it is not uncommon for people to express some feelings of loss or sadness when they bring to mind past experiences that they are nostalgic about, they also express a sense of happiness and appreciation for these cherished memories. The feelings of loss and sadness are outweighed by positive emotions.

One limitation of this particular study was that all of the nostalgic narratives were generated by undergraduate university students. Therefore, it is possible that the picture of nostalgia that is being painted by these college students is not an accurate reflection of how nostalgia is experienced more generally by adults. In a separate study, we (Wildschut et al., 2006) began to address this concern by drawing upon a broader adult sample. Specifically, we content analyzed narratives published in the periodical *Nostalgia*. The periodical invited readers to submit written narratives between 1,000 and 1,500 words in length of their own personal nostalgic stories. Contributors ranged in age from early 20s to late 80s. We selected a sample of issues of the periodical and trained judges to code these narratives. The results paralleled the effects of the study previously described. The most common objects of nostalgia were other people and momentous life events. Nostalgia narratives featured the self in a major role. Expressions of positive affect were significantly more common than expressions of negative affect and a redemptive sequence characterized the majority of narratives.

This initial content coding research provided the first systematic consideration of the experience of nostalgia. And the results were clear. Nostalgia is about the memories we hold dear and these memories are typically social in nature. This is perhaps not surprising considering that humans have a fundamental need to belong (Baumeister & Leary, 1995) and identify close relationships as a primary source of meaning in life (Lambert et al., 2013). But nostalgia is also about the self. When we engage in nostalgia we reflect on past experiences through the lens of the self. The experience is shared with others but recounted from our own vantage point. The memory is our own. Thus, the self is a central component of the nostalgic experience. Finally, nostalgia is an emotionally ambivalent experience: it involves both negative and positive emotions. However, these emotions do not enjoy equal space in the nostalgic memory. That is, nostalgic memories contain some elements of negative emotion, a tinge of sadness, longing, and loss. But these unpleasant feelings are overshadowed by positive ones. Nostalgic memories are about happy experiences, times of joy, celebration, and intimacy. When they do involve negative experiences, people are able to extract and highlight the positive or redeeming qualities. Perhaps the best way to illustrate the content of nostalgia is to provide some examples of nostalgia narratives. Below are some examples of nostalgia narratives selected from different studies my colleagues and I have conducted over the years.

This first example is from an American undergraduate student.

"My nostalgic moment was when I graduated from high school. I graduated first in my class so I was proud. I was graduating so high school was finally done so I was relieved. I miss the classes and all of my friends so there is longing. At the moment I graduated from high school I realized that was the last time I would see some of my friends. I also realized it was a new beginning and a new set of challenges for me advancing into college. For me this creates a feeling of longing to be back there. It also creates a feeling of accomplishment cause I was done.

In this narrative, the participant is reflecting on a culturally and personally valued event: high school graduation. The reflection prominently features the self, but it also refers to close relationships. She is proud that she finished first in her class, but she also recognizes the importance of her social connections. Again, highlighting the self, she also emphasizes how this life transition has implications for her own future pursuits (i.e., college). In addition, the individual highlights both positive and negative feelings. She longs for the friends she no longer sees, but she also feels a sense of pride and excitement about future opportunities."

The next example highlights the redemptive emotional sequence commonly found in nostalgia. It was also generated by an American undergraduate student.

"I felt really sad and upset when my aunt passed away in 2007. This is very sentimental to me because I know that I should take better control of my life than she did. I look up to her still, but many of the decisions that she made were not good. She had a good heart and when I try and think about her, all I can think about is the good that she would bring to her family. I try to forget about her mistakes because I like having a positive memory of her. Just thinking of the memories I had with her, I feel happy because I had a great time with her when she was still alive. I like to think that she is in a better place now and that she feels much better than she did before. I get sad to think that we can no longer have as many great memories that we once shared, but I think this was for the best."

In this example, the individual's experience of nostalgia starts with a feeling of sadness resulting from the death of a loved one. However, this sense of loss is redeemed as the individual expresses feelings of happiness because of the time shared with her aunt and the hope that she is in a better place. In addition, the memory is interpersonal in nature as it focuses on a close relationship. Yet, the self is also central. The individual focuses on how this time spent with a family member relates to and affects her own life.

The next example is an excerpt from a much longer nostalgia narrative provided by a UK resident.

"I was just 3 years old when the second world war started in 1939. My father was in a Scottish Regiment and for the first 3-4 years of the war was stationed in Scotland. My mother, in her early twenties, my younger brother and I followed him to wherever his base was. The furthest north was near the Moray Firth where the cold and the wind froze the washing on the line. Kilted soldiers marched to the sound of bagpipes, drums and band. When I see a film with Scottish soldiers or hear the bagpipes I am a child again, running out to watch them or march behind them with other children, like those who followed the Pied Piper.

When my father was on mountain training in the Scottish Highlands we returned to my grandparents in Bournemouth which had its share of air raids. The siren signaled an air raid warning and I would become aware of being carried down the road in the middle of the night to the safety of an air raid shelter with bunks on each side where we lay until the 'all clear' and being returned to our own beds. Sometimes we visited my father's parents in Wales. My Welsh grandparents were always old, always dressed in black, always serious and who always spoke in Welsh when they didn't want us to know their business. My uncles worked in the pits before there were showers at the pit head and came home in their blackened clothes and with faces covered in coal dust to bath in the galvanised baths in front of the range – and us! My sister was born on one of these visits and was left with an aunt and my grandmother while we went back to Scotland for the next 2 ½ years. Settling as a family on our return to Bournemouth was difficult. Our travels ceased when my father went with his unit to Europe.

There are so many memories. There was so much movement, so much upheaval, yet through it all there is a strong sense of belonging, of security, of family. My childhood was interrupted by war but I return to those years with nostalgia. A longing for the past? Perhaps, too, a realization of thankfulness."

In this narrative, the individual focuses on memories of childhood events that occurred during World War II. The narrative nicely captures the emotional ambivalence that is often found in nostalgic memories as well as the redemptive nature. The author explicitly highlights this sequence in the closing paragraph. The narrative also focuses on social connections and the security provided by these connections.

The next example was also provided by a UK resident.

"The birth of my first child. I was married for 7 years before she arrived. I was in hospital for 5 months before she was born and for 3 weeks after she was born.

She made me feel totally fulfilled. My parents were alive then and able to share this with me. It was the culmination of a great deal of treatment, etc., and all things considered, was the happiest time of my life. When I think about that time of my life I count my blessings and consider that my 'guardian angel' has been good to me."

This narrative focuses on the birth of a child, which the author describes as the happiest moment of her life. In the narrative, the author insinuates that there were some negative aspects of the experience as she required hospital care for many months prior to the birth of her daughter. However, clearly, the memory is redemptive. And again, though the self was central, the memory also involved others, e.g., parents, a new baby.

In all, these few examples illustrate the experience of nostalgic reflection. The details of the memories are unique. Each person has her or his own distinct life experiences. However, the memories share common themes. Most notably, nostalgic memories are social, and often involve close bonds with family and good friends. The memories also contain some negative feelings or experiences, but predominantly feature feelings of accomplishment, thankfulness, and happiness. And these memories represent meaningful life experiences such as graduation and the birth of a child or consequential life events such as the death of a loved one or living through a war. Nostalgic memories are momentous memories.

Distinguishing Nostalgia

The research on the content of nostalgia paints a picture of what characterizes the nostalgia experience. However, it does not reveal how nostalgia is distinct from other past-oriented reflections. How does the content of nostalgia compare to the content of other autobiographical memories? We (Abeyta, Routledge, Wildschut, & Sedikides, in press) conducted a study to begin to address this question. We asked a sample of North American university students to write about an experience they were nostalgic about or an ordinary experience from their past and then these narratives were content analyzed by trained coders. The results from this study indicate that nostalgic memories contain unique features.

First, nostalgia is uniquely emotional. More precisely, when people describe nostalgic memories they use significantly more positively-valenced emotional words than when they describe ordinary autobiographical memories. However, the reverse pattern was observed for negative emotions: participants who wrote about a nostalgic memory used fewer negative emotion words when describing their memory than participants who wrote about an ordinary autobiographical memory. In addition, replicating the findings of Wildschut et al. (2006), nostalgic memories contained more positive than negative emotional content. There was not a significant difference in the amount of positive relative to negative emotional content in ordinary autobiographical memories. Nostalgia can thus be distinguished from other autobiographical memories in terms of emotional content.

Content coding also revealed that nostalgic memories are more social than ordinary autobiographical memories. That is, participants used significantly more social-related words in the nostalgia compared to ordinary autobiographical narrative writing condition. Wildschut et al. (2006) established that nostalgia is highly interpersonal: nostalgic memories typically feature close ones. By comparing nostalgia narratives to narratives about non-nostalgic memories, the results of this study indicate that nostalgia is a uniquely relationship-focused experience.

The results from these content-analysis studies, as well as the lay conception studies previously discussed, are inconsistent with the historical portrayal of nostalgia as an illness. When people engage in nostalgia, they bring to mind personally meaningful experiences shared with loved ones. And critically, these memories are largely positive in emotional tone. They feature more positive than negative emotional content and, compared to other non-nostalgic memories, are more emotionally positive but not more emotionally negative.

Other research has further elucidated the content of nostalgia by considering some of the cognitive features that distinguish it from other autobiographical memories (Stephan, Sedikides, & Wildschut, 2012). According to construal level theory (CLT) (Kyung, Menon, & Trope, 2010; Liberman, Trope, & Stephan, 2007; Trope & Liberman, 2010), psychological distance contributes to how people think about events. Events that seem close to the current self (proximal events) tend to be thought of or construed in concrete terms, whereas events that seem far from the current self (distal events) tend to be construed in more abstract terms. In other words, the more distal an event is, the more that event is construed in terms of abstract, coherent, and super-ordinate mental representations or, what is referred to in CLT as higher-level construal. Imagine, for example, you ran a marathon. From the perspective of CLT, if this experience is perceived as distal perhaps because you ran the race ten years ago, then when reflecting on the event you are more likely to think about it in abstract terms, highlighting the gist of the experience, the central features. For instance, you might think about how the race was very challenging but finishing it gave you a great sense of personal accomplishment. However if this experience is perceived as proximal, perhaps because you ran the race yesterday, then when reflecting on the event you are more likely to think about it in concrete terms, focusing on the particulars. For instance, you might think about how hot and dehydrated you felt once you reached the twelfth mile or the specific aches and pains you had in your feet and knees as you closed in on the final few miles.

The same idea applies to events that have yet to happen. If you plan to run a marathon within the next several years, you are more inclined to think about this future ambition abstractly. You may contemplate the fact that the race will be rather difficult and require you to be in good physical shape. However, if you plan to run a marathon within the next few weeks or months you are more likely to be considering the details of this race. You may be thinking about the exact pace you should be running each mile as well as the amount of calories and water you should be consuming at various points throughout the race.

Stephan et al. (2012) proposed that nostalgia, compared to other autobiographical memories, would possess a unique construal make-up. Specifically, they proposed that people think about the actual experience they are nostalgic about in more abstract, higher-order terms. But they also predicted that when engaging in nostalgia, people would seek to connect the past experience to the present self and when doing this, they would use more concrete terms. In other words, Stephan and colleagues proposed that nostalgia involves both higher and lower-level construals. In their first study in this package, participants wrote narratives about an experience of nostalgia or an ordinary autobiographical experience. The researchers then content analyzed the narratives in terms of frequency of abstract and concrete language as well as psychological distance (both temporal and spatial distance).

Compared to ordinary autobiographical memories, nostalgic memories were described in more abstract terms. Further, when participants mentioned in their narratives any relevance the past experience had for the current self, they used more concrete terms in the nostalgia compared to non-nostalgia autobiographical narrative condition. Finally, nostalgia narratives were higher on coded psychological distance than ordinary autobiographical narratives. That is, people in the nostalgia condition mentally travelled further back in time and in geographical distance than people in the ordinary autobiographical memory condition.

A second study sought to replicate this pattern of results and also consider an additional type of autobiographical memory. In this study, participants wrote about a nostalgic, ordinary, or positive memory. The same coding methods were applied. And the same general pattern of results emerged. When people discussed the core nostalgia experience, they used more abstract terms. But when they described how this core experience relates to the present self, they used more concrete terms. And this pattern distinguished nostalgia from both ordinary and positive memories. In terms of psychological distance, replicating the first study, nostalgic memories involved both more temporal and spatial distance than ordinary memories. However, nostalgic memories did not differ significantly from positive memories in terms of temporal or spatial distance.

How Common Is Nostalgia?

Research has now established that nostalgia is conceptualized and experienced similarly among people. And these conceptualizations and experiences of nostalgia are at odds with the historical treatment of nostalgia as an illness or psychological vulnerability. But what about the idea put forth previously by scholars and practitioners that nostalgia is confined to specific groups of people? Is nostalgia a rarely experienced condition that is restricted to a few marginalized groups such as soldiers fighting wars far from home, as was thought in centuries past? Or is nostalgia something experienced by most people? Clearly, based on the research already described, it appears that nostalgia is an experience that many people can identify with. But just how prevalent is it? How frequently do people tend to engage in nostalgic reflection?

To begin to answer this question, my colleagues and I (Wildschut et al., 2006) asked undergraduate students to indicate how frequently they become nostalgic. Participants were specifically instructed to tick one of seven options reflecting nostalgia frequency: at least once a day, three to four times a week, approximately twice a week, approximately once a week, once or twice a month, once every couple of months, once or twice a year. The modal response (which included 26 percent of participants) was three to four times a week. In all, 79 percent of participants reported experiencing nostalgia at least once a week and another 17 percent indicated that they experienced nostalgia once or twice a month. Only 4 percent of participants reported experiencing nostalgia less frequently than once a month. This initial assessment of the regularity of nostalgia suggested that, even among relatively young adults, nostalgia is a common experience.

Other studies have similarly evidenced that nostalgia is frequently experienced across different ages and cultural groups. For example, my colleagues and I (Hepper et al., 2015) considered the frequency of nostalgia across the adult lifespan among a sample of British participants ranging in age from 18 to 91. We first considered the potential relationship between age and nostalgia. There was not a linear relationship between these two variables, but a small quadratic effect was detected. Nostalgia was highest among younger and older adults with a slight dip in mid-adulthood. We then sought to describe the general frequency of nostalgia across age groups so divided the sample into five age categories: 18–30, 31–45, 46–60, 61–75, and 76–91. We found that nostalgia is regularly experienced by people in all age categories. Specifically, over 55 percent of participants in every age category reported being nostalgic at least once a week. Consistent with the observed quadratic effect, the median response for the youngest (18–30) and oldest (76–91) groups was twice a week, whereas the median response for every other group was once a week. Overall, however, clearly it is commonplace for people to engage in nostalgia. By comparing different age groups, these findings also challenge the common stereotype that nostalgia is an emotion confined largely to older adults. Echoing our earlier findings (Wildschut et al., 2006), approximately 74 percent of participants age 18–30 reported experiencing nostalgia at least once a week and only 15 percent of people in this age group indicated that they are nostalgic less than once a month.

In all, people of all ages frequently engage in nostalgia. Indeed, in studies involving Chinese children and young adults, Zhou, Sedikides, Wildschut, and Gao (2008) reported that even school children as young as eight were familiar with the word *huaijiu* (nostalgia in Mandarin Chinese). As will be discussed later in Chapter 3, there are specific experiences or situations that tend to trigger nostalgic feelings. Thus, the frequency of nostalgia may result, in part, from how frequently people experience these triggers. That being said, clearly, nostalgia is not rare, nor is it confined to certain groups of people.

Summary: The Rebranding of an Old Emotion

We don't have time machines so we are not able to travel to the past to determine if lay conceptions of nostalgia have changed over time. It seems hard to imagine, however, that the emotional experience we now refer to as nostalgia has not always existed. Humans are self-reflective animals who have the ability to think temporally. Thus, we have probably always revisited our pasts through the lens of nostalgia. Yet, historical scholarly treatments of nostalgia do not match how people currently understand and experience it. People all over the globe have a strikingly similar conception of what nostalgia involves. In addition, studies exploring the content of nostalgic memories reveal that this past-focused emotional experience hardly seems like a source of distress. In the next chapter, I discuss why historical scholarly views may be inconsistent with contemporary research. In the present chapter, however, I described research that identifies nostalgia as a relatively positive emotional experience concerning personally meaningful past experiences involving close ones, but also prominently featuring the self. As discussed, nostalgic memories can also be distinguished from other autobiographical memories along different affective and cognitive dimensions. And finally, adults of all ages frequently feel nostalgic and even young children are familiar with this experience. The next questions then are what makes people nostalgic and what, if anything, do they get out of it? I explore these questions over the next several chapters. In Chapter 3, I start with the question: what makes people nostalgic?

3
WHAT MAKES PEOPLE NOSTALGIC?

In Chapter 2, I discussed research indicating that nostalgia is a common experience. Most people, regardless of age, regularly take nostalgic trips down memory lane. But why? Our lives are full of challenges and opportunities that keep us focused on the present and the future. Why then do we often turn our attention to the past and revisit experiences that are long gone? In other words, what inspires nostalgia?

The present chapter focuses on this question and in doing so begins to reveal why nostalgia may be an important component of healthy living. Specifically, in this chapter I review a growing body of research indicating that nostalgia is triggered by psychological threat or negative affective states and may thus be a resource people turn to in order to regulate distress or cope with a number of life's challenges. Of course, as most of us can attest, nostalgia can also be instigated by a range of familiar sights, sounds, and smells that remind us of days gone by. Thus, in this chapter I will also review research highlighting the many sensory triggers of nostalgia.

Are the Symptoms Actually the Cause?

Hofer determined that nostalgia was a disease because the patients that were longing for home were experiencing a significant amount of distress (see Routledge et al., 2013; Sedikides et al., 2015b). Anxiety, insomnia, disordered eating, and sadness were common symptoms of nostalgia. In Chapter 1, I discussed how the conception of nostalgia might have shifted over time. The symptoms that Hofer and his contemporaries believed were the result of nostalgia might have actually been the consequence of what we now distinguish as homesickness. Indeed, Hofer and other physicians of the time as well as psychologists and scholars long after very much viewed nostalgia as akin to homesickness. There is another possibility however. Perhaps some of the patients that were experiencing distressing symptoms were in fact nostalgic in the way we think about nostalgia today. Maybe Hofer was correct, at least in some cases, in recognizing an association between certain unpleasant symptoms and a sentimental longing for the past. But maybe he was incorrect in his understanding of the causal nature of this association.

Hofer argued that nostalgia was causing distress. When soldiers were nostalgically reflecting on the past, the result was a wide range of physical and mental health problems. But as any person who has taken a basic research methods course can confirm, correlation is not causation. Another possibility then is that nostalgia is the consequence not the cause of distress. Perhaps some of Hofer's patients were experiencing distress for other reasons. Considering that they were fighting in wars on foreign soil far from home, I can think of a few explanations as to why their mental and physical health might have been compromised. Perhaps then they were engaging in nostalgia as a result of this distress. That is, maybe Hofer got the directionality of the relationship between nostalgia and distress wrong. Nostalgia might be a response to distress, not the cause. If this assertion is true, then nostalgia might serve as a coping mechanism or regulatory resource that people employ to counter negative states.

From this perspective, nostalgia is not problematic as Hofer and many others believed. In fact, it may be adaptive. Nostalgia may serve important psychological and perhaps even physical health functions. So which is it? Does nostalgia cause distress or does distress cause nostalgia? The research discussed in Chapter 2 on the experience of nostalgia casts serious doubt on the assertion that nostalgia triggers distress. Nostalgic memories tend to be on the whole happy and personally meaningful – cherished memories of times spent with loved ones (Abeyta et al., 2015d; Wildschut et al., 2006). In addition, lay conceptions of nostalgia are at odds with the notion that nostalgia causes pain and suffering (Hepper et al., 2012, 2014). However, just because nostalgic memories tend to be good memories and people view nostalgia as a generally positive experience does not mean that it does not have ill effects. After all, there are many things in life that are enjoyable (e.g., drug use, unprotected casual sex) but also have a number of negative consequences for health and well-being. In order to truly understand the causal relationship between nostalgia and outcomes associated with mental and physical health, experimental research is needed testing the triggers and consequences of nostalgia. In Chapters 4 to 7, I review the ever-growing literature concerning the effects of nostalgia on psychological health and well-being. In the present chapter, however, I address the possibility that nostalgia may result from, not cause, distress.

Negative Mood Makes People Nostalgic

In an initial exploration of whether or not distress triggers nostalgia, my colleagues and I (Wildschut et al., 2006) simply asked participants to reflect on and describe the circumstances in which they tend to become nostalgic. You can try this exercise yourself. Think about your own experiences of nostalgia. Under what circumstances are you most likely to feel nostalgic about the past? Coders then categorized these descriptions. The most common category was negative emotion. Nearly 40 percent of participants indicated that they tend to feel nostalgic when they are experiencing unpleasant emotions. For example, one participant wrote "Generally I think about nostalgic experiences when things are not going very well – lonely or depressed". The categories "social interactions" and "sensory inputs" were the next most common circumstances associated with nostalgia, accounting for 24 percent and 19 percent of participant descriptions, respectively. I will return to these triggers later in this chapter. In addition, it is worth noting that only 3 percent of participants indicated that they are nostalgic when they are happy. Thus, nostalgia is far more likely to be experienced when people are distressed than when they are happy or content. But does distress in fact cause nostalgia?

To test the potential for distress to trigger nostalgia, we (Wildschut et al., 2006) conducted an experiment in which we induced different mood states. Participants in a negative mood condition read a news story about the wide destruction caused in coastal regions of Asia and Africa by the 2004 Indian Ocean tsunami. Participants in a positive mood condition read an uplifting story about the birth of a polar bear at the London Zoo. Who doesn't love baby polar bears? Participants in a neutral mood condition read a story about the landing of the Huygens unmanned probe on Titan, Saturn's largest moon. After reading one of these randomly assigned stories, all participants were instructed to write down five key words that represented the emotions they felt when reading the article and to spend a few minutes reflecting on those emotions. Participants then completed positive and negative affect scales (as manipulation checks) and two measures of nostalgia. One measure was the Batcho Nostalgia Inventory, where individuals rate the extent to which they miss various aspects of their past, e.g., their family, friends, holidays, the way things were (Batcho, 1995). The second measure was a face-valid nostalgia scale my colleagues and I constructed consisting of items such as "Right now I am feeling nostalgic".

The results were consistent with the assertion that distress triggers nostalgia. First, and importantly, the mood manipulations successfully instigated the intended mood states. Participants in the tsunami condition evidenced significantly higher negative affect than participants in either the polar bear or Titan probe conditions. Had the negative mood manipulation not worked, I might have lost my faith in humanity. And participants in the polar bear condition evidenced significantly higher positive mood than participants in either the tsunami or Titan probe conditions. Critically, participants who read the tsunami story were significantly more nostalgic (on both measures) than participants in either the polar bear or Titan probe conditions. Participants in the Titan probe and polar bear conditions did not significantly differ from one another on nostalgia. With this experiment, we had found the first experimental evidence that negative mood triggers nostalgia. The inclusion of a positive mood condition was important as it demonstrates that it is not the case that any type of emotion induction increases nostalgia. Nostalgia is specifically triggered by negative affective states. More resent research on music-evoked nostalgia converges with these experimental findings: when listening to music that was popular during their youth, participants were more likely to report that the music made them nostalgic if they were in a negative mood prior to listening to the music (Barett, 2010). Negative mood inspires nostalgia, but what about other distressing psychological states?

Loneliness as a Potent Trigger of Nostalgia

As previously discussed, in our initial exploration of nostalgia triggers, we (Wildschut et al., 2006) observed that nearly 40 percent of participants indicated that they typically feel nostalgic when they are experiencing negative mood. Interestingly, within the category, we observed that of the participants who identified a discrete emotional experience, loneliness was by far the most common experience (59 percent of this category). This finding suggests that though negative emotions in general promote nostalgia, loneliness may be a particularly potent nostalgia instigator. Therefore, we (Wildschut et al., 2006) then experimentally tested the effect of loneliness on nostalgia. Do people turn to nostalgia when their belongingness needs are compromised?

In this experiment, we had participants complete a loneliness inventory including items taken from the UCLA Loneliness Scale (Russell, Peplau, & Cutrona, 1980). However, to create a convincing loneliness manipulation, we altered the loneliness scale for each group in the experiment. For participants who were randomly assigned to a high loneliness condition, we phrased the items so as to elicit general agreement, e.g., "I sometimes feel isolated from others". Most people would agree with this kind of statement as most of us occasionally experience feelings of loneliness. For participants who were randomly assigned to a low loneliness condition, we phrased the items so as to elicit general disagreement, e.g., "I always feel isolated from others". Far fewer people would agree with this statement as most of us, thankfully, are not chronically in a state of loneliness. In other words, we worded the questions in a way that would assist us in presenting believable feedback to participants when we manipulated loneliness.

After completing this inventory, participants were led to believe that the experimenter was scoring their questionnaire in order to provide them with feedback. The feedback was then provided to participants on a form. Participants in the high loneliness condition were informed that, relative to their university peers, they had scored high (in the 62nd percentile) on the loneliness inventory. Participants in the low loneliness condition were informed that they had scored low (in the 12th percentile) on loneliness. Again, this feedback was made more believable because of the way we worded the loneliness questionnaires that provided the basis for this feedback.

Next, participants completed measures of state loneliness and nostalgia. Confirming that the manipulation was successful in inducing high versus low levels of loneliness, participants in the high loneliness condition reported significantly higher levels of loneliness than those in the low loneliness condition. Critically, high loneliness participants also reported significantly higher levels of nostalgia than their low loneliness counterparts. Experimentally induced loneliness triggered feelings of nostalgia.

Zhou, Sedikides, Wildschut, & Gao (2008) further tested the effect of loneliness on nostalgia with Chinese participants. They first considered the correlation between trait loneliness and trait nostalgia. Do lonely individuals more frequently engage in nostalgia? One interesting feature of this study was that participants were migrant children ranging in age from 9 to 15. In a pilot study, Zhou and colleagues confirmed that Chinese elementary school children were familiar with the concept of *huaijiu*, the term for nostalgia in Mandarin Chinese. Even young children are able to experience nostalgic. Participants completed the UCLA loneliness scale, which consists of items such as "I feel isolated from others" and "I have nobody to talk to" (Russell, 1996). They then completed the Southampton Nostalgia Scale (Routledge, Arndt, Sedikides, & Wildschut, 2008), a measure of nostalgia proneness, e.g., "How often do you experience nostalgia?". Loneliness was positively associated with nostalgia. In another study in that series, Zhou and colleagues replicated this effect with a sample of Chinese adult factory workers. Lonely people are more prone to nostalgia.

Of course, given the correlational nature of these findings, it remains possible that nostalgia proneness makes people feel lonely as opposed to loneliness increasing nostalgia. Such an interpretation would be inconsistent with our previous findings (Wildschut et al., 2006) but consistent with historical views on nostalgia. Since this was the first examination of the relation between nostalgia and loneliness within a non-Western sample, experimental evidence was needed. Therefore, Zhou et al. (2008) sought to replicate our previous findings (Wildschut et al., 2006) that induced loneliness triggers nostalgia with a sample of Chinese undergraduate students. The results confirmed that loneliness inspires nostalgia. Participants who were given false feedback that they scored high, relative to low, on a loneliness inventory reported significantly higher levels of nostalgia. In two distinct cultural samples, experimentally induced loneliness increased nostalgia.

In a series of follow-up studies, my colleagues and I (Seehusen et al., 2013) sought to further elucidate the relationship between negative feelings associated with a lack of social connections and nostalgia. In particular, we investigated the potential for nostalgia to result from a belongingness motivation. Since loneliness triggers nostalgia, people with a high need to belong (i.e., people who especially do not want to be alone) should be prone to nostalgia. To test this proposal, we administered to participants (Dutch adults from the community in this instance) a need-to-belong scale (Leary, Kelly, Cottrell, & Schreindorfer, 2006; sample item: "I try hard not to do things that would make other people avoid or reject me") and the Southampton Nostalgia Inventory (Routledge et al., 2008). As predicted, higher need to belong was associated with higher nostalgia proneness.

In our next study, we (Seehusen et al., 2013) replicated the relationship between the need to belong and nostalgia with a British sample. In addition, we extended our analysis by considering two distinct types of belongingness motivation: deficit reduction and growth orientations (Lavigne, Vallerand, & Crevier-Braud, 2011). A deficit reduction belongingness orientation reflects a desire to be socially accepted and avoid rejection, whereas a growth orientation reflects an interest in interpersonal relations without a focus on fear of rejection. We measured need to belong and nostalgia as before and also measured deficit reduction and growth orientations with the Belongingness Orientation Scale (Lavigne et al., 2011). The deficit reduction dimension of the scale consists of items such as "My relationships are important to me because they fill a void in my life" and the growth dimension consists of items such as "My relationships are important to me because they allow me to learn about myself". The results confirmed a relation between the need to belong and nostalgia: those high in the need to belong tended to also be highly nostalgia prone. In addition, though both the deficit reduction and growth dimensions of belongingness orientation were significantly and positively associated with nostalgia, the effect of deficit reduction was larger than the effect of growth. This finding is consistent with the relationship between loneliness and nostalgia. The people seeking belongingness out of concern for rejection were more inclined to be nostalgic than those that were seeking belongingness to grow as an individual. Interpersonal distress promotes nostalgia.

In the final two studies of this package we sought to find experimental evidence for the proposal that a need to belong, and threatened belongingness in particular, triggers nostalgia. We manipulated social exclusion (Twenge, Baumeister, Tice, & Stucke, 2001) and measured nostalgia. Specifically, participants completed a personality assessment (Eysenck & Eysenck, 1975) and then were given feedback to manipulate social exclusion. Participants were first presented with accurate information regarding their level of extraversion in order to bolster the credibility of the feedback. Then, half of the participants were presented with feedback suggesting that their personality scores indicate that they are at great risk for ending up alone later in life (exclusion condition). The other half of the participants were presented with feedback suggesting that they would likely have great success with relationships later in life (Study 3) or with no feedback at all regarding their future relationship outlook (Study 4). Numerous published studies demonstrate that this manipulation of social exclusion is effective in undermining feelings of belongingness and triggering attitudes and behaviors associated with countering or regulating threatened belongingness (e.g., Baumeister, DeWall, Ciarocco, & Twenge, 2005; Twenge, Baumeister, Tice, & Stucke, 2001; Twenge, Catanese, & Baumeister, 2003). Next, participants completed a nostalgia questionnaire.

The results confirmed that threatened belongingness motivates nostalgia. Participants in the future alone condition were significantly more nostalgic than those in the control conditions. When people feel like their chances of having lasting and fulfilling relationships in the future are slim, they turn to the past for comfort. In all, loneliness is clearly a powerful trigger of nostalgia. Considering that nostalgic memories tend to be highly social in nature, perhaps these results are not surprising. When people feel alone, they may desire to mentally time travel to a point in which they had relationship success. Nostalgia may offer a means to affirm belongingness needs. In Chapter 5, I focus on this issue in detail.

An Existential Void Generates Nostalgia: Meaninglessness and Boredom

My scholarly interest in nostalgia actually began with an existential question. Do people long for the past, in part, because of their awareness of future mortality and the perceptions of meaninglessness that this awareness may promote (Routledge & Arndt, 2005)? A number of scholars have discussed at length the existential implications of the advanced cognitive capacities that humans possess (e.g., Becker, 1971, 1973; Florian & Kravetz, 1983; Greenberg, Pyszczynski, & Solomon, 1986; Lifton, 1979). Humans are highly self-aware and are able to project the self in time. We can think about the future and this can be a very useful ability as it allows us to engage in long-term goal-planning. Our ancestors were able to successfully inhabit and dominate much of this planet, in part, because they could regulate their behavior in the service of future goals. As an inhabitant of one of the coldest states in the US (North Dakota), I often think about the Europeans who immigrated to this part of the country to farm. Had they not adequately planned for the brutal winters they would face, they would not have survived. And I am sure a number of them did not survive. But many did and this region of the nation is now a thriving agricultural sector. Temporal consciousness has proven vital to the success of our species.

Yet, this ability to think in terms of time also allows humans to contemplate the inescapable reality of mortality. Just as we can think about our future existence, we can think about our future non-existence. And as many scholars have noted (see Greenberg *et al.*, 1986), such thoughts have the potential to cause a significant amount of distress. For example, thinking about mortality can decrease perceptions of meaning in life and satisfaction with life and increase anxiety (Routledge *et al.*, 2011). Thus, when people are reminded of their mortal nature, they engage in efforts to affirm and defend the beliefs, institutions, and relationships that give their lives existential meaning (see Burke, Martens, & Faucher, 2010).

Nostalgic reflection is an activity that also requires temporal consciousness. That is, nostalgia involves projecting the self in time. It entails travelling backwards in time though, not forwards. And as discussed in Chapter 2, nostalgic memories tend to be about personally cherished life experiences. In other words, nostalgic memories are meaningful memories. They concern the autobiographical experiences that reassure us that our lives have been worthwhile. Thus, people might use the same cognitive capacities that make them vulnerable to threatened meaning to bolster meaning. The ability to think about the future may contribute to perceptions of meaninglessness because it allows people to contemplate death. However, the ability to think about the past may contribute to perceptions of meaning. Does threatened meaning inspire nostalgia?

To test the assertion that people turn to nostalgia in response to threatened meaning, my colleagues and I (Routledge et al., 2011) conducted an experiment in which we induced meaninglessness and measured nostalgia. Specifically, participants were randomly assigned to read one of two philosophical essays. One essay concerned the cosmic insignificance of humans. It served to remind participants that human life is extremely short and that, relative to the timeline of the universe or even our own planet, humans have existed for but a brief moment. It also explicitly asserted that humans are no more objectively meaningful than any other form of biological life. In other words, humans are cosmically insignificant. The other essay (the control condition) concerned the limitations of computers. In a pilot study, we found that both essays were judged to be equal in the extent to which readers found them to be engaging, interesting, and original. However, the meaning-threatening essay decreased perceptions of meaning relative to the control essay.

After participants read one of the two essays, they completed a nostalgia questionnaire. The results confirmed that threatened meaning triggers nostalgia. Participants who read an essay about the insignificance and meaninglessness of human life reported higher levels of nostalgia than participants who read an essay about the limitations of computers.

In a subsequent series of studies, van Tilburg, Igou, and Sedikides (2013) further explored meaninglessness as an instigator of nostalgia. They specifically focused on the experience of boredom as a threat to meaning that leads to nostalgia. Research indicates that boredom fosters feelings of purposeless and motivates people to seek out meaning (van Tilburg & Igou, 2011; van Tilburg & Igou, 2012). But does boredom trigger nostalgia?

In their first study, van Tilburg et al. (2013) induced boredom by having participants copy ten references about concrete mixtures (high boredom condition). Participants in a low boredom condition were only asked to copy two references. They then responded to a manipulation check item ("To what extent was the task you just completed boring?"). Subsequently, participants were asked to bring to mind a past memory. Half of the participants were specifically instructed to bring to mind a nostalgic memory and half were instructed to bring to mind a past memory (the word nostalgia was not used). All participants then completed a nostalgia questionnaire. The researchers proposed that high boredom would inspire people to become nostalgic when thinking about their past.

The results supported this proposal. First, participants found the high boredom task significantly more boring than the low boredom task. Turns out that copying references regarding concrete mixtures is not particularly stimulating. Not surprisingly, participants who were specifically instructed to bring to mind a nostalgic memory reported higher nostalgia than participants in the unspecified memory reflection task. Critically though, the boredom induction moderated this effect. In the low boredom condition, participants in the nostalgia memory condition felt significantly more nostalgic than participants in the unspecified memory condition. However, in the high boredom condition, participants in the unspecified memory condition felt just as nostalgic as participants in the nostalgia memory condition. In addition, within the unspecified memory condition, high boredom participants were significantly more nostalgic than low boredom participants.

In two additional experiments using a different boredom task, the researchers replicated this effect. Participants asked to trace a line through nine spirals (high boredom condition) became more nostalgic when bringing to mind an unspecified past experience than participants asked to trace a line through three spirals (low boredom condition). The researchers also tested and confirmed that participants were in fact bored when they completed the high boredom task (Study 3) and that this effect of boredom on nostalgia was not the result of negative mood (Study 2). When people are thinking about the past, boredom inspires them to revisit the experiences that generate nostalgia.

The researchers then endeavored to further establish that the need for meaning in life was indeed responsible for the effect of boredom on nostalgia. Participants were randomly assigned to a high or low boredom task (i.e., copying ten or two references about concrete mixtures), responded to items assessing the extent to which they would currently like to do something meaningful or purposeful (search for meaning), and then completed a nostalgia measure. The high boredom condition increased the search for meaning and nostalgia. Further, search for meaning fully mediated the relationship between boredom and nostalgia.

The researchers then replicated this pattern of results with dispositional measures. That is, participants responded to items indicative of trait boredom (e.g., "How often do you experience boredom?"), completed a search for meaning scale (e.g., "I am looking for something that makes my life feel meaningful"; Steger *et al.*, 2006), and finally, completed the Southampton Nostalgia Scale (e.g., "How often do you experience nostalgia?"; Routledge *et al.*, 2008). Replicating the experimental findings, trait boredom predicted search for meaning and nostalgia proneness. Further, the relationship between boredom and nostalgia was mediated by search for meaning.

Boredom has existential implications. When people are bored, they are not engaged in activities that they find fulfilling or worthwhile. Thus, boredom can undercut feelings of purpose and meaning. As a result, boredom promotes the search for meaning. People want to restore a sense of meaning in life when they are experiencing boredom. They long to do something that has purpose. The research by van Tilburg *et al.* (2013) indicates that boredom invoked search for meaning triggers nostalgia.

In all, a number of studies demonstrate that the existential threat of meaninglessness triggers nostalgia. Life is full of experiences that make us wonder whether or not our existence is meaningful. And these experiences increase nostalgia. But does nostalgia facilitate perceptions of meaning? I consider this question in detail in Chapter 7.

Self-Discontinuity Triggers Nostalgia

Self-discontinuity is a sense of disruption or disjointedness between one's past and present self (Davis 1979; Parfit, 1971) and is problematic for psychological health. For example, self-discontinuity is associated with negative affect and anxiety (Milligan, 2003), ineffective coping with difficult life transitions (Sadeh & Karniol, 2012), and even suicide (Chandler & Proulx, 2008). The sociologist, Fred Davis (1979) proposed that nostalgia is instigated by self-discontinuity. He asserted that "the nostalgic evocation of some past state of affairs always occurs in the context of present fears, discontents, anxieties, and uncertainties" and that "it is these emotions that pose the threat of identity discontinuity that nostalgia seeks, by marshalling our psychological resources for continuity, to abort or at least deflect" (ibid., pp. 34–35).

Best and Nelson (1985) were the first to test the potential for self-discontinuity to trigger nostalgia. Specifically, they re-analyzed US national survey data from 1968, 1974, 1976, and 1980 to determine if indicators of self-discontinuity were positively associated with indicators of nostalgia. The surveys they re-analyzed included a number of items indicative of life circumstances often associated with self-discontinuity (e.g., "deteriorating life circumstances such as divorce and health problems" and "work interruptions") and several items they believed to be indicative of nostalgia (e.g., "people had it better in the old days"). Are people who experience more life disruptions more apt to be nostalgic? The results from this study were mixed. One indicator of self-discontinuity (i.e., "deteriorating life circumstances such as divorce and health problems") was positively associated with nostalgia, but the remaining indicators were not. This study, however, had a number of limitations including a reliance on existing items that may or may not have best captured the constructs of self-discontinuity and nostalgia.

Qualitative investigations have provided some supporting evidence for discontinuity-triggered nostalgia. For example, Milligan (2003) observed and interviewed employees of a coffee shop before and after the business moved to a new location. She was particularly interested in how the relocation of the coffee shop would affect employees. Therefore, she conducted a participant observation study in which she took a job at the coffee shop prior to its relocation and observed her fellow employees for nearly two years (four months at the old coffee shop and 18 months at the new coffee shop). She worked at the shop at least ten hours per week but often 30 to 40 hours per week. While working, she would observe and engage in conversations with her fellow employees. Following the observation period, she conducted a number of in-depth interviews to further determine the effects of the coffee shop relocation. Milligan found support for discontinuity-induced nostalgia as she observed that employees often engaged in nostalgia following the relocation of the coffee shop. They would specifically talk among themselves about being nostalgic for the old location. They would also share stories about particular memories from the old shop. Drawing on ideas proposed by Davis (1979), Milligan concluded that nostalgia helped employers adjust to their new work setting. And in this way, nostalgia helped restore a sense of identity. It facilitated self-continuity.

Similarly, in another qualitative study, Goodson, Moore, and Hargreaves (2006) reported that teachers sometimes became nostalgic when experiencing unwanted organizational change. Though these different studies provided some evidence in support of Davis' assertion that self-discontinuity is a trigger of nostalgia, further empirical investigation was needed.

My colleagues and I (Sedikides, Wildschut, Routledge, & Arndt, 2015a) conducted a series of empirical studies investigating the potential for discontinuity to inspire nostalgia. In our first study, we sought to determine if people who have experienced more discontinuity in life are more nostalgic than those who have not experienced much discontinuity. Adults ranging in age from 34 to 61 years from a British community completed questionnaires assessing discontinuity and nostalgia. Specifically, first, as a measure of discontinuity, participants completed an abbreviated version of the Social Readjustment Rating Scale (SRRS) (Holmes & Rahe, 1967). The SRRS consists of life events that represent discontinuity. These events range from high ("divorce") to low ("change in eating habits") severity. Weights are attached to the SRRS events according to their relative impact or severity, with the most severe event ("death of a spouse") receiving a weight of 100. For each event, participants were instructed to indicate whether it had occurred over the past two years. Participants then completed the nostalgia proneness inventory previously discussed (Routledge *et al.*, 2008), e.g., "How often do you experience nostalgia?".

To start, we assessed the correlation between number of discontinuity events and nostalgia proneness. In support of the assertion that discontinuity leads to nostalgia, the results indicated that the greater number of life disruptive events people had experienced in the last two years, the more they tended to be nostalgic. In addition, this relationship remained significant when the life events were weighted according to the Holmes and Rahe (1967) weights.

In addition, we examined the relationship between each life event and nostalgia. What disruptive life events in particular appear to inspire nostalgia? The events that were significantly and positively associated with nostalgia were "change in living conditions", "change in residence", "change in sleeping habits", and "change in eating habits". Though not quite significant, "death of a close family member" also appeared to be associated with greater nostalgia. Disruptive life events that tend to be viewed as positive such as "gain of a new family member" and "outstanding personal achievement" were unrelated to nostalgia.

Though this study provided more direct evidence than past research in support of the assertion that self-discontinuity leads to nostalgia, it was correlational in nature. Thus, in a second study we (Sedikides et al., in press) sought to experimentally test the proposal that self-discontinuity triggers nostalgia. In addition, we sought to determine if the valence of self-discontinuity matters. Does any type of life change that affects the self-inspire nostalgia or is it the changes that aversely impact the self in particular that motivate people to nostalgically revisit the past? Based on the findings of the first study, other findings that negative states trigger nostalgia, and the theorizing of Davis (1979), we believed that negative discontinuity in particular would increase nostalgia. In this study, undergraduate UK student participants were randomly assigned to read one of three essays regarding the implications of transitioning to life as a university student. One essay was written to induce feelings of negative self-discontinuity. It asserted that the university years are a time of difficult change in which students are often confronted with overwhelming challenges that can make them question their values, goals, and beliefs. One essay was designed to induce feelings of positive self-discontinuity. It also asserted that the university years are a time of change. However, it suggested more positive transformations: becoming more independent and exploring new opportunities. The one remaining essay was written to induce feelings of self-continuity. It asserted that the university years are a time of stability. Participants then responded to a manipulation check item ("The university years are a time of change") and completed a measure of nostalgia (Batcho, 1995).

The results supported the assertion that self-discontinuity triggers nostalgia. First, both the positive and negative self-discontinuity manipulations successfully induced feelings of discontinuity. Participants in these two conditions were significantly more likely to agree with the assertion that the university years are a time of change than participants in the self-continuity condition. However, only negative self-discontinuity influenced nostalgia. That is, participants in the negative self-discontinuity condition were significantly more nostalgic than participants in the positive self-discontinuity and self-continuity conditions. These latter two conditions did not differ on levels of nostalgia.

In addition, we explored the data further to determine if the effect of negative self-discontinuity was particularly impactful on social nostalgia. That is, the Batcho (1995) nostalgia inventory consists of a range of items reflecting nostalgia for people, objects, places, feelings, and experiences. Therefore, we separated the social-relevant items (e.g., "family", "the way people were", and "having someone to depend on") from the non-social items (e.g., "feelings I had", "childhood toys", and "my pets") and re-analyzed the data. Negative self-discontinuity increased both social and non-social nostalgia. However, the effect of negative self-discontinuity was larger on social compared to non-social nostalgia. When people experience negative self-discontinuity, they generally become nostalgic, but especially for experiences involving close ones. This finding is perhaps not surprising considering that research indicates that when people engage in nostalgia, they typically bring to mind experiences that are highly social in nature (Abeyta et al., 2015d; Wildschut et al., 2006).

In all, emerging evidence is providing support for the assertion made by Davis (1979) that self-discontinuity causes nostalgia. Though a number of studies over the years have provided some support for this proposal (Best & Nelson, 1985; Goodson et al., 2006; Milligan, 2003), the research we (Sedikides et al., 2015a) conducted provided the first experimental evidence as well as the first evidence that it is negative self-discontinuity in particular that triggers nostalgia. This finding is consistent with the notion that nostalgia is a response to distress. Life transitions that are viewed as positive or indicative of personal growth and exploration do not incline people to turn to nostalgia. Instead, it is the experiences of discontinuity associated with negative psychological states (e.g., sadness, loss, anxiety, loneliness) that motivate nostalgia.

Summary: Distress Causes Nostalgia

Taken together, research clearly indicates that distressing or psychologically threatening experiences inspire nostalgia. Historically, nostalgia was believed to be the cause, not the effect, of distress (see Routledge et al., 2013). As previously discussed, one reason past scholars held this view was because nostalgia was conceptualized as being akin to homesickness and homesickness can lead to negative psychological states. An additional possibility, however, is that physicians and clinicians observed a co-variation between nostalgia and distress and concluded that nostalgia causes distress. In some instances perhaps people were engaging in what we would now refer to as nostalgia and were doing so in response to unpleasant life experiences. We do not have time machines so we cannot truly know for certain what the relationship was between symptoms of poor physical and mental health and experiences of nostalgia as conceptualized by people like Hofer. However, an ever-growing body of research concerning current views of nostalgia indicates that distressing experiences such as negative mood, loneliness, meaninglessness, and negative self-discontinuity increase feelings of nostalgia. The question then becomes, how does nostalgia influence psychological health and well-being? I address this question in Chapters 4 to 7. However, now I consider other, non-threat related, triggers of nostalgia.

Social and Sensory Triggers of Nostalgia

Thus far I have discussed research indicating that psychologically distressing situations inspire nostalgia. Research has also identified nostalgia triggers that are not associated with distress or psychological threat. That is, there are a number of experiences and stimuli that remind people of the past, and particularly experiences from that past that provide the content of nostalgic memories. In other words, though people recruit nostalgia in response to unpleasant feelings such as loneliness and meaninglessness, they also become nostalgic when a particular situation, social interaction, or sensory input cues a nostalgic memory.

Social interactions are a particularly potent nostalgia cue. When we get together with friends and family, it is common to communally engage in nostalgic reflection. We love to revisit past experiences with those who were there and even share these experiences with those who were not. And with the growing presence of social media in our lives, the opportunities of social interaction triggered nostalgia are abundant. Consider, for example, a growing trend on the popular social networking website Facebook referred to as "Throwback Thursday". This popular activity typically involves posting old photographs and providing a comment regarding the events surrounding that particular memory. Also, it is common for people to tag in the post other Facebook users who are also featured in that photo and thus part of that nostalgic memory. Essentially, "Throwback Thursday" is the Internet version of a reunion with family or friends. It provides a venue for socially-motivated nostalgia. People are thinking about close friends or family members and as a result become nostalgic and wish to share those memories with others and potentially revisit those memories with the individuals who were part of that cherished experience. Of course, Facebook is not alone. A growing number of other social media websites similarly provide a platform for socially-induced nostalgia. These sites afford friends and family who live far from one another or are unable to easily get together in person an opportunity to engage in the kind of social interactions that often lead to nostalgia.

Research supports the assertion that interacting with others often leads to nostalgia. For example, as previously discussed, in one study, my colleagues and I (Wildschut et al., 2006), asked participants to describe the situations that make them feel nostalgia. I already discussed the finding that negative affect and, in particular, loneliness were the experiences that were most commonly reported as nostalgia triggers. However, we also found that social interactions were the next most frequently identified category. Nearly a quarter of participants described a social experience as a nostalgia trigger. In this category, it was common for people to describe some type of experience that involved meeting up with family or friends and subsequently talking about a shared past event that generated feelings of nostalgia.

Nostalgic memories tend to be highly social: when people engage in nostalgia they typically revisit past experiences shared with close ones (Abeyta et al., 2015d; Wildschut et al., 2006). Thus, it is not surprising that interacting with close ones commonly instigates nostalgia, and, in particular, social nostalgia – discussing shared meaningful past experiences with others.

Sensory inputs also trigger nostalgia. We (Wildschut et al., 2006), found that nearly 20 percent of participants identified some type of sensory input as a cause of nostalgia. For example, one participant wrote "I find some of the strongest triggers are smells and music". When people see, smell, or hear something that reminds them of the past, feelings of nostalgia often follow.

Studies have explored the distinct sensory inputs that can trigger nostalgia. Focusing specifically on the sense of smell, Hirsch (1992) reported results from a survey indicating that around 85 percent of participants experienced olfactory-evoked nostalgia. More recent studies have explored in greater detail scent-evoked nostalgia. Reid, Green, Wildschut, and Sedikides (2014) proposed that smells may be a particularly potent elicitor of nostalgia because the olfactory bulb is linked to neurological structures associated with emotion and memory: the amygdala and hippocampus. To test the potential for scent-evoked nostalgia, Reid and colleagues first collected a large sample of pleasant and neutral scented oils and asked participants to smell each scent and indicate how nostalgic it made them feel. About half of the selected scents produced mean nostalgia ratings about the midpoint of the nostalgia scale. In addition, a number of these scents were judged to evoke nostalgia by many of the participants. Participants agreed that scents such as eggnog, pumpkin pie spice, cotton candy, and flowers triggered nostalgia. In addition, the researchers also asked participants to rate how arousing, familiar, and autobiographically relevant each scent was to them. Each of these dimensions predicted felt nostalgia. That is, the more arousing, familiar, and autobiographically relevant the scent was, the more it generated nostalgia. In addition, participants completed measures of generalized state nostalgia. This allowed the researchers to determine if scent-evoked nostalgia (i.e., the extent to which a specific scent makes one nostalgic) leads to more generalized nostalgia (i.e., the extent to which one broadly feels nostalgic about the past). Scent-evoked nostalgia significantly predicted generalized state nostalgia. Participants who reported high levels of scent-evoked nostalgia also reported higher levels of generalized nostalgia. Smells that remind people of the past trigger nostalgia.

Marketers and consumer psychologists have understood the link between sensory inputs and nostalgia for some time. Scholars, for example, have argued that nostalgia is regularly utilized in advertising: a common marketing strategy is to promote a product in a way that reminds people of fond memories from their childhood or youth (Havlena & Holak, 1991). Indeed, as discussed in Chapter 1, studies indicate that products (e.g., clothing, music, films) that were popular during an individual's youth have a lifelong impact on consumer behavior (Schindler & Holbrook, 2003). For example, Holbrook and Schindler (1994) observed that preferences for movie stars peak at around age 14 and preferences for movies peak around age 27, thus suggesting that people's attitudes about entertainment are formed during adolescence and early adulthood. Exposure to stimuli that remind people of films from their youth may thus inspire nostalgia and consumption of products associated with these films. It is not surprising then that motion pictures are frequently re-released, rebooted, or turned into lasting franchises involving multiple prequels and sequels, as well as other product tie-ins such as toys and video games. In fact, a recent news article argued that 2013 was the year of the sequel (Allen, 2012). Evidently, a record 31 sequels and 17 movie reboots were scheduled for release in 2013. The growing number of such nostalgia-inspired films has led to many discussions and debates about the loss of originality, creativity, and risk-taking in the film industry. But movie making is, at its core, a business. Companies that produce movies want to sell movie tickets. And, evidently, nostalgia sells.

This effect of product-induced nostalgia extends beyond movies. Holbrook and Schindler (1994), for example, found that people, particularly males, have a preference for automobiles from their youth. The potency of this effect was recently exhibited when a sinkhole opened up and swallowed a number of classic (as well newer) Corvettes at Kentucky's National Corvette Museum. This event became a national news story and one that prompted much discussion about the importance of cherishing and celebrating the cars that defined a particular generation. Many car enthusiasts as well as those who merely had fond memories involving a Corvette, articulated feelings of sadness upon hearing about the harm that came to these classic vehicles when they fell into the sinkhole. Ford Car Company is currently seizing on the potential for product-induced nostalgia as it celebrates the 50th birthday of the Mustang and attempts to capitalize on the warm feelings associated with the Mustang brand to market its newest version of the classic car.

In short, sensory experiences such as watching a movie or a car commercial that bring to mind experiences from our youth can trigger the sentiment of nostalgia. And, as consumer psychologists and marketing researchers have observed, corporations that are in the business of selling consumer products have long exploited sensory-input induced nostalgia. Companies such as Coca-Cola, PepsiCo, Ford, McDonald's, General Mills, Nintendo, and many others have created advertising campaigns asking people to nostalgically travel back in time. The goal of this advertisement-induced trip down memory lane is, of course, to inspire liking for and purchasing of brands associated with nostalgia.

One sensory input that has received a fair amount of empirical attention is music. Holbrock and Schindler (1989), for example, found evidence that nostalgia is a potentially powerful predictor of music preferences. In their study, they asked participants ranging in age from 16 to 86 to evaluate excerpts from popular songs dating back to 1932. The results from this study indicated that people prefer music that was released in their late teens and early twenties. These findings converge with similar research by these scholars regarding movie preferences (Holbrock and Schindler, 1994, 1996). If people prefer music that was popular in their youth, then music from one's past may lead to feelings of nostalgia.

In support of the proposal that music can trigger nostalgia, Juslin, Lilkestrom, Vastfjall, Barradas, and Silva (2008) found that when people are listening to music, nostalgia is one of the most common emotions experienced. This finding is consistent with other studies indicating that nostalgia is a frequently experienced emotion when listening to music (Zentner et al., 2008). But what is it about music that inspires nostalgia? Barret et al. (2010) considered this issue by examining characteristics about songs that predict nostalgia. In this study, participants listened to samples of songs that were popular (i.e., ranked on the Billboard Top 100) during their adolescent and teenage years. After listening to each sample, they rated the extent to which the song made them nostalgic. Participants also rated how familiar and autobiographically-relevant the song was to them. Further, they indicated the extent to which listening to the song led to arousal, positive emotions, negative emotions, and mixed emotions. The results indicated that the more familiar, autobiographically-relevant, and arousing music is, the more it triggers nostalgia. In addition, all of the emotions that music inspires influence nostalgia. That is music-triggered positive, negative, and mixed emotions were all significant predictors of music-triggered nostalgia. It is worth noting, however, that positive emotions derived from music more strongly predicted nostalgia than negative or mixed emotions derived from music. In all, music from one's youth leads to nostalgia if it is familiar and relevant to one's autobiographical experiences. Furthermore, arousal and emotion are also important elements of music's capacity to trigger nostalgia. Based on the research connecting nostalgia to music, a number of experimental studies have now used music to induce feelings of nostalgia (e.g., Cheung et al., 2013; Routledge et al., 2011). Music is a potent trigger of nostalgia.

Are there other sensory-relevant experiences that may promote feelings of nostalgia? Zhou et al. (2012) considered the potential for temperature to influence nostalgic feelings. Specifically, they proposed that nostalgia may be triggered by cold temperatures, especially if the cold temperature is unpleasant. In their first assessment of this possibility, participants reported how nostalgic they felt each day over a period of 30 days. The researchers also kept track of daily temperatures. The results indicated that people were more nostalgic on colder days. In a second study, the researchers experimentally manipulated the temperature of the laboratory. Participants were randomly assigned to complete materials in a cold (20°C), neutral (24°C), or warm (28°C) room. Participants in the cold room reported significantly higher levels of nostalgia than participants in the neutral or warm room. These latter two conditions did not differ significantly. In other words, it was not simply that nostalgia increased as temperature decreased. Nostalgia appeared to only be triggered when the temperature was cold enough to be considered unpleasant. As previously discussed, nostalgia is triggered by psychologically unpleasant experiences. This research identifying cold temperatures as a trigger of nostalgia suggests that physically unpleasant experiences may also influence the experience of nostalgia.

Closing Thoughts

In all, there appear to be two general classes of nostalgia triggers. First, people turn to nostalgia in response to affectively negative or psychologically threatening experiences. Specifically, research has identified negative affect, loneliness, meaninglessness, and self-discontinuity as states that increase nostalgia. It is worth noting that the list of psychologically unpleasant nostalgia-inducing states discussed in this chapter is probably incomplete. Future research will likely elucidate other unpleasant psychological states that inspire people to nostalgically reflect on the past. Critically, the research to date clearly indicates that a range of distinct psychologically threatening experiences increase nostalgia. These findings provide partial evidence suggesting that nostalgia is the result, not the cause, of distress. However, to fully understand the relation between nostalgia and psychological health and well-being, experimental research considering the effect of nostalgia on indicators of psychological health and well-being is required. Distress may lead to nostalgia, but how does nostalgia influence psychological health? It is this question that I turn to over the next several chapters.

Second, social encounters and sensory inputs that serve as reminders of the past, also frequently trigger feelings of nostalgia. When people connect with close ones, either in person or via social media, nostalgia often results. Likewise, sensory experiences that remind people of the past are also potent nostalgia triggers. These include smells, visual-based media such as movies and video games, and music.

4
THE AFFECTIVE CONSEQUENCES OF NOSTALGIA

In Chapter 2, I described research concerning lay conception of nostalgia (Hepper *et al.*, 2012). When research participants listed the characteristics that they believed defined nostalgia they frequently used the word happiness. This finding was noteworthy in the context of historical views on nostalgia that typically invoked negative emotions. Lay people, at least in the present day, disagree with historical treatments of nostalgia. They view nostalgia as more of a positive than negative emotional experience. Research on the content of nostalgic narratives further elucidated the emotional landscape of nostalgia. Nostalgic narratives contained more positive than negative emotion-related words (Abeyta *et al.*, 2015d; Wildschut *et al.*, 2006) and the overall emotionality of these narratives typically followed a redemptive sequence (Wildschut *et al.*, 2006).

But how does engaging in nostalgia actually make people feel? People might view nostalgia as a happy experience but this does not necessarily mean that nostalgia actually makes people happy. Likewise, the content of nostalgic memories may be largely positive but this does not inherently mean that a person reflecting on positive experiences from the past will experience positive emotions in the present. In fact, consistent with the thinking of past physicians and clinicians, there are compelling reasons to suspect that nostalgia may actually lead to negative emotions. For example, if nostalgia involves longing for past experiences or relationships, then it may trigger feelings of loss and ultimately sadness. Similarly, nostalgia might involve comparing an idealized past to a less than ideal present which could foster feelings of discontent and even frustration (Verplanken, 2012). In this way, nostalgia may leave people dissatisfied with their current life and thus prevent them from enjoying the present and looking forward to the future. In short, by orienting people towards personally cherished bygone days, nostalgia may leave people vulnerable to negative affective states.

However, there are also compelling reasons to posit that nostalgia enhances positive emotions. Since nostalgia involves mentally time travelling to personally treasured past experiences, it may allow individuals opportunities to re-experience the pleasant emotions felt during those times. For example, think about a time in which you looked through an old photo album. How did it make you feel? I keep on my desk at work a picture that my wife took of me with our two kids standing in front of a mural on the south bank of the Thames River in London. Our kids were around the ages of four and six and we were taking a day trip to London (we lived just south of London at that time). Every time I look at that picture it makes me nostalgic. And it also puts a smile on my face. I enjoy being reminded of that time and cherish that memory. I know that I cannot recreate that experience now, but to me that is part of what makes it so special. Revisiting that experience makes me happy, not sad. And I suspect that the positive emotions I experience when looking at old family photos are not unique. Also, as I will discuss in more detail in subsequent chapters, revisiting the past nostalgically may make us feel closer to the ones we love and reminds us that we have lived meaningful lives. And of course, these kinds of feelings of belongingness and meaningfulness should inspire positive emotions.

So which is it? Does nostalgia lead to negative or positive emotional states? Is it an experience that reminds us of what we have lost or is it an experience that makes us happy about the lives we have lived. There are now a number of studies that answer this question. In the current chapter, I discuss the research on the emotional consequences of nostalgia. I also discuss the need for future research to more fully elucidate the many ways that nostalgia may influence affective states.

Does Nostalgia Increase Negative Affect?

Let us first consider the potential for nostalgia to increase negative affect. Nostalgia is, as already discussed, a complex emotional experience. That is, nostalgic memories involve mixed emotions (Wildschut et al., 2006). And lay conceptions of nostalgia tend to recognize a component of loss or longing (Hepper et al., 2012). But does engaging in nostalgia elevate negative affect? That is, does the tinge of sadness and loss present in nostalgic memories actually make people feel bad? My colleagues and I (Wildschut et al., 2006) tested this possibility in two studies. In both of these studies we randomly assigned participants to one of two autobiographical conditions. In the nostalgia condition, participants were instructed to "bring to mind a nostalgic event in your life. Specifically, try to think of a past event that makes you feel most nostalgic". In the control condition, participants were instructed to "bring to mind an ordinary event in your daily life – an event that took place in the last week". In one study, participants then responded to a number of items, including questions related to negative mood. Specifically, participants were asked to indicate to what extent thinking about the nostalgia or ordinary event made them feel "sad" and "blue". In the other study, after the nostalgia or ordinary writing task, participants completed a validated measure of positive and negative affect (the Positive and Negative Affect Schedule or PANAS) (Watson, Clark, & Tellegen, 1988).

In both of these studies, nostalgia did not influence negative mood. That is, participants in the nostalgia condition did not report significantly higher negative mood than those in the control condition. Nostalgia may reflect a longing for the past and nostalgic memories may contain some bittersweet elements; however, engaging in nostalgia does not appear to elevate negative mood.

Results from other studies converge with these findings. For example, across several studies, Zhou, Wildschut, Sedikides, Shi, & Feng (2012) used the same method we (Wildschut et al., 2006) employed: they manipulated nostalgia with an autobiographical writing task and measured mood with the PANAS (Watson, Clark, & Tellegen, 1988). An important distinction, however, is that the research conducted by Zhou and colleagues involved more culturally diverse samples. Whereas our research was conducted using relatively young undergraduate British students, the research by Zhou and colleagues was conducted using adult participants from a number of different countries (e.g., China, Russia, the US). Across several studies, Zhou and colleagues found no evidence that nostalgia increases negative affect. Other studies similarly find no difference between nostalgia and non-nostalgia conditions on negative affect (e.g., Cheung et al., 2013).

Stephan, Sedikides, and Wildschut (2012) went a step further and, in addition to assessing general negative affect with items such as "makes me feel sad" and "makes me feel unhappy", they also considered the level of arousal in affective states by assessing specifically activated versus deactivated negative affect (Barrett & Russell, 1998). Activated negative affect was assessed with items such as "makes me feel disturbed" and deactivated negative affect was assessed with items such as "makes me feel tired". Perhaps nostalgia does promote negative mood but maybe more specificity is needed to elucidate such an effect. Stephan and colleagues also included an additional comparison condition. Specifically, some participants were asked to write about a positive memory. Results were generally consistent with previous findings with one exception. Specifically, participants in the nostalgia condition did not differ from those in the ordinary or positive memory conditions on general negative affect or deactivated negative affect. However, a significant effect was observed on activated negative affect. Participants in the nostalgia condition reported significantly higher activated negative affect than participants in either the ordinary or positive memory conditions. In other words, nostalgia appeared to increase the high arousal dimension of negative affect.

Though it was only a single study, the results observed by Stephan et al. (2012) that nostalgia may increase activated negative affect, warrant further investigation as most of the existing research on nostalgia has failed to find negative effects of nostalgia on variables related to affect or well-being. Were these results a fluke? Or might nostalgia, at least in some contexts or for some individuals lead to negative affective states? In Chapter 8, I consider in more detail the potential role that individual differences may play in influencing the affective consequences of nostalgia. For now I will simply note that specific traits associated with chronic negative affect may have important implications for how nostalgia impacts emotion.

It is also worth noting that there is little existing evidence that nostalgia decreases negative affect. That is, in most of the research in which negative affect is measured as an outcome of nostalgia there is simply no observed effect of nostalgia on negative affect. Nostalgia does not increase or decrease negative affect. That being said, some findings hint at the possibility that nostalgia can decrease negative affect. For example, in one study, Lasaleta, Sedikides, & Vohs (2014) found a marginal trend ($p < .10$) indicating that participants in a nostalgia condition reported lower levels of negative affect than participants in a neutral condition. But the bulk of research in which nostalgia is induced and then negative affect is assessed does not provide evidence that nostalgia decreases negative affect. It is important to note, however, that such studies do not provide a true test of nostalgia's potential to decrease negative affect because, without provocation, people do not generally experience negative affective states (Diener & Diener, 1996). Therefore, to test whether or not nostalgia decreases negative affect, researchers would need to experimentally induce negative affect before manipulating nostalgia and measuring subsequent changes in affect. We know that people become nostalgic as a response to negative affective states (e.g., Wildschut et al., 2006), but does nostalgia in turn decrease negative affect? Future research is needed to test this possibility.

In all, research to date indicates that nostalgia typically does not lead to affectively negative states. The emotional content of nostalgic memories can be ambivalent. That is, nostalgia often involves happy thoughts tinged with sadness or loss. However, reflecting on these bittersweet memories does not put people in a bad mood. Empirical studies therefore contradict historical views that nostalgia leads to distress (Routledge et al., 2013). But why is this? If nostalgic memories contain some negatively valence affective themes, why do these memories not tend to lead to the experience of negative emotions? One possible explanation relates to the affective sequence of nostalgic memories. As discussed in Chapter 2, though nostalgic memories contain both negative and positive emotional themes, these narratives tend to follow a redemptive sequence (Wildschut et al., 2006). Negative feelings typically give way to a positive conclusion. Therefore, when people engage in nostalgic reflection, any negative emotions felt might be muted by the redemptive outcome. Likewise, positive and negative emotions do not share equal space in nostalgic memories: the presence of positive emotions far outweighs the presence of negative emotions (Abeyta et al., 2015d). Therefore, the potential for negative affect may be squashed by the overall positive emotional tone of the memory. However, additional research is needed to test these and other possibilities. For example, future research could examine the relation between amount of positive and negative affective information in nostalgic memories and present affective states. In addition, future research is needed to more fully consider the potential for nostalgia to elicit negative affect. Research to date has relied on explicit self-report measures of affect. Might nostalgia have more subtle effects on affective states that people are unable to report?

Nostalgia may not typically cause negative affect, but how does it influence positive affect? Does nostalgia decrease or increase positive mood? Or does nostalgia simply have no significant impact on people's emotional lives?

Nostalgia and Positive Affect

As previously discussed, nostalgic memories, though bittersweet, are more sweet than bitter. When people return to the past nostalgically, they tend to reflect on experiences that were personally meaningful and joyous (Abeyta et al., 2015d; Wildschut et al., 2006). But how does reflecting on treasured past experiences impact positive emotions in the present? A number of studies have examined this question.

First, when we (Wildschut et al., 2006) assessed negative affect after an experimental induction of nostalgia, we also assessed positive affect. In one study, after bringing to mind and writing about a nostalgia or ordinary event, participants were asked to indicate to what extent thinking about this event made them feel "happy" and "content". In another study, participants completed the PANAS (Watson, Clark, & Tellegen, 1988). Across both studies, nostalgia, relative to the control condition, increased positive affect. In short, we found that though nostalgia did not influence negative affect, it did increase positive affect. The general finding that bringing to mind and writing about a nostalgic experience, relative to an ordinary experience, increases positive affect has now been replicated a number of times (e.g., Baldwin & Landau, 2014; Chueng et al., 2013; Lasaleta et al., 2014; Wildschut, Sedikides, Routledge, Arndt, & Cordaro, 2010).

In one study, Chueng et al. (2013) did not find an effect of nostalgia on positive affect, but it is worth noting that this was likely due to the control condition serving as a positive affect induction. Specifically, the researchers wanted to control for positive affect as an alternative explanation of nostalgia's potential effect on optimism, a topic I will return to in a later chapter. The researchers also wanted to employ an experimental manipulation that capitalized on music's capacity to induce nostalgia. Thus, in this study, participants were presented with one of two songs that had previously been established as distinct in the level of nostalgia they generated (high versus low) but similar in how much positive affect they produced. Not surprisingly then, in this study, participants did not differ on a measure of positive affect as a function of listening to one of these songs. Participants in both conditions listened to happy songs. And listening to a nostalgic song did not boost positive mood to a greater extent than listening to a non-nostalgic but affective pleasant song.

However, in a subsequent study in that package, Cheung et al. (2013) did test the potential for nostalgic music to elevate positive affect. Specifically, in this study, as part of a pre-study, participants were given the definition of nostalgia (i.e., "nostalgia is a sentimental or wistful affection for the past") and asked to list the titles and artists of three songs that made them nostalgic (Routledge et al., 2011). During the experimental session, which occurred at least three weeks after the pre-study session, participants in the nostalgia condition were presented with the lyrics from one of the songs they listed as nostalgia-inducing. Participants in the control condition were yoked to participants in the nostalgia condition. That is, each control participant was presented with the nostalgia lyrics of a participant in the nostalgic condition. The researchers ensured that these lyrics were not identified as nostalgia-related for the control participants. In short, participants in both conditions received matched music lyrics, but only participants in the nostalgia condition were presented with the lyrics that evoked nostalgic feelings. Participants were then asked to indicate the extent to which reading the lyrics made them feel "happy" and "in a good mood". Results supported the assertion that nostalgia increases positive affect: participants who read the lyrics from songs they had previously indicated made them nostalgic reported greater positive mood than participants who read someone else's nostalgia lyrics.

Other studies using distinct methodologies similarly suggest a positive mood-enhancing function of nostalgia. For example, in their examination of the prototypical features of nostalgia, Hepper et al. (2012) tested the effect of nostalgia on positive affect using an experimental induction distinguishing central from peripheral characteristics of nostalgia. Specifically, participants in a high nostalgia condition were presented with words reflective of characteristics central to the experience of nostalgia (e.g., "memory", "the past", and "longing/yearning") and participants in the low nostalgia condition were presented with words reflective of characteristics peripheral to the experience of nostalgia (e.g., "homesickness", "mixed feelings", and "comfort/warmth"). Participants then responded to items assessing positive mood (e.g., "makes me feel happy"). Consistent with the research discussed thus far, nostalgia increased positive affect. That is, participants experienced a greater level of positive mood if they had been presented with words that are central to the construct of nostalgia.

Stephan et al. (2012) also considered positive affect in their exploration of nostalgia's effects on activated and deactivated affect. After a nostalgia, ordinary, or positive memory induction, participants responded to two items assessing general positive affect ("makes me feel happy" and "puts me in a great mood"), two items assessing activated positive affect ("makes me feel active" and "makes me feel ecstatic") and two items assessing deactivated positive affect ("makes me feel calm" and "makes me feel relaxed"). Replicating previous findings, participants in the nostalgia condition reported significantly higher general positive affect than participants in the ordinary memory condition. Not surprisingly, participants in the nostalgia and positive memory conditions did not differ on generalized positive affect. Interestingly, though nostalgia increased generalized positive affect relative to reflecting on an ordinary memory, no significant effects were observed on activated or deactivated positive affect.

Despite the evidence that nostalgia has an enhancing effect on positive mood, other studies have produced more mixed results. For example, across several studies involving participants from multiple countries (e.g., China, Russia, the US), Zhou et al. (2012) found that nostalgia sometimes, but not always, increases positive affect as measured with the PANAS (Watson, Clark, & Tellegen, 1988). Further, my colleagues and I (Stephan et al., 2014) found no effect of nostalgia on positive (or negative) affect as measured by the PANAS across two experiments.

In sum, using distinct nostalgia manipulations and measures of positive affect, much of the research to date suggests that nostalgia has an enhancing effect on positive affect. However, the fact that some studies find no effect on positive mood indicates that additional research is needed to fully elucidate how nostalgia influences positive affective states. It is worth noting that though in some studies nostalgia did not increase positive mood; it also did not decrease it. In those studies, nostalgia simply did not influence positive affect. One possibility is that participants find some of the control conditions such as the ordinary autobiographical writing task to be pleasant. Indeed, we (Stephen et al., 2014) observed that in both the nostalgia and ordinary autobiographical writing tasks, positive affect scores were significantly higher than negative affect scores.

Closing Thoughts

In Chapter 3, I discussed research demonstrating that negative affect triggers nostalgia. When people are in a bad mood or experiencing a psychological state associated with negative affect (e.g., loneliness), they turn to nostalgia. The results discussed in the current chapter suggest that nostalgia serves a mood-repair function (see Sedikides et al., 2015b). That is, negative affect leads to nostalgia and nostalgia leads to positive mood. However, additional research is needed to fully test the mood-repair potential of nostalgia. For example, as previously mentioned, researchers have yet to manipulate mood and nostalgia in a single experiment to determine how nostalgia influences affect after a negative mood induction. Since negatively-valenced affective experiences trigger nostalgia and nostalgia generally increases positive affect, nostalgia should serve to both decrease negative and increase positive affect after a negative mood induction.

Research on affect regulation indicates that people are motivated to engage in mood-repair following affectively negative experiences (for reviews see Gross, 1998; Koole, 2009; Larsen, 2000; Thayer, 1997). Studies have identified a wide range of activities that people can engage in to repair mood such as mindfulness-based stress reduction (Grossman, Niemann, Schmidt, & Walach, 2004), meditation (Rubia, 2009), physical exercise (Stathopoulou, Powers, Berry, Smits, & Otto, 2006) and art-making (Dalebroux, Goldstein, & Winner, 2008). Some such activities may relate to nostalgia. For example, researchers have found that listening to music is a common method of mood regulation (Thayer, Newman, & McClain, 1994). As previously discussed, music is a potent trigger of nostalgia

(Barret *et al.*, 2010) and thus perhaps nostalgia-inducing music helps people counter negative emotions. Research also indicates that people often recruit positive memories following a sadness induction as a method of mood repair (Josephson, 1996). Such research further suggests that nostalgia may serve a mood-regulation function. Future research is needed to test the potential for nostalgia to regulate mood and help people cope with the life challenges and stressors that lead to negative affective states.

5
THE SOCIAL FUNCTIONS OF NOSTALGIA

Humans are social animals. Our entire lives, we depend on others. Babies and small children require the caregiving of their parents to survive and thrive. As we develop and become more physically independent, we continue to rely on our parents as well as other adults to educate and prepare us for adult life. And as fully developed adults we often still benefit from the mentorship of others and are at our best when we are working cooperatively within teams or groups in pursuit of common goals. Humans have been able to dominate the planet, in part, by collectively harnessing our intellectual capacities – by working together. Thus, even when we are at the height of our individual abilities as healthy adults, we need other people. We also require others or at least one other to pass on our genes. So even at the most basic level of genetic replication, our survival depends on other human beings. Therefore, much of what we do in our lives is driven by a strong desire to find and maintain social bonds. We need to belong.

In this chapter, I discuss how nostalgia contributes to people's efforts to meet belongingness needs. First, to set the stage for how nostalgia relates to social pursuits, I provide a brief overview of literature that illustrates the importance of interpersonal relationships for adaptive functioning. I then consider research testing the assertion that nostalgia is useful in helping people meet their belongingness needs. As discussed in Chapter 3, belongingness threats (e.g., loneliness) trigger nostalgia. But how does nostalgia impact perceived social connectedness and how people think about and treat others? Subsequently, I describe emerging research linking nostalgia to social goals and behavior. Nostalgia involves reflecting on the past, often past interpersonal experiences, so how does this activity impact current and future social pursuits? Does nostalgia, by orienting people towards days gone by, inhibit present and future relational opportunities? Or does nostalgia mobilize the social self?

Humans as Social Animals

Considering the importance of social bonds, it is not surprising that a considerable amount of human behavior is driven by belongingness needs (Baumeister & Leary, 1995; Maslow, 1954). In fact, within the field of social psychology there is an extensive and ever-growing literature on the many ways that social needs influence attitudes, emotions, motivation, behavior, and health. Collectively, this research demonstrates that attaining and maintaining close interpersonal bonds is critical for both psychological and physical health (Baumeister & Leary, 1995; Cacioppo & Hawkley, 2003). When people feel loved and supported by others, they are happier and healthier (Cohen, 2004). They are more able to cope with life's challenges (Thoits, 1995), better at self-regulating (Dewall, Baumeister, & Vohs, 2008), and more motivated to take on new challenges and explore the world around them (Green & Campbell, 2000). Relationships may even influence longevity. People live longer if they are socially involved (House, Landis, & Umberson, 1988; Steptoe, Shankar, Demakakos, & Wardle, 2013).

Likewise, when people experience social rejection or loneliness, they perceive life as less meaningful (Stillman *et al.*, 2009), are less empathetic towards others (DeWall & Baumeister, 2006), more inclined to make poor choices (Baumeister, DeWall, Ciarocco, & Twenge, 2005), and generally less motivated (Twenge, Catanese, & Baumeister, 2003). Feeling ostracized or alone is also a significant risk factor for mental illness (Hawkley & Cacioppo, 2010). In short, people need social connections. We are wired to seek out relationships with others. And these relationships are crucial for adaptive functioning.

How Does Nostalgia Affect Perceived Social Connectedness?

Nostalgia clearly has social implications. First, as discussed in Chapter 2, nostalgic memories are highly social in nature. When people reflect nostalgically on the past, they typically bring to mind experiences that involve close ones (Abeyta *et al.*, 2015d; Holak & Havlena, 1992; Wildschut *et al.*, 2006). Nostalgic memories are often focused on family holidays and vacations, weddings, graduation ceremonies and parties, dances, romantic dates or getaways, team-based sporting events, and social outings with close friends. It is rare for a nostalgic memory to not involve close ones. Think about the experiences from your own life that make you nostalgic. My guess is that most of these nostalgic memories involve family, romantic partners, or good friends.

Second, as discussed in Chapter 3, threats to belongingness inspire nostalgia. When people are asked to describe the circumstances under which they become nostalgic, it is common for them to report experiences of feeling lonely (Wildschut *et al.*, 2006). Similarly, loneliness is positively correlated with trait nostalgia: lonely people are nostalgia prone (Zhou *et al.*, 2008). Likewise, the need to belong positively correlates with trait nostalgia: people who prioritize or are especially motivated by belongingness needs are nostalgia prone (Seehusen *et al.*, 2013). In other words, those whose belongingness needs are not being met and those who are highly sensitive to those needs tend to be highly nostalgic. Further, experimental manipulations that induce feelings of loneliness (Wildschut *et al.*, 2006; Zhou *et al.*, 2008) and social exclusion (Seehusen *et al.*, 2013) trigger nostalgia.

People turn to nostalgia when their social needs are not being met, but what does nostalgia do in relation to those needs? Is nostalgia merely an attractive distraction to take people's minds off of their social struggles? Might nostalgia actually be problematic and intensify feelings of loneliness because it reminds people of social connections from the past that are not presently available? Or is nostalgia good for social health? That is, does it help resolve belongingness concerns by making people feel socially connected? A number of studies have now addressed these questions.

Scholars have identified two distinct types of belongingness compensatory strategies: direct and indirect (Gardner, Pickett, & Knowles, 2005). Direct strategies are employed when people are afforded opportunities to interact with others. That is, direct strategies involve efforts to meet belongingness needs by connecting to other people. When given the chance, people will attempt to form, maintain, and repair relationships to meet belongingness needs. Indirect strategies are employed when people are not afforded opportunities to interact with others. These strategies involve the use of mental representations of social bonds to affirm belongingness.

Sedikides *et al.* (2004) proposed that nostalgia may operate as an indirect belongingness strategy by allowing people to revisit interpersonally fulfilling experiences from the past. That is, nostalgia provides people an opportunity to reassure themselves that they have had interpersonal successes and that they are loved and valued by others. In three studies, my colleagues and I (Wildschut *et al.*, 2006) provided the first empirical test of this proposal.

In our first study testing this social function of nostalgia, we manipulated nostalgia by having participants briefly write about and reflect on an experience of nostalgia or an ordinary experience from the recent past. Next, participants responded to items related to felt social connectedness, e.g., "Thinking about this event makes me feel loved". Results supported the assertion that nostalgia helps meet belongingness needs. Participants in the nostalgia condition reported feeling more socially connected than participants in the control condition.

In our second test of this function, after the nostalgia or ordinary recent event conditions, we administered a measure of interpersonal attachment, the Revised Experience in Close Relationships Scale (ECR-R) (Fraley, Waller, & Brennan, 2000). The ECR-R assesses the extent to which people perceive themselves as worthy of love and support (attachment-related anxiety; e.g., "I worry that romantic partners won't care about me as much as I care about them") and perceive others as responsive to their distress (attachment-related avoidance; e.g., "I am very uncomfortable with being close to romantic partners"). Though these two dimensions are largely stable over time as they represent underlying relational schemas (Scharfe & Bartholomew, 1994), we considered the possibility that nostalgia could at least temporarily influence people's attitudes about social bonds. If nostalgic memories involve interpersonal success, revisiting them might positively influence people's schemas about relationships. Results supported this idea. Participants in the nostalgia condition reported lower levels of attachment-related avoidance and anxiety than participants in the control condition.

Next, we tested the potential for nostalgia to positively impact feelings of interpersonal competence. Since nostalgic memories tend to involve experiences of interpersonal success, does reflecting on these experiences make people feel like they are competent interpersonally? To test this possibility, we induced nostalgia or an ordinary autobiographical memory as before and administered the Initiation, Disclosure, and Emotional Support subscales from the Interpersonal Competence Questionnaire (Buhrmester, Furman, Wittenberg, & Reis, 1988) to assess perceived competence in initiating social interactions and relationships (e.g., "Going to parties or gatherings where you don't know people well in order to start up new relationships"), self-disclosing personal information (e.g., "Telling a close companion how much you appreciate and care for him or her"), and providing emotional support to others (e.g., "Helping a close companion get to the heart of a problem he or she is experiencing"). Results indicated that nostalgia does inspire perceived interpersonal competence. Participants in the nostalgia condition scored higher on all three subscales than participants in the control condition.

A number of studies further demonstrate that nostalgia affirms feelings of belongingness. For example, Zhou *et al.* (2008) conducted a study in which Chinese undergraduate students brought to mind either a nostalgic or ordinary autobiographical experience and then completed the 12-item Multidimensional Scale of Perceived Social Support (Zimet, Dahlem, Zimet, & Farley, 1988), e.g., "I can count on my friends when things go wrong". As an additional measure of belongingness, participants were also asked to estimate how many friends they think would volunteer to participate in a study to help them get additional credit. Participants who engaged in nostalgia reported greater perceptions of social support than participants in the control condition. In addition, participants in the nostalgia condition listed a greater number of friends as being willing to help them get additional credit than participants in the control condition. These findings provided further confirmation in a distinct cultural context that nostalgia helps people meet belongingness needs.

Other research has further demonstrated a social function of nostalgia using distinct nostalgia cues. As discussed in Chapter 3, it is common for people to report that familiar smells that remind them of their childhood or youth make them feel nostalgic. But does scent-evoked nostalgia serve psychological functions? Most relevant for the present chapter, does it increase feelings of social connectedness? To test this, Reid *et al.* (2014) presented participants glass tubes containing oils selected from a pilot study and instructed them to smell each oil, indicate how nostalgic that scent made them feel, and complete measures which included two items assessing social connectedness ("connected to loved ones" and "loved"). Higher levels of scent-evoked nostalgia were associated with higher social connectedness.

As previously discussed in Chapter 3, music is a common trigger of nostalgia (Barret et al., 2010). When people hear songs from their youth it promotes feelings of nostalgia and people often purposely listen to such music because they enjoy these nostalgic feelings. But does nostalgic music bolster feelings of connectedness? Cheung et al. (2013) explored this possibility. In Chapter 4, I described the music manipulation utilized by Cheung and colleagues. As a reminder, each participant provided a list of songs that made her or him nostalgic and then the researchers used these lists to generate appropriate nostalgia stimuli for subsequent laboratory sessions (Routledge et al., 2011). In the lab session, participants in the nostalgia condition received lyrics from music they had previously indicated as nostalgic and participants in the control condition received another participant's nostalgic lyrics. To measure social connectedness, the researchers administered a measure in which participants were asked to indicate the extent to which these song lyrics made them feel socially connected, e.g., "connected to loved ones". Results revealed that nostalgic music promotes feelings of connectedness to others. Participants in the nostalgic music condition, relative to those in the control music condition, indicated that the song lyrics made them feel more socially connected. My colleagues and I (Routledge et al., 2011) found the same pattern of music-induced nostalgia increasing social connectedness and I describe this research in more detail in Chapter 7 when discussing the existential functions of nostalgia.

In addition, Hepper et al. (2012) tested for a social connectedness function of nostalgia in their research using an experimental induction distinguishing central from peripheral characteristics of nostalgia (see Chapter 4). As a reminder, participants in a high nostalgia condition were presented with words representing characteristics central to the experience of nostalgia (e.g., "memory", "the past", and "longing/yearning") and participants in the low nostalgia condition were presented with words representing characteristics peripheral to the experience of nostalgia (e.g., "homesickness", "mixed feelings", and "comfort/warmth"). Participants then responded to items assessing social connectedness (Routledge et al., 2011; Wildschut et al., 2010). Echoing the other findings already discussed, nostalgia increased feelings of connectedness.

These are just a few examples of the many studies representing different age and cultural groups demonstrating that nostalgia increases feelings of social connectedness (see Sedikides et al., 2015b). Nostalgia does not undermine a sense of belongingness. It makes people feel loved, supported, and socially competent.

Zhou and colleagues further considered a social function of nostalgia by testing the proposition that loneliness leads to nostalgia and nostalgia in turn counteracts loneliness by bolstering feelings of social support. In other words, based on the findings that loneliness triggers nostalgia and nostalgia increases perceived belongingness, Zhou and colleagues hypothesized a belongingness compensatory function of nostalgia. To test such a model, in one study, the researchers administered to migrant Chinese adolescents (mean age = 11) the UCLA Loneliness Scale (Russell, 1996), a nostalgia proneness scale (Routledge et al., 2008), and the 12-item Multidimensional Scale of Perceived Social Support (Zimet et al., 1988) used by Wildschut et al. (2006) to test the social function of nostalgia. Results supported the belongingness compensatory hypothesis. Not surprisingly, loneliness was negatively associated with perceived social support. Lonely people do not believe that others care about and want to support them. However, loneliness was positively associated with nostalgia. That is, consistent with the assertion that loneliness triggers nostalgia (Wildschut et al., 2006), lonely people tended to be highly nostalgic. Further, nostalgia was positively associated with perceived social support and, critically, the relationship between loneliness and perceived social support became significantly more negative when nostalgia was entered as a control variable. In other words, nostalgia suppresses the relationship between loneliness and perceived social support. Nostalgia helps lonely people restore feelings of belongingness.

In a subsequent study, Zhou and colleagues tested the belongingness compensatory model with an experimental induction of loneliness. Specifically, undergraduate Chinese students were randomly assigned to the loneliness manipulation used by Wildschut et al. (2006: see chapter 3). As a reminder, this manipulation involves having participants complete a loneliness questionnaire and then providing them with feedback suggesting that they are high or low (relative to their peers) in loneliness. Participants then completed measures of nostalgia (Routledge et al., 2008) and perceived social support (Zimet et al., 1988). Replicating the previous study, participants in the high loneliness condition evidenced increased feelings of nostalgia and decreased perceptions of social support relative to participants in the low loneliness condition. Loneliness makes people feel less connected, but it also inspires nostalgia. Critically, the effect of the loneliness induction on perceived social support was significantly stronger when nostalgia was entered as a control variable. Again, nostalgia countered the effects of loneliness on perceptions of social support.

In short, the available evidence supports the assertion that nostalgia serves an indirect belongingness function. Nostalgia generates feelings of connectedness, reinforces attachment security, bolsters perceived interpersonal competence, and elevates feelings of social support. Moreover, nostalgia counteracts belongingness threats. When people experience loneliness they utilize nostalgia which in turn reaffirms perceived connectedness. But just how far do the social benefits of nostalgia go?

How Does Nostalgia Influence Social Action?

As just discussed, a growing body of research demonstrates that nostalgia contributes positively to perceptions of belongingness. Though there are clearly benefits to having perceptions of social connectedness, perceiving that one has people he or she can turn to and depend on is not necessarily the same as actually having people to turn to and depend on. Indirect means of meeting social needs are temporary solutions. People ultimately benefit most from finding and maintaining actual relationships. People need to be part of a broader social fabric. This poses the question: how does nostalgia influence social motivation and behavior? Is nostalgia an experience that simply makes people feel loved and supported, or is it an experience that orients people towards social endeavors? Said differently, is nostalgia merely a psychological stopgap, a resource that temporarily mitigates the pain of thwarted belongingness? Or might nostalgia positively influence people's efforts to connect to others? A number of studies have now considered various ways that nostalgia can influence social motivation, goals, pro-social behavior, and intergroup attitudes. I now review these distinct lines of inquiry.

Social Motivation and Goals

An important question regarding the social utility of nostalgia is whether or not its interpersonal benefits go beyond the perception of belongingness. Sure, nostalgia makes people feel loved and socially valued, but do these feelings inspire social behavior? In popular culture nostalgia is often characterized as reflective of being stuck in the past. From this vantage point, one might propose that nostalgia would actually undermine social motivation. If mentally time travelling to personally cherished past interpersonal experiences serves the function of making people feel socially connected in the present, then perhaps engaging in nostalgia acts as a barrier to present and future social ambitions. Why go out and meet new people or pursue interpersonal goals if a dose of nostalgia can satiate your belongingness needs? In this way, nostalgia may prove problematic to our social lives. By focusing our attention on the past to meet interpersonal needs, nostalgia may prevent us from pursuing social opportunities in the present and laying the groundwork for future social successes.

However, another possibility is that nostalgia mobilizes the social self. When belongingness needs are threatened, people are motivated to seek out social connections (e.g., Maner, DeWall, Baumeister, & Schaller, 2007). However, threats to belongingness can also undermine social connectedness goals. For example, experiences of social exclusion can decrease motivation (Twenge, Catanese, & Baumeister, 2003), cooperation (Twenge *et al.*, 2007), and empathy towards others (DeWall & Baumeister, 2006). Social exclusion also depletes self-regulatory resources (Baumeister, DeWall, Ciarocco, & Twenge, 2005; Twenge, Catanese, & Baumeister, 2002) and may thus undermine people's ability to regulate their behavior in ways that would lead to positive social outcomes. Further, when people are lonely they often lack the social confidence needed to pursue social goals (e.g., Jones, Freemon, & Goswick, 1981). And loneliness is a risk factor for mental illnesses such as depression (e.g., Cacioppo, Hawkley, & Thisted, 2010;

Cacioppo *et al.*, 2006) which can undercut interpersonal pursuits. However, if nostalgia counteracts experiences of exclusion and loneliness by promoting feelings of social connectedness, then it may contribute positively to social motivation and behavior. That is, nostalgia might bring online the social self and push people towards others.

In a recent series of studies, we (Abeyta *et al.* 2015b) examined the effects of nostalgia on social goals and aspirations. In an initial study, we sought to determine if there was a relationship between nostalgia and interpersonal goals. We administered to a sample of American university students a measure of nostalgia (Batcho, 1995) and items assessing relationship aspirations (Kasser & Ryan, 1996). Specifically, the relationship aspirations measure involved having participants indicate the extent to which they find specific relationship goals (e.g., having good friends) to be important, the extent to which they believed they would succeed at these relationship goals in the future, and the extent to which they had already accomplished these relationship goals. We observed that nostalgia was significantly and positively correlated with how important people believe relationship goals are and how confident they are that they will accomplish these goals in the future. However, nostalgia was unrelated to people's beliefs that they have already accomplished relationship goals.

In a second study, we (Abeyta *et al.*, 2015b) found identical patterns with an experimental induction of nostalgia. Specifically, as in previous research (e.g., Wildschut *et al.*, 2006), we manipulated nostalgia by having participants bring to mind and briefly write about an experience that made them nostalgic or an ordinary experience. Subsequently, participants completed the relationship aspirations measure just described. Nostalgia increased how important people believed relationship goals are as well as the extent to which they believed they would accomplish these goals in the future. Nostalgia did not, however, influence the extent to which people believed they had accomplished relationship goals already. The results from these two studies suggest that nostalgia mobilizes the social self by making people prioritize relationship goals and increasing confidence that they can successfully complete these goals. However, nostalgia does not appear to bias people's views of past relationship accomplishments: in both studies nostalgia was unrelated to whether or not people believed they had already been successful in the interpersonal domain. In other words, nostalgia does not simply make people see their social lives in a more positive light, it specifically promotes a positive social view that could be helpful in present and future interpersonal pursuits.

Nostalgia promotes the pursuit of interpersonal goals. Thus, it appears that nostalgia triggers a social approach orientation. We (Abeyta *et al.*, 2015b) tested this assumption directly by experimentally inducing nostalgia and measuring social approach motivation. In this study, participants brought to mind and wrote about a nostalgic experience, an ordinary past experience, or a positive past experience. We included a positive past condition to help control for the possibility that nostalgia would increase social approach motivation by increasing positive mood. We then assessed social approach motivation with a state version of the friendship-approach subscale of the Elliot, Gable, and Mapes (2006) friendship approach/avoidance goal measure. This measure is based on Gable's (2006) hierarchical model of social approach/avoidance motivation which defines social goals as "lower-level cognitive representations that direct individuals toward potential positive relational outcomes or away from potential negative relational outcomes" (Elliot et al., 2006, p. 379). Specifically, this measure assesses four approach friendship goals (e.g., "Trying to deepen my relationships with my friends") and four avoidance friendship goals (e.g., "Trying to avoid disagreements and conflicts with my friends"). Participants were instructed to indicate how much they wanted to pursue each of the four friendship approach goals based on how they were currently feeling (e.g, "I feel that I want to move toward growth and development in my friendships"). Supporting the proposal that nostalgia increases social approach motivation, participants in the nostalgia condition reported significantly greater friendship approach motivation than participants in both the ordinary and past positive conditions.

As previously discussed, nostalgic memories tend to be social memories. Thus, perhaps a key feature of nostalgia's capacity to mobilize the social self is its sociality. That is, nostalgia for social-related past experiences may mobilize the social self to a greater extent than nostalgia for non-social related past experiences. In our next study, we (Abeyta et al., 2015b) explored this possibility. Specifically, we administered the Batcho nostalgia inventory (Batcho, 1995) and a measure of social goal striving to American undergraduate participants. For the social goal striving measure, participants were informed that the University Office of Student Life wanted to assess interest in a new student program designed to connect university students socially. Participants read a description of the program which provided examples of the events the program might host (e.g., game nights, concerts) and then responded to items assessing interest in the program.

In this study we chose the Batcho nostalgia inventory because it measures the extent to which people feel nostalgia in a number of distinct domains. Some of these domains are clearly social, e.g., "my family" and "someone I loved". Some of the domains are less social, e.g., "my childhood toys" and "TV shows/movies". Using this measure thus allowed us to examine more specifically the role of nostalgia for social aspects of the past in social approach motivation. First, further supporting the proposal that nostalgia motivates social approach, there was a positive and significant relationship between overall nostalgia (the entire Batcho scale) and interest in the university program designed to socially connect students. However, when the nostalgia scale was divided into high social and low social subscales, only the high social subscale remained as a significant predictor of social approach. The more participants reported being nostalgic for aspects of their past that were clearly social in nature, the more they were interested in the university program designed to socially connect students. The results of this study suggest that the sociality of nostalgia plays an important role in mobilizing the social self.

In our next study, we (Abeyta et al., 2015b) wanted to replicate this effect with a non-student sample and a more behavioral measure of social approach. In this study, we recruited adult participants for an online study. Participants completed the Batcho nostalgia inventory (Batcho, 1995) and a measure of social motivation. We designed this measure to get us closer to actual social behavior. Specifically, participants were informed that we wanted to gauge interest in and promote future research studies we planned to conduct. We then provided them with a description of four different studies they could potentially participate in. Two of the studies were social in nature. One was titled "Personality and Social Interaction" and the other was titled "Solving Problems with Others". The descriptions of these studies indicated that participants would be interacting with other people as part of the study. The remaining two studies were non-social. One was titled "Cognitive Problem Solving" and the other was titled "Personality and Opinions about Music". The descriptions of these studies indicated that participants would work alone during the study. After each study description, participants responded to items assessing their interest in being recruited for the study.

Results from this study further indicated that nostalgia mobilizes the social self. Higher nostalgia scores were significantly associated with interest in participating in future social, but not non-social, research studies. Consistent with the previous study, when the nostalgia scale was divided into high and low social dimensions, only highly social nostalgia was significantly associated with interest in participating in social research studies. When people are nostalgic about aspects of their past that are highly social in nature, they are motivated to pursue future opportunities to interact and work with others.

After evidencing a relationship between nostalgia and indicators of social approach motivation and specifying that it is social nostalgia in particular that mobilizes the social self, we (Abeyta et al., 2015b) endeavored to elucidate the process through which nostalgia motivates social approach by assessing social efficacy as a potential mediator. Since we had previously found that nostalgia increases confidence in one's ability to successfully accomplish a social goal, we proposed that it is the feelings of social efficacy that people gain by revisiting past interpersonal experiences that motivates the pursuit of interpersonal goals in the present. Therefore, in our next experiment, we manipulated nostalgia, measured social efficacy, and assessed interpersonal goal motivation.

In this study, to manipulate nostalgia, we created a novel induction. Specifically, we recruited adult participants to take part in an online study and asked them to search Youtube for a song. In the nostalgia condition, we instructed participants to find and listen to a song from their past that made them feel nostalgic. In the control condition, we asked participants to find and listen to a song that they really liked but only recently heard for the first time. The control condition was designed to rule out the possibility that any effect may be due to listening to music or being exposed to positive mood inducing stimuli. A nostalgia manipulation check ensured that this induction was successful: participants in the nostalgia song condition reported significantly higher levels of state nostalgia than participants in the control condition.

Following the manipulation, participants completed a measure of social efficacy that was modeled after similar domain specific self-efficacy scales, e.g., "Rate your confidence in your ability to maintain social relationships". Finally, participants completed a measure of motivation to pursue a social goal. Specifically, participants were asked to list a social goal that they would like to achieve and then responded to items assessing their motivation for pursuing the listed goal, e.g., "How motivated are you to pursue this goal?", "How much time will you dedicate to attaining this goal?". As predicted, participants in the nostalgia condition reported being significantly more motivated to pursue an interpersonal goal than participants in the control condition. Participants in the nostalgia condition also reported significantly higher levels of social efficacy than participants in the control condition. Further, the effect of nostalgia on social motivation was mediated by social efficacy. Thus, nostalgia appears to inspire social motivation because it increases people's confidence in their social abilities.

Belongingness needs can be challenged by interpersonal conflict. We (Abeyta et al., 2015b) therefore sought to further test the social motivational power of nostalgia by examining the potential for nostalgia to increase motivation to resolve a relationship conflict. Further, we again wanted to test the potential for social efficacy to serve a mediating role. In this study, we randomly assigned American university student participants to the nostalgic or control Youtube music search task previously described. Next, participants completed the social efficacy measure previously described. Finally, participants were presented with a friendship conflict task. Specifically, in this task, participants were instructed to imagine getting into a disagreement with a close friend, the type of conflict that would cause a significant amount of distress and interpersonal distance between them. In other words, we wanted participants to imagine a relationship conflict that could threaten feelings of belongingness. After imagining this conflict, participants responded to items assessing how optimistic they felt about being able to resolve such a conflict (e.g., "I would feel optimistic that my close friend and I could completely resolve this conflict") and items assessing their motivation to proactively resolve such a conflict (e.g., "I would dedicate myself to solving this conflict").

Results further evidenced a social motivating function of nostalgia. Participants who engaged in nostalgia, compared to those in the control condition, reported greater optimism about resolving an interpersonal conflict as well greater motivation to proactively resolve the conflict. In addition, both of these effects were mediated by social efficacy. Nostalgia contributes to people's social confidence, which in turn makes them optimistic about resolving and motivated to resolve interpersonal conflicts.

Having established that nostalgia mobilizes the social self, we (Abeyta et al., 2015b) then sought to determine if nostalgia is a resource that people naturally turn to when they are struggling with interpersonal goals. That is, if nostalgia increases social efficacy and motivation, might people utilize nostalgia when they are failing to meet interpersonal aspirations?

As a first step to test this possibility, we considered whether or not relationship pessimism triggers nostalgia. To test this, we conducted an experiment in which American university students were randomly assigned to one of two pessimism conditions. Specifically, participants were told that they were going to complete a perspective taking task. In one condition, they were presented with information suggesting that were good reasons to be pessimistic about their future relationships. After reading this information, participants were instructed to take the writer's perspective and write down five reasons why they should be pessimistic about future relationships. In the control condition, participants completed a similar exercise regarding pessimism about future technology. That is, in both conditions, participants were asked to take on a pessimistic outlook. However, what varied was whether or not this outlook was related to social ambitions. Finally, participants completed a state measure of nostalgia. We predicted that since nostalgia is a social focused experience, it would be triggered to a greater extent by a social threat. Results supported this prediction. Participants in the relationship pessimism condition were significantly more nostalgic than participants in the technology pessimism condition. When relationship aspirations are under threat, people turn to nostalgia.

The next question we (Abeyta et al., 2015b) asked was whether or not nostalgia effectively restores social motivation when people have pessimistic outlooks about their future relationships. To test this, we focused on the trait of loneliness. Lonely individuals want social connections, but feel like they lack them (Hawkley & Cacioppo, 2010; Weiss, 1973). As a result, people high in loneliness tend to be pessimistic about their relationship prospects and tend to adopt avoidance goals aimed at preventing loss of affiliation rather than approach goals aimed at achieving affiliation (Gable, 2006). As previously discussed, loneliness triggers nostalgia and in turn nostalgia restores feelings of social connectedness (Zhou et al., 2008). Thus, nostalgia might serve as a motivating resource for lonely individuals by making them more optimistic about their future relationships.

To investigate this possibility, we assessed trait loneliness (Russell, 1996) in an American undergraduate sample, assigned participants to the nostalgia or control Youtube music task previously described, and measured relationship optimism by altering the wording of an established general optimism measure, i.e., the Revised Life Orientations Test (LOT-R) (Scheier, Carver, & Bridges, 1994) to focus on relationship-oriented optimism, e.g., "I'm feeling optimistic about my future interpersonal relationships". Results supported the proposal that nostalgia counteracts the effects of loneliness on relationship optimism. Specifically, as one would predict, in the non-nostalgic control condition, there was a significant negative relationship between loneliness and relationship optimism: lonely people are not optimistic about the future interpersonal ambitions. However, this effect became non-significant in the nostalgia condition. Nostalgia offers lonely people hope that they will have success in the interpersonal domain.

In a recent study, my colleagues and I (Stephan et al., 2014) found behavioral evidence that nostalgia mobilizes the social self. Chinese undergraduate university students were randomly assigned to write about a nostalgic or ordinary past experience (Wildschut et al., 2006). Next, they were informed that as part of the study they would have a brief conversation with another participant. Participants were then asked to help prepare the room for the social interaction by setting up a couple of chairs in the room while the experimenter went to fetch the other participant. After each participant placed the chairs, the experimenter returned to the room and measured the distance between the chairs. We proposed that if nostalgia promotes social motivation then those asked to reflect on an experience of nostalgia, relative to those in the control condition, would place the chairs closer together. That is, nostalgia would increase approach-oriented social behavior. The results supported this prediction. Participants in the nostalgia condition placed the chairs closer together than participants in the control condition.

In all, a number of studies demonstrate that the social function of nostalgia is not merely about the perception of social connectedness. Nostalgia promotes social goal pursuit. When people nostalgically reflect on the past, they prioritize relationship aspirations, feel more confident about their social abilities, hold more optimistic beliefs about future relationships, are more motivated to pursue interpersonal opportunities, feel more confident about resolving relationship conflicts, and demonstrate social approach-oriented behaviors. Further, when people are struggling to meet belongingness needs they become nostalgic, which in turn restores a needed sense of optimism about future interpersonal opportunities.

Nostalgia and Pro-Social Behavior

Feelings of belongingness can increase people's willingness to help others (e.g., Mikulince & Shaver, 2001; Pavey, Greitemeyer, & Sparks, 2011). Since nostalgia increases feelings of belongingness, it might also promote pro-social behavior. In a series of studies, Zhou et al. (2012) explored this possibility. First, they tested whether or not nostalgia would increase people's willingness to donate their time and money to a charity that helped people in need. Undergraduate Chinese students brought to mind a nostalgic or ordinary experience and then wrote down four keywords related to this experience (Wildschut et al., 2006). To measure intentions to donate to a charity, the researchers presented to participants a one-page description of a fictitious non-profit organization that existed to help young victims of the May 2008 Wenchuan earthquake. After reading the description of the charity, participants were instructed to write down the number of hours and amount of money they would be willing to donate to this charity. Results indicated that nostalgia increased self-reported willingness to donate time and money to a charity that helps people in need.

In a second study, Zhou and colleagues sought to replicate the effect of nostalgia on charitable intentions and considered the potential for this effect to be mediated by feelings of empathy. The researchers induced nostalgia as before and then administered an emotional state assessment that contained items related to empathy (e.g., "sympathetic", "compassionate", "soft-hearted", "tender"; e.g., Batson, Fultz, & Shoenrade, 1987). Finally, participants indicated their willingness to donate time and money to the charity. As in the first study, nostalgia increased charitable intentions. In addition, nostalgia increased feelings of empathy. Finally, feelings of empathy mediated the effect of nostalgia on charitable intentions. Nostalgia makes people more charitable because it promotes empathy.

In two additional studies, Zhou and colleagues replicated the mediation path of nostalgia increasing charitable intentions via empathy using a different fictitious charity (to show that the effect was not specific to one charitable outlet; Study 3) and a broader sample (people ranging in age from 16 to 62 and representing a range of nationalities; Study 4). In all, these findings demonstrate that nostalgia not only makes people feel connected to others, it makes them feel empathic towards others and more willing to help others.

In a final study, Zhou and colleagues sought to determine if they could use what they learned about nostalgia increasing charitable intentions to fashion a charity appeal that would persuade people to engage in charitable behavior. First, though asking people to bring to mind and write about a nostalgic experience is an effective way to induce feelings of nostalgia in the laboratory, this procedure does not represent how nostalgia is normally experienced in people's daily lives and may not be the most pragmatic way of employing nostalgia to promote pro-social behavior in an applied setting. Further, feeling empathic towards others and expressing a willingness to help does not necessarily mean that one will engage in helping behavior (Batson, 1991). Thus, the researchers wanted to test more directly whether or not nostalgia would lead to charitable behavior and if they could produce this effect with a nostalgia induction that would better lend itself to real-world application.

To accomplish these goals, the researchers created two versions of a charity appeal to be distributed to participants. Both versions contained information, including pictures, about a charity to help young earthquake victims. In one condition, however, the charity appeal contained wording intended to activate feelings of nostalgia. For example, this appeal contained the statement "Those Were the Days: Restoring the Past for the Children in Wenchaun". In the control condition, the charity appeal did not make any reference to the past. Instead, it contained statements such as "Now is the Time: Build the Future for Children in Wenchaun". A pilot study confirmed that the nostalgia charity appeal elevated state nostalgia relative to the non-nostalgic charity appeal.

The experiment involved undergraduate and graduate Chinese students completing a number of unrelated laboratory tasks that provided a reason for the researchers to compensate them financially. It was when participants believed the study was over and they were paid that the true experiment began. As participants left the laboratory, they encountered another individual (a research assistant) who handed them either the nostalgia or non-nostalgia flyer for the charity. There was also a collection box in the room to allow participants to make a financial donation to the charity. In support of the assertion that nostalgia increases charitable giving, participants who received the nostalgia-based charity flyer donated significantly more money to the charity than participants who received the non-nostalgia charity flyer. The findings of this study provide compelling evidence that nostalgia promotes pro-social behavior. Nostalgia increases empathy, charitable intentions, and charitable behavior.

Other research indicates that nostalgia more broadly makes people helpful. Specifically, in an experiment my colleagues and I (Stephan et al., 2014) conducted, we created a situation to afford participants an opportunity to help someone. Undergraduate Chinese students completed the nostalgia or ordinary autobiographical event writing tasks (Wildschut et al., 2006). Following this task, a research assistant entered the laboratory room carrying a box of pencils and a folder of papers. In what appeared to be an accident, the experimenter spilled the box of pencils on the floor. We were interested in the extent to which participants would help the experimenter pick up the pencils. Does nostalgia inspire people to help others? Results indicate that the answer is yes. Participants in the nostalgia condition picked up more pencils than participants in the control condition.

Nostalgia and Intergroup Attitudes

Considering that nostalgia increases social approach and pro-social behavior, it might also have consequences for intergroup relations. Researchers have recently considered this possibility. In two studies, Turner, Wildschut, and Sedikides (2012) considered the potential for nostalgia to increase positive attitudes towards a stigmatized group. They specifically proposed that having people reflect on a nostalgic experience that involved interacting with an overweight individual would increase positive attitudes towards people who were overweight.

In the first study, British university students who were not visibly overweight were asked to bring to mind and briefly write about a nostalgic experience involving an interaction with an overweight person or an ordinary past experience involving an interaction with an overweight person. Participants then completed a measure of inclusion of the outgroup in the self (Aron, Aron, & Smollan, 1992) which involved selecting from a list the pair of overlapping circles that best represented their relationship with the outgroup (i.e., overweight people). The idea is that the greater the overlap between the circles, the more the individual is including the outgroup in the self. Next, participants completed a measure of outgroup trust (adapted from Tam, Hewstone, Kenworthy, & Cairns, 2009) that included items such as "Right now, I am able to trust an overweight person as much as any other person". Finally, participants completed an outgroup attitudes questionnaire that included three components: affective, cognitive, and behavioral. The affective component involved participants indicating their feelings towards overweight people, e.g., cold-warm, hostile-friendly (Wright, Aron, McLaughlin-Volpe, & Ropp, 1997). The cognitive component involved participants reporting their beliefs about the extent to which people have personal control over their weight, e.g., "People have control over their weight". The behavioral component involved participants indicating their behavioral intentions toward overweight people, e.g., "Right now, when thinking of overweight people I want to avoid them" (Mackie, Devos, & Smith, 2000). Responses on these subscales were highly correlated. Thus, the researchers combined them to create a single index reflecting attitudes towards the overweight.

The results indicated that, as predicted, reflecting on a nostalgic experience that involved an overweight individual led to more positive attitudes toward people who were overweight. In addition, the researchers found that this effect was mediated by inclusion of the outgroup in the self and outgroup trust. When one's nostalgic experience includes a member of a stigmatized group, the nostalgic individual perceives that group as more similar to themselves, is more trusting of that group, and generally holds more positive attitudes about that group.

In a second study, the researchers replicated the effect of nostalgia on attitudes towards overweight individuals and also considered additional mediators. Specifically, after the nostalgia or control induction, participants again completed measures of inclusion of the outgroup in the self and outgroup trust. They then also completed an assessment of intergroup anxiety that involved rating how they would feel (e.g., "awkward", "relaxed") if they had to interact with an unknown overweight person (Stephan & Stephan, 1985) as well as a measure of common ingroup identity (e.g., "To what extent do normal weight people and overweight people feel like members of the same group?").

As in the previous study, reflecting on a nostalgic experience that involved an overweight individual led to more positive attitudes toward people who were overweight. In addition, inclusion of the outgroup in the self, intergroup anxiety, and common ingroup identity were all significant mediators of the effect of nostalgia on outgroup attitudes when considered individually and simultaneously. Outgroup trust was a significant mediator when considered individually, but did not remain significant when considered simultaneously with the other mediators.

In two other studies, Turner, Wildschut, Sedikides, & Gheorghiu (2013), tested the effect of nostalgia on intergroup attitudes among British university students using a different stigmatized group, mentally ill individuals. In their first study, Turner and colleagues utilized a manipulation created by Hepper et al. (2012) and discussed earlier in this chapter. Specifically, participants were told they were going to receive a list of several features that characterized experiences and memories from one's life. Participants in the nostalgia condition were presented with words that represent central features of nostalgia and participants in the control condition were presented with words that represented peripheral features of nostalgia. Prior to receiving the nostalgia or control induction, participants were instructed to recall an interaction with a person who they knew well and who had a mental illness.

Following the nostalgia or control induction, participants were instructed to think about an experience involving this individual that could be characterized as relevant to the words they just received. Said differently, nostalgia participants were to bring to mind an experience high in the central features of nostalgia that involved an interaction with someone close who had a mental illness. Control participants also brought to mind a past experience with someone close who had a mental illness, but this experience involved features more peripheral to nostalgia. All participants wrote a brief description of this experience.

Subsequently, participants completed a nostalgia manipulation check (Routledge et al., 2008), the inclusion of the outgroup (i.e., people with a mental illness) in the self-measure previously described, and a feeling thermometer in which they reported how positively they felt toward people with mental illness (Haddock, Zanna, & Esses, 1993). Results indicated that the manipulation of nostalgia was successful. Participants who received the list of words central to nostalgia reported significantly higher state nostalgia than participants who received the list of words that were peripheral to nostalgia. Critically, conceptually replicating the work by Turner et al. (2012) on attitudes towards overweight individuals, results indicated that nostalgia increased the inclusion of the outgroup in the self and positive attitudes toward people with mental illness. Further, the effect of nostalgia on outgroup attitudes was mediated by inclusion of the outgroup in the self.

In their second study, Turner et al. (2013) sought to replicate this effect but also broaden the analysis to more explicitly measure an element of the relationship between nostalgia and outgroup attitudes that they assumed existed. Specifically, because nostalgia typically inspires feelings of social connectedness, the researchers assumed that such feelings contribute to the effects of nostalgia on the variables that lead to positive attitudes about outgroups, e.g., inclusion of the outgroup in the self. However, this assumed relationship had yet to be tested. The researchers induced nostalgia. In this study, nostalgia was manipulated with the method utilized by Turner et al. (2012), in which participants were presented with the definition of nostalgia and asked to bring to mind a nostalgic experience that involved interacting with someone who had a mental illness. Participants in the control condition were asked to bring to mind an ordinary experience involving someone with a mental illness. Subsequently, they assessed social connectedness with items such as "Thinking about this interaction makes me feel connected to loved ones", inclusion of the outgroup in the self, outgroup trust, and attitudes toward people with mental illness (adapted from Wright et al., 1997).

Turner et al. (2013) hypothesized that nostalgia would increase feelings of social connectedness which would in turn contribute to inclusion of the outgroup in the self and outgroup trust, which would in turn predict positive attitudes toward people with a mental illness. A serial mediation model supported this proposal. Also, results from structural equation modeling indicated that this model had an excellent fit. The feelings of social connectedness that nostalgia generates not only benefit the person engaging in nostalgia, but also benefit members of stigmatized groups. Nostalgia expands the self in a way that promotes positive attitudes towards people who are often the victims of prejudice and discrimination.

Concluding Thoughts

In all, a number of studies utilizing distinct manipulations and measures indicate that nostalgia serves critical social functions. Nostalgic memories are typically social in nature and revisiting those memories increases perceptions of social connectedness. In this way, nostalgia is a potent indirect belongingness compensatory strategy. When people feel lonely or excluded, nostalgia helps restore feelings of connectedness. However, nostalgia is much more than an indirect compensatory strategy. Recent research indicates that nostalgia inspires behaviors that directly promote social connections. Nostalgia increases the prioritization of social goals as well as the confidence that one will achieve these goals. And this social confidence in turn increases social approach-oriented behavior. Nostalgia also inspires pro-social behavior as well as positive attitudes towards members of stigmatized groups. In this way, nostalgia does not simply make people feel connected. It inspires people to connect to, empathize with, and help others. Nostalgia brings online the social and pro-social self.

With these benefits in mind, future research should seek to further elucidate the many potential social functions of nostalgia. For instance, future research should consider whether nostalgia can mitigate negative outcomes associated with social exclusion. As previously discussed, experiences of social exclusion can decrease motivation (Twenge et al., 2003), cooperation (Twenge et al., 2007), and empathy towards others (DeWall & Baumeister, 2006). Such effects may result from the depletion of self-regulatory resources (Baumeister et al., 2005; Twenge et al., 2002). If nostalgia restores feelings of belongingness and social support following social exclusion, might it serve to preserve or restore self-regulatory resources? If so, nostalgia may offer a powerful intervention for social exclusion and loneliness.

Might nostalgia also prove useful for romantic relationships? If nostalgia expands the self, perhaps couples who regularly engage in relationship-oriented nostalgia will feel more intimately connected, more satisfied with their relationships, and benefit from greater feelings of trust (Simpson, 2007). In Chapter 8, I touch on this topic when discussing how individual differences in attachment-related avoidance interact with nostalgia to influence romantic relationship outcomes. However, to date, research has yet to consider nostalgia in romantic couples.

Similarly, future research should probe the potential for nostalgia to influence family bonds. Does feeling nostalgic about family and sharing nostalgic experiences with family members have positive effects on the family? For example, since nostalgia increases perceptions of social support (Zhou et al., 2008) as well as the prioritization of social goals (Abeyta et al., 2015b), might it help people feel more supported by and be more supportive of family? In this way, nostalgia may serve as social glue that helps keep families feeling connected.

6
THE SELF-RELATED FUNCTIONS OF NOSTALGIA

Humans are unique in their high level of self-awareness. Of course, there are other animals that have the capacity for self-awareness. However, as far as we know, no other organism matches the introspective abilities of people. We are not merely animals aware of our physical existence. We are animals highly invested in symbolic conceptions of self (Becker, 1973). We have identities. To this end, people spend a considerable amount of time and energy constructing, maintaining, and defending their conceptions of self (Sedikides & Gregg, 2003).

Further, our capacity for temporal consciousness facilitates a wide range of self-focused psychological processes (Routledge & Arndt, 2005). We are able to reflect on our past selves, to think about who we used to be. Likewise, we can draw upon past self-relevant experiences in our efforts to meet present self-related needs such as the need for self-esteem. We are also able to project the self into the future. That is, we can imagine the person we want to become or the person we fear becoming. To this end, we develop and pursue a number of self-relevant goals to invest in our future selves. When we ask our children what they want to do when they grow up, essentially we are asking them to identify a desired future self. In short, the human self is a self that involves time-related reflective processes. We do not merely exist in the present. We regularly mentally time travel to the past and future.

In this chapter, I discuss self-related functions of nostalgia. Since nostalgia involves bringing to mind cherished autobiographical experiences from one's past, it has important implications for a number of self-related motives: self-esteem, self-continuity, self-growth. In the following discussion, I consider each of these motives and the growing body of research elucidating how nostalgia serves them.

Nostalgia and Self-Esteem

Psychological research has long identified self-esteem as a fundamental human need (Pyszczynski et al., 2004). Perhaps more than any other self-related motive, people endeavor to self-enhance, to elevate their feelings of self-worth (Sedikides 1993). And this need for self-esteem has been demonstrated to be universal (Sedikides, Gaertner, & Toguchi, 2003). Further, self-esteem is a critical component of adaptive psychological functioning. Low self-esteem is associated with a wide range of psychological and physical health problems (see Sedikides & Gregg, 2008).

Considering the prevalence of self-esteem pursuit and the importance of a positive view of self for mental and physical health, much research in social psychology has been focused on identifying the various ways that people affirm a sense of self-worth (Crocker & Wolfe, 2001; Sedikides & Gregg, 2003). Numerous studies have also considered the ways that people respond to threats to self-esteem: when the self is threatened, people go to great lengths to defend it (Pyszczynski et al., 2004). Most relevant to the current analysis, recent research has identified nostalgia as a resource that people can turn to in their efforts to both enhance and defend the self.

The first consideration of how nostalgia impacts self-esteem came from our (Wildschut et al., 2006) examination of the content and functions of nostalgia. As previously discussed in Chapter 2, we observed that nostalgic memories focus both on the self and close others. However, the self plays a central role. Since the self is typically the protagonist in nostalgic memories and these memories are often focused on personally treasured or consequential life experiences, we (Wildschut et al., 2006) proposed that inducing nostalgia would increase self-esteem.

In two experiments, we (Wildschut et al., 2006) found support for this hypothesis. In both studies, university students from the UK were instructed to bring to mind and write about either a nostalgic or ordinary past experience. In the first experiment, participants then rated their agreement with statements reflective of positive self-regard ("I feel significant" and "I have high self-esteem"). In the second experiment, following the nostalgia or control condition, participants completed the Rosenberg Self-Esteem Scale, e.g., "I take a positive attitude towards myself" (Rosenberg, 1965). In both studies, participants who brought to mind a nostalgic experience reported higher self-esteem than participants who brought to mind an ordinary past experience.

Conceptual replications of these studies further demonstrate that nostalgia boosts positive self-regard. For example, Hepper et al. (2012) examined the effects of nostalgia on self-esteem using a prototype-based nostalgia induction. As previously discussed in Chapters 4 and 5, the researchers randomly assigned participants to receive a list of either central or peripheral features of nostalgia and then instructed them to bring to mind an event characterized by at least five of those features.

Participants then rated their agreement with a number of statements indicative of high self-esteem ("value myself", "have many positive qualities"). Participants in the central nostalgia features condition reported higher self-esteem than participants in the peripheral nostalgia features condition.

As previously discussed in Chapter 3, music is a common trigger of nostalgia (Barret et al., 2010). And music-related nostalgia increases positive affect and feelings of connectedness (see Chapters 4 and 5). However, does listening to the soundtracks of our youth benefit our self-esteem? Cheung et al. (2013) explored this possibility. They specifically sought to replicate the effect of nostalgia on self-esteem with a large and age-diverse (ages ranged from 14–67) Dutch community sample and a music-based nostalgia induction. Participants who were visiting a website of a popular Dutch radio and television program were invited to participate in a research study. If they were interested, they were directed to another website. Participants were randomly assigned to listen to either a nostalgic or control song performed by the Dutch artist, Wim Sonneveld. The songs were determined to be nostalgic or not in a pilot study using a different sample of Dutch participants. In the pilot study, participants listened to both songs and rated them on nostalgia. Results supported the use of the two songs as nostalgic and non-nostalgic music. In the experiment, after participants listened to one of the songs, they completed a manipulation check item and, as in previous studies (Wildschut et al., 2006), responded to items assessing self-esteem. Participants who listened to the nostalgic song reported significantly higher levels of nostalgia than participants who listened to the non-nostalgic song. Critically, listening to the nostalgic song, compared to the non-nostalgic song, elevated self-esteem.

In a follow-up study, Cheung et al. (2013) further tested the effect of nostalgic music on self-esteem. As discussed in Chapters 4 and 5, participants received lyrics from songs that either they (nostalgia condition) or another participant (control condition) had indicated as being nostalgic (Routledge et al., 2011). Participants subsequently responded to self-esteem items similar to those previously described. Participants in the nostalgia condition reported higher self-esteem than participants in the control condition. Music-evoked nostalgia elevates self-esteem.

A recent study (Reid et al., 2014) further demonstrated the self-enhancing potential of nostalgia by revealing that scents that serve as nostalgia cues can increase self-esteem. The nature of this study was described in Chapter 5. Participants smelled different oils and indicated how nostalgic that smell made them feel. They then completed measures which included two items assessing self-esteem ("feel good about myself" and "value myself"). Higher levels of scent-evoked nostalgia were associated with higher self-esteem. In all, a number of studies using a wide range of nostalgia inductions evidence that people can turn to the past to boost the present self. Nostalgia enhances the self.

Building on the idea that nostalgia boosts positive self-views, my colleagues and I (Vess et al., 2012) sought to further consider how nostalgia might influence self-relevant cognition. We proposed that nostalgia would increase the cognitive accessibility of positive self-attributes. To test this hypothesis, American university students were randomly assigned to a nostalgia or control condition. Nostalgia participants were instructed to bring to mind a nostalgic experience and participants in the control condition were instructed to bring to mind a positive event in their future. This control condition was utilized to ensure that any observed effect on the accessibility of positive self-attributes was not merely the result of bringing to mind any kind of positive self-relevant thoughts. Participants in both condition were asked to write down four keywords associated with this experience and to spend a few moments thinking about how this experience made them feel. These instructions remained on the computer screen for 30 seconds for all participants.

For the dependent measure, participants completed a Me/Not Me task (Markus, 1977) that has been used in recent research on self-concept accessibility (e.g., Schlegel, Hicks, Arndt, & King, 2009). Specifically, a series of personality traits were individually displayed to participants on a computer screen. When each trait was presented, participants were instructed to press the "Z" key (labeled Me) if the trait was descriptive of them or the "/" key (labeled Not Me) if the trait was not descriptive of them. The traits were presented in random order and remained on the screen until they were categorized. After each trait was categorized, a blank screen was presented for one second. Response latency from stimuli onset to categorization was recorded. Shorter latencies represent greater concept accessibility (Bargh & Chartrand, 2000). That is, the faster someone categorizes a trait as self-descriptive, the more accessible that trait is assumed to be because accessible traits should be easier to identify. After a number of practice trials, participants categorized 13 positive and 20 neutral traits. The positive traits were taken from a list of positive evaluative items (e.g., smart, worthy, valued) used in past work to develop an Implicit Association test of self-esteem (Greenwald & Farnham, 2000). Neutral traits were taken from those rated in the middle range of Anderson's (1968) likeability ratings of 555 personality traits, e.g., cautious, serious, talkative.

We then calculated a positive self-attribute accessibility index that controlled for individual differences in general categorization speed. Results supported the hypothesis that nostalgia increases the accessibility of positive self-attributes. Participants in the nostalgia condition evidenced faster response latencies to positive self-attributes than participants in the future positive event condition.

This research further supports the notion that nostalgia enhances the self. After nostalgic reflection, positive characteristics of the self are more accessible. Thus far, I have discussed a number of studies that provide evidence for a self-enhancing function of nostalgia. Nostalgia boosts current levels of self-esteem. However, are the self-enhancing benefits of nostalgia restricted to appraisals of one's current self? Might nostalgia also contribute to optimistic views about one's future self?

In his theoretical consideration of nostalgia, sociologist Fred Davis (1977) suggested that nostalgia may contribute to an optimistic outlook on life. Specifically, he first proposed that nostalgia enhances people's sense of current self-worth. This assertion was of course empirically validated by the research just described indicating that nostalgia elevates self-esteem. Davis went on though to argue that people's current perceptions of worth prove diagnostic for how they view the future. That is, when people make judgments about what they can expect in the future, they are likely to base these predictions, in part, on how they assess their current lives. Thus, by enhancing positive attitudes about the self in the present, nostalgia may promote positive attitudes about one's future. Indeed, research indicates that perceptions of past experiences contribute to positive future outlooks (e.g., Carnelley & Janoff-Bulman, 1992).

The research by Cheung et al. (2013) assessed the relation between nostalgia and optimism. In one study, the researchers had British undergraduate participants spend five minutes writing about either a nostalgic or ordinary experience. Subsequently, the researchers analyzed the content of these writing conditions with Linguistic and Word Count software (LIWC) (Pennebaker, Booth & Francis, 2007). They specifically focused on the proportion of words that LIWC categorized as relating to optimism, e.g., optimistic, hope, determined. In support of the assertion that nostalgia fosters optimism, results indicated that nostalgic narratives contained a significantly higher proportion of optimism-related words than non-nostalgic narratives. Relative to other types of autobiographical memories, nostalgic memories appear to involve a greater sense of optimism.

Having established that nostalgic memories often feature feelings of optimism, Cheung and colleagues conducted further studies to test whether or not engaging in nostalgia increases optimism and to explore potential mediators of this effect. In one study, participants wrote about a nostalgic or ordinary past experience (Wildschut et al., 2006) and then responded to items assessing the extent to which thinking about that experience made them optimistic about the future, e.g., "makes me feel optimistic about my future" and "gives me a feeling of hope about my future". Results supported the assertion that nostalgia inspires optimism. Bringing to mind a nostalgic experience led to greater feelings of optimism about the future than bringing to mind a non-nostalgic autobiographical experience.

Their next study was the Dutch Internet-based music study previously discussed. In this study, listening to nostalgic music increased self-esteem. After measuring self-esteem in that study, the researchers assessed optimism about the future. In addition to elevating self-esteem, music-evoked nostalgia increased optimism. Since nostalgia increased self-esteem and optimism, the researchers explored the potential for self-esteem to serve as a mediator of the relationship between nostalgia and optimism. Results supported this possibility. It is of course important to recognize that self-esteem and optimism correlate, so this mediation model is speculative. This study does, however, demonstrate that when self-esteem is elevated by nostalgia, so is optimism about the future, which is further evidence that nostalgia enhances the self.

As previously discussed, in another study involving UK undergraduate students, Cheung et al. (2013) found that presenting participants with lyrics from songs they had previously identified as nostalgic increased self-esteem. In this study, the researchers also assessed optimism. In addition, to further explore potential mediators, the researchers assessed social connectedness (discussed in Chapter 5) by asking participants to rate the extent to which the lyrics of the song made them feel "connected to loved ones", "protected", "loved", and "trust others". As predicted, participants who received the nostalgic song lyrics reported significantly higher levels of optimism than participants who received the non-nostalgic song lyrics. In addition, mediation analyses explored a number of possible models of the relationship between the measured variables. The model that best fit the data was one in which nostalgia led to higher social connectedness, which in turn elevated self-esteem, which in turn increased optimism. Again, one must use caution when interpreting these types of mediation models, but critically, this study indicates that nostalgia enhances attitudes about the present and future self. And these positive attitudes may result, in part, from nostalgia's capacity to make people feel connected to and valued by others.

Nostalgia enhances the self. However, does it offer a viable defense when the self is threatened? In other words, can people employ nostalgia to counter experiences in life that undermine positive self-views? Based on the finding that nostalgia increases the accessibility of positive self traits (Vess et al., 2012) as well as research indicating that nostalgia boosts self-esteem (e.g., Wildschut et al., 2006), we (Vess et al., 2012) proposed that nostalgia, by affirming the self, would decrease the need to employ other self-protective tactics when the self is threatened. That is, we argued that nostalgia serves a self-defensive function.

One common response to self-esteem threat is an attributional bias in which individuals are more inclined to take credit for their successes and less inclined to take credit for their failures (e.g., Campbell & Sedikides, 1999). Attributional bias can have negative consequences including reducing the likelihood of self-improvement (Alicke & Sedikides, 2009; Sedikides & Strube, 1997). How can a person grow if he or she is unwilling to take responsibility for poor performance? Might nostalgia offer an alternative means of protecting the self, thus reducing the need to be biased in a self-serving manner? We examined this possibility.

First, following previous research (McFarlin & Blascovich, 1984), we randomly assigned American university students to a difficult (negative feedback condition) or easy (positive feedback condition) purported test of analytic reasoning (The Remote Associates Test or RAT) (Mednick, 1962). Specifically, participants were given three minutes to solve 10 RAT items and upon completion of the test were provided with a scoring key to allow them to see how they performed relative to other students. That is, the scoring key provided the correct answers to each RAT item and indicated how one's score compared to other university students (scores of 0–4 labeled "*below average for University students*", 5–6 was "*average*," and 7–10 was "*above-average*"). In other words, the manipulation was set up so that participants in the difficult RAT condition would likely receive negative performance feedback (i.e., below average) and participants in the easy condition would likely receive neutral to positive feedback (average or above average). The manipulation was successful. Participants in the negative feedback condition scored significantly worse than participants in the positive feedback condition and mean scores in these conditions were in line with the intended feedback. Specifically, the mean score in the negative feedback condition (M = 1.36) fell within the below average for university students range and the mean score in the positive feedback condition (M = 6.43) fell between the average to above average for university students ranges.

Next, participants were randomly assigned to a nostalgia or control condition. Specifically, participants were instructed to bring to mind and write about a nostalgic experience or an ordinary experience from the last week (Wildschut et al., 2006). Finally, participants responded to the question: "To what extent was your performance on the Remote Associates Test caused by your ability?" (1 = not at all; 7 = totally). Higher scores reflect a stronger internal attribution for one's performance.

We hypothesized that nostalgia would reduce attribution bias. Results supported this hypothesis. Consistent with previous research (Alicke & Sedikides, 2009; Campbell & Sedikides, 1999), in the absence of nostalgia (i.e., the ordinary past condition), participants in the negative feedback condition attributed their performance less to their ability than participants in the positive feedback condition. However, nostalgia reduced this difference. For participants who were in the negative feedback condition, there was a significant difference in attribution such that those who engaged in nostalgia were more inclined to attribute their poor performance to their own ability than those who reflected on a non-nostalgic autobiographical event. Nostalgia reduced the need to defend the self.

Threats to the self can lead to a range of personally and socially problematic outcomes. For example, following experiences that undermine the self, individuals are more likely to engage in prejudice (Fein & Spencer, 1997), self-handicapping (Berglas & Jones, 1978), and even aggressive behavior (Baumeister, Smart, & Boden, 1996). The research we conducted suggests that nostalgia may offer an alternative and less problematic means of protecting the self. When people engage in nostalgia, they bring to mind experiences that affirm a positive view of self. And when self-security is maintained in this way, people may be less in need of resorting to other means of self-defense.

In all, research demonstrates that nostalgia contributes to positive self-views. Nostalgic memories involve the variables that are known to enhance the self: close relationships, personal triumphs, significant rites of passage, and culturally valued events. In addition, self-esteem increases following nostalgic reflection and this may be due to nostalgia's capacity to increase the accessibility of positive self-attributes. Relatedly, nostalgia inspires optimism. It gives people a reason to be hopeful about the future. Finally, nostalgia offers a viable means of defending the self from threat. Further research should be conducted to determine the potential for nostalgia to mitigate a wide range of self-related threats as our (Vess et al., 2012) work only considered one type of threat: negative performance feedback. Research has demonstrated that nostalgia does counter existential threats to the self and I discuss this research in detail in Chapter 7. However, more work is needed to determine the extent to which nostalgia can insulate people from the many experiences that can compromise feelings of self-worth.

Nostalgia and Self-Continuity

Self-continuity reflects a sense of connection between one's past self and present self (Parfit, 1971; Vignoles, 2011). Scholars have proposed that self-continuity is an important human need (Vignoles, 2011; Vignoles, Regalia, Manzi, Golledge, & Scabini, 2006). Indeed, self-continuity is positively associated with psychological well-being (King, Scollon, Ramsey, & Williams, 2000; McAdams, Reynolds, Lewis, Patten, & Bowman, 2001) and physical health (Anderzén & Arnetz, 1999; Chandler, Lalonde, Sokol, & Hallett, 2003). Self-continuity also helps people regulate psychological threat (Landau, Greenberg, & Solomon, 2008). Further, as previously discussed, self-discontinuity, a sense that one's past and present self are disjointed, is associated with psychological distress (Milligan, 2003), difficulty coping with challenging life transitions (e.g., job loss, Sadeh & Karniol, 2012), and even suicide (Chandler & Proulx, 2008).

In short, self-continuity is generally good and self-discontinuity is generally bad. People strive to have a continuous, stable conception of self. The question then is how are people able to attain and maintain perceptions of self-continuity, that who they were in the past is connected to who they are now? Davis (1979) proposed that nostalgia helps people manage threats to continuity and restore self-continuity by "encouraging an appreciative stance toward former selves; excluding unpleasant memories; reinterpreting 'marginal, fugitive, and eccentric facets of earlier selves' in a positive light; and establishing benchmarks of one's biography" (ibid., pp. 35–36). From this perspective, nostalgia may prove vital to people's efforts to form and preserve a consistent self-narrative.

As discussed in Chapter 3, when discontinuity is negative or undermines one's sense of self-stability, it motivates nostalgia (Sedikides et al., 2015a). This supports the assertion (e.g., Davis, 1979) that people are using nostalgia to regulate the threat of discontinuity, that nostalgia is a means of restoring self-continuity. We (Sedikides et al., 2015a) directly tested this possibility. We hypothesized that inducing nostalgia would heighten perceptions of self-continuity. In one study, undergraduate participants from a Midwestern American university were randomly assigned to bring to mind and briefly write about either a nostalgic or ordinary autobiographical experience (Wildschut et al., 2006). Participants then responded to items assessing personal and temporal continuity. All items were preceded with the stem; "Thinking about this event makes me feel ...". The personal continuity items included statements such as "connected with my past" and "important aspects of my personality remain the same across time". The temporal continuity items included statements such as "the past merges nicely into the present" and "the present is a mere continuation of the past". Results indicated that nostalgia increased personal but not temporal continuity. Nostalgia promotes feelings of continuity. Moreover, the continuity that nostalgia inspires is most related to one's sense of self. Nostalgia makes people feel like they have a self that is continuous and stable across time.

In a subsequent study, we (Sedikides et al., 2015a) sought to replicate the findings that nostalgia enhances self-continuity with an additional control condition that would help rule out the alternative explanation that it is positive affect, as opposed to nostalgia specifically, that is responsible for the observed effect. In this study, undergraduates from a UK university were randomly assigned to one of three conditions: nostalgia, ordinary autobiographical event, positive autobiographical event. In the nostalgia condition, participants were instructed to bring to mind an experience of nostalgia. In the ordinary condition, participants were instructed to bring to mind an ordinary experience from the past. In the positive condition, participants were instructed to bring to mind a past experience that was positive. Participants in each condition were instructed to think about and briefly describe in writing how this event made them feel. Participants then completed a brief measure of positive affect (e.g., "Thinking about this event makes me happy"), the measure of personal continuity used in the previous study and a nostalgia manipulation check.

First, as predicted, the nostalgia condition increased feelings of nostalgia relative to both the positive and ordinary autobiographical event conditions. These latter two conditions did not differ on state nostalgia. In addition, the positive autobiographical event condition increased positive affect relative to both the nostalgia and ordinary past conditions. The nostalgia and ordinary past conditions did not differ in terms of generating positive affect. As noted in Chapter 4, previous research has generally but not always found that nostalgia leads to increased positive affect relative to other reflective conditions. Critically, nostalgia increased self-continuity relative to both positive and ordinary autobiographical reflection. Participants in these latter two conditions did not differ on self-continuity. Moreover, the effect of nostalgia on self-continuity remained significant when controlling for positive affect. The self-continuity function of nostalgia cannot be explained by positive affect.

In another series of studies, my colleagues and I (Sedikides et al., 2015) sought to further consider the potential for nostalgia to contribute to self-continuity and ultimately psychological well-being. In the first study, we sought to replicate the effect of nostalgia on self-continuity and also consider social connectedness as a mediator. In a sample of British university students, we manipulated nostalgia using the music induction previously described (Routledge et al., 2011) and then measured social connectedness with items such as "Right now, I feel connected to loved ones" (Wildschut et al., 2006). We then assessed self-continuity (e.g., "I feel connected with my past"; Sedikides et al., 2015a). As predicted, nostalgia increased both feelings of social connectedness and self-continuity. Further, the effect of nostalgia on self-continuity was mediated by social connectedness. In additional studies we (Sedikides et al., 2015) observed the same pattern of results with samples from non-Western cultures and using distinct nostalgia manipulations and control conditions. Nostalgia functions to promote self-continuity.

Our (Sedikides et al., 2015) next goal was to consider the potential for nostalgia-induced self-continuity to benefit psychological well-being. We specifically focused on the construct of eudaimonic well-being: the extent to which people perceive themselves as functioning at optimal and meaningful levels (Deci & Ryan, 2001). We first conducted a study in which we experimentally manipulated self-continuity and measured well-being. Specifically, American adult participants were randomly assigned to a self-continuity or control condition. In the self-continuity condition, participants were asked to think of themselves as they were three years ago and to spend some time writing about how they felt connected with their past selves. In the control condition, participants were also asked to think about themselves as they were three years ago (and to write about this), but they were not instructed to make any connections to their past selves. Participants then responded to the self-continuity items previously described and completed a measure of eudaimonic well-being: the Subjective Vitality Scale (Ryan & Frederick, 1997). This scale assesses the extent to which people feel alive and vital with items such as "I have energy and spirit".

First, the results indicated that the manipulation was successful. Participants in the continuity condition scored significantly higher on measured self-continuity than participants in the control condition. Critically, the results provided support for the assertion that self-continuity benefits well-being. Participants in the self-continuity condition reported significantly higher levels of vitality than participants in the control condition. In addition, measured self-continuity mediated this effect.

Having established experimentally that self-continuity improves well-being, we (Sedikides et al., 2015) then wanted to test the full causal model of nostalgia improving well-being via increased social connectedness and self-continuity. Specifically, in an adult sample of American participants, we manipulated nostalgia with the established writing task (Wildschut et al., 2006) and subsequently measured social connectedness, self-continuity, and vitality with the measures previously described. Mediation analyses supported the proposed model. That is, the data were consistent with the assertion that nostalgia contributes to feelings of social connectedness which in turn promote self-continuity which in turn boosts psychological well-being.

In all, studies indicate that nostalgia helps people feel connected to their pasts and as if part of who they are remains stable across time. In this way, nostalgia may prove vital in people's effort to form and maintain a strong sense of identity. Life is full of experiences that can lead to self-doubt and uncertainty. And when people experience these episodes of discontinuity, they may naturally turn to nostalgia as a means to restore continuity. Further, the continuity that nostalgia provides contributes to adaptive psychological functioning. Future research should further probe the potential role that nostalgia may play in the development and maintenance of the self-concept.

Nostalgia and Self-Growth

The True Self

The research described thus far establishes nostalgia as a resource for the self. Nostalgia enhances views of the current self and promotes optimism for the future. Nostalgia also connects the past self to the present self to facilitate continuity of self. A number of scholars from the humanistic and positive psychological traditions have argued that people are not only motivated to protect and enhance their positive views of self. They are also motivated by a desire for self-growth, to explore their full potential and discover fully the pursuits that intrinsically fulfill them (see Deci & Ryan 2000). There are now a number of studies indicating that nostalgia contributes to growth-oriented pursuits. Below, I discuss this research.

One important facet of self-growth relates to "the true self", authenticity, or the intrinsic self (Kernis & Goldman, 2006; Ryan & Deci, 2000). When people feel like they know or are in touch with who they really are, they are psychologically healthier (Schlegel, Hicks, King, & Arndt, 2009). Nostalgic memories are focused on the personal experiences that people hold dear (Wildschut et al., 2006). In addition, nostalgia promotes self-continuity in the face of experiences that could undermine people's confidence that they know themselves (Sedikides et al., 2015a). Finally, nostalgia reduces people's external attributions of failure (Vess et al., 2012). Nostalgia may therefore contribute to feelings of authenticity.

Stephan et al. (2012) were the first to explore empirically nostalgia's potential to increase feelings of authenticity. In their experiment, participants were randomly assigned to write about a nostalgic, ordinary, or positive past event. Subsequently, as part of a larger questionnaire, participants indicated the extent to which the experience they described reflected the person who they truly were. Nostalgic relative to ordinary or positive autobiographical experiences reflected feelings of authenticity. When people bring to mind events from their past, it is the experiences they are nostalgic for that contribute to an authentic sense of self. Lenton, Bruder, Slabu, and Sedikides (2013) provided further support for this assertion. Specifically, they asked participants to write about an experience that made them feel most like their true or real self or an experience that made them feel least like their true or real self. Subsequently, participants responded to a number of items assessing current psychological states. One of these items specifically assessed nostalgia ("Do you feel nostalgic about the time you described?"). Participants who wrote about an experience that made them feel most like their true self reported feeling more nostalgia about that experience than participants who wrote about an experience that made them feel least like their true self. When people are reviewing the life experiences that identify the true self, they bring to mind the events from their past that generate feelings of nostalgia.

Building on these initial findings, Baldwin, Biernat, and Landau (2015) further explored nostalgia's potential to reveal the true self. They started with a study assessing the relation between state nostalgia and measures related to the true self. Specifically, participants from an online community sample were asked to bring to mind one memory from their past and to think about it for a few minutes. They were not instructed to bring to mind a particular type of memory. The instructions read "people have all sorts of memories so there are no rules for the kind of memory you think about". Next, they responded to items assessing how nostalgic thinking about this memory made them feel, e.g., "This memory makes me feel nostalgic" and "This memory makes me feel a longing for my past". Participants then completed the Authenticity Inventory (Kernis & Goldman, 2006) which assesses the extent to which people feel their current lives are authentic, e.g., "For better or for worse I am aware of who I truly am" and "I am aware of when I am not being my true self". They also completed the Extrinsic Contingency Focus Scale (Williams et al., 2009) which assesses the extent to which people are focused on living up to extrinsic sources of self-worth, e.g., "I work hard at things because of the social approval it provides" and "I have an image to maintain".

Baldwin and colleagues proposed that if nostalgia brings online the true (authentic) self, then the more people reported feeling nostalgic in the memory reflection task, the higher they would score on the authenticity measure and the lower they would score on the extrinsic contingency measure. Results supported these predictions. When people feel nostalgic, they feel more authentic and are less concerned about meeting external standards of value.

In a second study, Baldwin and colleagues sought experimental evidence for their predictions. In an online experiment, they randomly assigned participants to bring to mind and write about a nostalgic or ordinary past experience (Wildschut et al., 2006). Participants were then instructed to bring to mind a picture of who they were at the time of the recalled event and to keep that image of their past self in mind while completing the next measure which was an adapted version of the Authenticity Inventory (Kernis & Goldman, 2006) previously described. In this adapted version of the measure, items were reworded to refer to the past self, e.g. "For better or for worse I was aware of who I truly was". Participants then completed the Extrinsic Contingency Focus Scale (Williams et al., 2009) as previously discussed and were specifically instructed that their responses to this scale should reflect the current conception of self.

Participants in the nostalgia condition rated their past selves as more authentic than participants in the ordinary past condition. In addition, participants in the nostalgia condition reported lower extrinsic self-focus than participants in the ordinary past condition. In addition, past self-authenticity mediated the effect of nostalgia on current extrinsic self-focus. Nostalgia offers people a means to connect to a past authentic self and doing so may reduce concerns about extrinsic contingencies in the present.

Next, the researchers tested the potential for nostalgia to render the true self more cognitively accessible. In an online experiment, participants were randomly assigned to bring to mind and briefly write about a nostalgic or ordinary experience (Wildschut et al., 2006). Next, participants were randomly assigned to write about their true self or their everyday self. Specifically, in the true self condition, participants were instructed to "take some time to think about all the things that are important to you, such as your goals and aspirations" and to "think about who you really are". Participants then spent a few minutes writing about themselves. Participants in the everyday self-condition were asked to describe their current lifestyle.

The researchers then coded the content of the essays. First, the researchers assessed the length of (word count) and amount of time spent writing the essay. Second, the researchers used LIWC (Pennebaker et al., 2007) to assess participants' use of cognitive words (e.g., because, think, know) in their self-descriptions. The researchers hypothesized that when participants were writing about their true selves, nostalgia would facilitate increased accessibility. That is, participants in the nostalgia condition would write more words and use more cognitive words in their true self-descriptions. The results supported these predictions. Nostalgia helped people elaborate about their true selves.

These and other studies conducted by Baldwin et al. (2015) further establish that nostalgia is an experience that brings out the true self. Nostalgia makes people feel authentic. It renders accessible the core aspects of one's identity. Scholars have long argued that self-authenticity has important implications for psychological health and well-being. For instance, when people pursue goals that represent their intrinsic interests, they experience greater well-being and goal success (Deci & Ryan, 2000). Nostalgia may thus promote well-being, in part, because it activates the true self which many ultimately lead to life choices that best match people's intrinsic values and interests. Indeed, Baldwin et al. (2015) observed that high levels of trait nostalgia were associated with higher levels of self-reported authenticity which in turn was associated with greater psychological well-being.

Exploration

Psychological growth requires exploration, the pursuit of new experiences and ideas and the willingness to be open to alternative ways of thinking. A number of studies demonstrate that nostalgia promotes growth, in part, by inspiring exploration. For example, Baldwin and Landau (2014) discovered that nostalgia increases people's curiosity and interest in learning about or experiencing new things. In two studies, participants were randomly assigned to bring to mind and write about a nostalgic or ordinary past event (Wildschut et al., 2006). Participants then completed a number of self-report measures including measures of exploration. Specifically, participants completed the Curiosity and Exploration Inventory (Kashdan et al., 2009) which includes statements such as "I am the kind of person who embraces unfamiliar people, events, and places" and "I frequently seek out opportunities to challenge myself and grow as a person". They also completed the Exploration Inventory (Green & Campbell, 2000) which includes statements such as "I would like to explore someplace that I have never been before" and "I would like a job that was unusual or different". In both studies, results confirmed that nostalgia inspires growth-oriented exploration. Participants in the nostalgia condition, relative to participants in the ordinary past event condition, reported higher levels of exploration on both scales.

Baldwin and Landau (2014) also assessed other psychological functions of nostalgia prior to measuring exploration in order to test for possible mediators. Specifically, they assessed perceptions of social connectedness, self-esteem, and meaning in life. Replicating previous research, they found that nostalgia significantly increased each of these psychological states. Further, self-esteem (but not connectedness or meaning) was found to mediate the relationship between nostalgia and exploration. This finding suggests that by bolstering feelings of self-worth, nostalgia facilitates self-growth via exploration.

Creativity

Other research also identifies a self-growth function of nostalgia in the domain of creativity. Social psychological research indicates that psychological security enhances creative expression (Routledge, Arndt, Vess, & Sheldon, 2008). Creativity involves distinguishing oneself from others and thus, people may feel more comfortable and be more willing to individuate themselves creatively if they have a sense of psychological security. Indeed, studies indicate that secure attachment is associated with explorative thought processes (Green & Campbell, 2000) and curiosity (Mikulincer, 1997). And nostalgia offers feelings of security (e.g., increased social connectedness) and increases exploration (Baldwin & Landau, 2014). Thus, nostalgia may provide a foundation for creative expression.

Ye, Ngan, and Hui (2013) tested this possibility. They randomly assigned students from a university in Hong Kong to bring to mind and write about a nostalgic experience (Wildschut et al., 2006) or to describe in writing the schedule and activities from the previous day. To assess creativity, participants were given the Alternative Uses Task (Wallach & Kogan, 1965) which involves generating a list of possible uses of three common objects. Specifically, participants were instructed to think of and list as many possible uses they could think of for a brick, shoe, and newspaper. Participants were given three minutes per object. Participants were also instructed that there uses could be creative. Researchers summed the total number of generated ideas and used this score as an indicator of fluency of creativity. Results supported the prediction that nostalgia inspires creativity. Participants in the nostalgia condition generated more uses of common objects than participants in the control condition.

Taken together, a body of literature evidencing a self-growth function of nostalgia is beginning to take shape. Nostalgic memories appear to capture the experiences from our past that generate feelings of authenticity. That is, nostalgia keeps us in touch with our true selves, the people we believe we are deep down.

Nostalgia also promotes growth by encouraging explorative processes. That is, nostalgia increases people's curiosity and desire to seek out new experiences and ideas. Not surprisingly then, nostalgia contributes positively to creative expression.

Closing Thoughts

Nostalgia involves personally cherished autobiographical memories and therefore has a number of implications for the self-system. In this chapter, I described research elucidating some of these implications. Nostalgia bolsters the self. When people engage in nostalgia they are revisiting past experiences that serve to enhance their feelings of self-worth. Self-esteem striving can come at the expense of others (Fein and Spencer, 1997) and sometimes even one's own health (e.g., Routledge, Arndt, & Goldenberg 2004; Arndt et al., 2009). Nostalgia thus may offer a more personally and socially healthy means of meeting esteem needs. Indeed, as discussed, nostalgia reduces defensiveness following self-esteem threat. Future research is needed to determine if nostalgia can mitigate other self-threatening experiences. Studies should also test whether or not people naturally recruit nostalgia when self-esteem is under threat.

Nostalgia also promotes self-continuity. When people experience discontinuity in their lives they evidence increased nostalgia, which in turn increases feelings of self-continuity. Further, nostalgia induced self-continuity contributes positively to psychological well-being. People strive to maintain feelings of self-stability and continuity throughout their lives and nostalgia appears to play an important role in these efforts. Future research should further explore, perhaps in longitudinal designs, the role that nostalgia plays in helping people navigate the many life experiences that potentially threaten perceptions of self-continuity. Is nostalgia a self-continuity resource that people regularly access when coping with difficult life changes and disruptions?

Finally, nostalgia promotes psychological growth. Nostalgic memories help people maintain a sense of authenticity. In this way, nostalgia reveals the true self. In addition, nostalgia motivates exploration and creativity. In popular culture, it is common to see nostalgia being associated with a lack of creativity. Revisiting the past is often considered to be unoriginal and uninspired. The past is the old and to be creative is to embrace the new. However, research suggests that people may draw creative inspiration from revisiting their own past nostalgically. Future research is needed to more fully consider how nostalgia can influence creativity. When people bring to mind their own experiences of nostalgia, they subsequently evidence more creative fluency on idea generation tasks. However, does nostalgia facilitate more creative works of art or novel (but useful) solutions to problems? Much work is needed in this domain.

7
THE EXISTENTIAL FUNCTIONS OF NOSTALGIA

Humans are existential animals. As discussed in the previous chapter, we are highly self-aware. This awareness of self, combined with other advanced cognitive capacities, allows us to ask the heavy questions (Becker 1971). Why are we here? What purpose do we serve? What happens to us when we die? Once our ancestors began to grapple with these kinds of existential concerns, they started to look like the cultural animals that we are today (Solomon et al., 2004). That is, existential questions drove our ancestors to start focusing on more than concerns of the body. Humans do not simply want to survive. We want to live lives of meaning. We want to feel like we are making contributions to the world that will transcend our mortality.

A number of scholars have argued that existential motives for meaning and symbolic permanence play a central role in human life (Becker, 1973; Baumeister, 1991; Frankl, 1997; Greenberg, Pyszczynski, & Solomon, 1986; Wong & Fry, 1998; Yalom, 1980). Consistent with this assertion, a large body of research demonstrates that meeting existential needs is critical for both psychological and physical health. People who perceive their lives as meaningful are better able to cope with life challenges (Park, 2010; Updegraff, Silver, & Holman, 2008). And those who suffer from meaning deficits are more likely to develop mental illness (Wong, 1998), engage in risky behavior such as problem drinking, gambling, and drug abuse (Marsh, Smith, Piek, & Saunders, 2003; Orcutt, 1984; Padelford, 1974; Waisberg & Porter, 1994), and be at risk of suicide (Harlowe, Newcomb, & Bentler, 1986). In addition, meaning in life is a significant predictor of health outcomes: across all adult age groups, higher meaning in life is associated with lower risk of death (Hill & Turiano, 2014). Clearly, perceiving one's life as meaningful is critical for adaptive functioning.

In the present chapter, I discuss a growing body of research indicating that nostalgia plays an important role in people's efforts to find and maintain perceptions of meaning in life. I specifically discuss research demonstrating that nostalgia (1) is associated with and increases perceptions of meaning, (2) mitigates the effects of existential threat, and (3) helps those who have meaning deficits cope with stressful experiences.

Nostalgia Inspires Meaning

Check out the self-help section of any major bookstore and it becomes apparent that there is a big market for meaning. People want to perceive their lives as meaningful and are looking for the tools that will help them accomplish this goal. So what is it that makes life meaningful? A considerable amount of research in psychology has explored this question. Not surprisingly, meaning can be derived from all sorts of endeavors. Anything that makes someone feel important, loved, and symbolically immortal (i.e., making a contribution that will transcend physical death) can generate meaning (Hicks & Routledge, 2013). We (Routledge & Arndt, 2005) and others (Sedikides, Wildschut, & Baden, 2004) proposed that nostalgia is a meaning-making resource.

Content analyses of nostalgia narratives provided early empirical evidence that nostalgia promotes meaning (Wildschut et al., 2006). Specifically, nostalgic memories tend to be focused on personally cherished or consequential life events, e.g., weddings, holiday traditions. In addition, nostalgic memories prominently feature close ones and research indicates that feelings of belongingness provide perceptions of meaning (Stillman et al., 2009). Feeling loved and needed makes one feel meaningful. Thus, based on the nature of people's nostalgic memories, there are good reasons to suspect perceptions of meaning are garnered from these memories. Nostalgic memories offer snapshots of the personally treasured life experiences that make life meaningful. Of course, these cherished life experiences cannot occur every day. Thus, nostalgic reflection may offer a means by which people can regularly tap into these meaning-providing experiences. Consistent with this idea, as discussed in Chapter 3, threats to meaning in life trigger nostalgia. When people experience situations that call into question life's meaning, they turn to nostalgia. They revisit the life experiences they most cherish. But does nostalgia generate meaning?

A number of correlational studies suggest that nostalgia increases meaning. For example, in two studies my colleagues and I (Routledge et al., 2011) observed that higher nostalgia is associated with greater levels of perceived meaning. In the first study, American undergraduate participants completed the nostalgia proneness scale described in previous chapters (Routledge et al., 2008) and two measures of the perceived presence of meaning in life: the Purpose in Life scale, e.g., "My personal existence is purposeful and meaningful" (McGregor & Little, 1998) and the Presence of Meaning in Life subscale, e.g., "I have a good sense of what makes my life meaningful" (Steger, Frazier, Oishi, & Kaler, 2006). Nostalgia proneness was positively and significantly correlated with both meaning measures. The more people engage in nostalgia, the more they perceive their lives as being full of meaning and purpose.

In our next study, we (Routledge et al., 2011) recruited Dutch nationals ranging in age from 10 to 71 to take part in an online study. Participants listened to popular songs on their computers and rated how nostalgic each song made them feel. As an indicator of meaning, they also rated the extent to which each song made them feel that life is worth living. The results again supported a link between nostalgia and meaning. The more people reported that music made them feel nostalgic, the more they reported that the music made them feel like life is worth living. In addition, the pattern was consistent across all ages. When people feel nostalgic while listening to music they also feeling meaningful, that life is worthwhile.

Reid et al. (2015) found a similar pattern of results with scent-evoked nostalgia. As discussed in previous chapters, in this research participants were presented with tubes containing scented oils and instructed to smell each oil and indicate how nostalgic the scent made them feel. In addition to assessing other states, e.g., belongingness, self-esteem, the researchers asked participants to indicate the extent to which each scent made them feel "life is meaningful" and "life has a purpose". The more a scent generated nostalgia, the more participants reported that it made them feel like life has meaning and purpose. Studies such as these establish a relationship between nostalgia and meaning. However, they do not clarify the direction of this relationship. I already discussed studies evidencing that threatened meaning triggers nostalgia, but does nostalgia, in turn, elevate meaning?

Experimental studies establish the directionality of the relation between nostalgia and meaning by evidencing that induced nostalgia increases perceived meaning. We (Routledge et al., 2011) utilized multiple nostalgia inductions to establish a causal effect on meaning. In one study, as in similar research described in previous chapters, UK undergraduate student participants received nostalgic or non-nostalgic song lyrics. Specifically, participants received lyrics from songs that either they (nostalgia condition) or another participant (control condition) had indicated as being nostalgic. Subsequently, participants completed the Presence of Meaning in Life subscale (Steger et al., 2006). The results confirmed the hypothesis that nostalgia increases meaning: participants who received nostalgic song lyrics reported higher meaning in life than participants who received non-nostalgic lyrics.

We (Routledge et al., 2012) demonstrated the same effect with the nostalgia writing induction. American university students were given a dictionary definition of nostalgia and asked to bring to mind and write down four keywords concerning an experience of nostalgia (Wildschut et al., 2006). Participants in a control condition were asked to bring to mind and write down key words related to a desired future event. All participants then completed the Presence of Meaning in Life subscale (Steger et al., 2006). Again, nostalgia increased meaning. Importantly, this effect occurred when nostalgia was contrasted with a desired future event induction.

This finding speaks to the potential potency of nostalgia-induced meaning. University students presumably have a number of meaningful major life events ahead of them, e.g., graduation, finding a career, marriage, starting a family. And thinking about these future desired events could bolster perceptions of life as meaningful. Thus, finding that nostalgia generates meaning relative to a desired future event condition provides strong evidence that the past is an important existential resource. Thinking about the experiences we have already had bolsters meaning more than thinking about the experiences we want to have.

We (Routledge et al., 2012) further tested the effect of nostalgia on meaning with an experiment including, in addition to nostalgia, control conditions related to a future desired event and a recent positive event. Positive emotions increase perceived meaning in life (Hicks, Schlegel, & King, 2010). Thus, this experiment allowed for a further test of the potency of nostalgia. Does nostalgia increase meaning relative to an affectively positive recent experience? In addition, this study added to the study of nostalgia and meaning by measuring the search for meaning instead of the presence of meaning. Since meaning is an important psychological need, when people lack meaning in life, they are motivated to search for it (Juhl & Routledge, 2012; Park, 2010; Steger, Kashdan, Sullivan, & Lorentz, 2008; Vess et al., 2009). Specifically, after receiving one of the three experimental conditions (nostalgia, future desired event, recent positive event), American university student participants completed the Search for Meaning in Life subscale, e.g., "I am looking for something that makes my life feel meaningful" and "I am seeking a purpose or mission for my life" (Steger et al., 2006). In support of the assertion that nostalgia provides meaning, participants in the nostalgia condition reported significantly lower scores on search for meaning than participants in the future desired and recent past positive event conditions. Nostalgia enhances meaning and thus reduces the need to further search for it.

In a sample of UK residents, Hepper et al. (2012) found additional evidence that nostalgia increases meaning using the prototype nostalgia induction described in previous chapters. Specifically, the researchers randomly assigned participants to receive a list of either central or peripheral features of nostalgia and then instructed them to bring to mind an event characterized by at least five of those features. Participants then rated their agreement with a number of statements indicative of meaning in life, e.g., "makes me feel life is meaningful" and "makes me feel there is a greater purpose in life". A similar pattern emerged such that participants in the central features condition tended to reported greater meaning in life than participants in the peripheral features condition.

Studies have also sought to establish potential mediators of the relationship between nostalgia and meaning. As previously discussed, nostalgic memories involve personally cherished life experiences, the types of experiences that people would describe as meaningful. These experiences may differ in many ways from person to person. For example, one person may describe her or his wedding day as a meaningful experience. Another person may describe a particular family vacation as especially meaningful. And so on. Critically, despite the unique features of people's life histories, a commonality is that most of the life events that individuals describe as meaningful involve other people. That is, meaning tends to be found in our connections to others. And nostalgic memories are typically social in nature. Even experiences that involve personal success often involve close ones. For instance, when actors win Academy Awards, in their acceptance speeches, they are quick to thank all the people that helped them succeed and often indicate that they share that award with those people. The individual successes and triumphs that people are nostalgic about are rarely solitary events. Thus, feelings of social connectedness may contribute to the perceptions of meaning that nostalgia generates.

In support of this possibility, we (Routledge et al., 2011) found in two studies that feelings of connectedness mediated the effects of nostalgia on meaning. In the study in which Dutch nationals listened to popular songs and rated the song for nostalgia and meaning, they also rated the song for social connectedness by indicating the extent to which the song made them feel "loved". Mediational analyses revealed that the relationship between nostalgia and meaning was mediated by social connectedness. In the experimental study involving the nostalgia musical lyrics induction, we (Routledge et al., 2011) found a similar effect. Specifically, after receiving the nostalgia or non-nostalgic music lyrics and prior to completing the meaning measure, participants completed the Social Provisions Scale (Cutrona & Russell, 1987), a 24-item measure assessing six provisions of social relationships: Guidance (e.g., "There is someone I could talk to about important decisions in my life"); Reliable Alliance (e.g., "There are people I can count on in an emergency"); Reassurance of Worth (e.g., "There are people who admire my talents and abilities"); Nurturance (e.g., "There are people who depend on me for help"); Attachment (e.g., "I have close relationships that provide me with a sense of security and emotional well-being"); and Social Integration (e.g., "I feel part of a group of people who share my attitudes and beliefs"). The effect of nostalgia on meaning was mediated by social connectedness. Nostalgia increased scores on the Social Provisions Scale which in turn predicted meaning in life.

In sum, a number of methodologically diverse studies establish a clear association between nostalgia and meaning. Nostalgic memories pertain to the life experiences that people hold dear. Nostalgic memories are meaningful memories. And when people bring to mind these memories, they perceive their present lives as full of meaning and purpose. Further, the feelings of love and connectedness to others that nostalgia reinforces appear to be at least partially responsible for the meaning nostalgia provides. Future work is needed to explore other possible mediators. For example, self-continuity is a viable candidate. Reflecting on past meaningful experiences might generate meaning in the present by fostering meaningful connections between past and present selves.

When meaning is threatened people turn to nostalgia. In addition, as just discussed, nostalgia increases perceptions of meaning in life. Combined, these findings suggest that people use nostalgia to counter existential threat. Next, I turn to the question of whether or not nostalgia successfully mitigates the negative effects of existentially threatening experiences. Does nostalgia help people maintain psychological health and adaptive functioning in the face of existential concerns?

Nostalgia Counters Threats to Meaning

In Saul Bellow's *Mr. Sammler's Planet* (1970), one of the characters, Wallace, argues the existential benefit of nostalgic memories: "They keep the wolf of insignificance from the door" (p. 190). Davis (1979, p. 41) similarly asserted that nostalgia "quiet[s] our fears of the abyss". Consistent with this idea, Routledge and Arndt (2005) proposed that nostalgia might prove to be an important resource for regulating existential threat and protecting meaning. Routledge and Arndt's proposal was based upon ideas from terror management theory (TMT) (Greenberg et al., 1986). Like all animals, humans strive for self-preservation in the service of genetic replication. However, humans are uniquely able to project the self forward in time and thus uniquely able to realize that, despite all efforts to thrive, death is a certain future outcome. This realization, according to TMT, has the potential to generate a great deal of personal distress or terror. The theory proposes that people are able to, for the most part, avoid the terror associated with the awareness of their future mortality by believing that their lives are meaningful. People know that their bodies will die, but to have meaning in life is to feel as if one has made an enduring mark. In this way, meaning offers symbolic death-transcendence.

In support of TMT, a large body of research demonstrates that heightened awareness of mortality leads to heightened investment in socially and culturally-derived meaning-providing structures (e.g., family, religion, social identities) and that such investment reduces the accessibility of death-related thoughts (Greenberg, Solomon, & Arndt, 2008) as well as psychological distress (e.g., anxiety, Routledge & Juhl, 2010; Routledge et al., 2010). We (Routledge & Arndt, 2005) proposed that nostalgia is a psychological resource that people can employ to reassure themselves that their lives are meaningful. In other words, when people are grappling with existential concerns about the future, they can mentally time travel to the past via nostalgia as a means to revisit the life experiences that affirm meaning.

My colleagues and I (Routledge et al., 2008) tested this proposal that nostalgia serves as a regulator of existential threat. We specifically hypothesized that if nostalgia is a meaning-providing resource then, like other meaning-providing resources, it will mitigate the effects of death-related cognition. We tested this hypothesis in three experiments. In the first study, we measured individual differences in nostalgia proneness (e.g., "How often do you engage in nostalgia?") and manipulated death-related cognition with a well-established mortality salience induction (Rosenblatt et al., 1989). In the experimental condition, participants were instructed to spend a few minutes reflecting on their mortality (e.g., "Briefly describe the emotions that the thought of your own death arouses in you"), whereas in the control condition participants pondered an unpleasant experience not related to death (e.g., "Briefly describe the emotions that the thought of dental pain arouses in you"). Next, participants completed a scale assessing meaninglessness, e.g., "All strivings in life are futile and absurd" (Kunzendorf & Maguire, 1995). We hypothesized that thinking about one's mortality would increase perceptions that life is meaningless, but only among individuals low in nostalgia proneness — those not disposed to reflect on meaning-providing past life experiences. The results confirmed the hypothesis. People who regularly wax nostalgic did not experience lowered meaning when thinking about their mortality. However, those who do not regularly employ nostalgia did exhibit mortality salience-induced deficits in meaning.

We then focused on the potential for nostalgia to reduce the accessibility of death thoughts following mortality salience. As noted, previous research demonstrates that, when mortality is made salient, investment in meaning-proving structures (e.g., religion) reduces the accessibility of death thoughts (Greenberg et al., 2008). We thus hypothesized that nostalgia would reduce the accessibility of death thoughts after such thoughts are activated via a mortality salience induction. In one study, we measured nostalgia proneness and then induced mortality salience as previously described. In another experiment, we manipulated nostalgia or ordinary autobiographical reflection with the writing tasks previously described (Wildschut et al., 2006). In both experiments, the dependent variable was death-thought accessibility. Specifically, participants received a list of incomplete words, some of which could be completed with death or non-death-related words, e.g., COFF_ _ could be COFFIN or COFFEE (Greenberg, Pyszczynski, Solomon, Simon, & Breus, 1994). Participants were instructed to complete each word stem. The more words that are completed to be death-related, the more death thoughts are accessible. Both studies provided support for the hypothesis. Mortality salience increased the accessibility of death-related thoughts, but only at low levels of nostalgia (when nostalgia proneness was measured) and in the "ordinary" condition (when nostalgia was manipulated). Nostalgia buffered the effects of mortality salience on increased death thoughts. When people are reminded of death, nostalgia counters these thoughts and reduces their cognitive accessibility.

In a subsequent investigation, we (Juhl et al., 2010) further considered nostalgia as a way to manage the existential threat of death awareness. Numerous studies indicate that death-related cognition contributes to intergroup conflict. People respond to mortality salience with ingroup bias and outgroup derogation (Greenberg et al., 2008). Group identities are a powerful source of meaning. They contribute to feelings of self-worth and they also help people feel like they have meaning that transcends death. Individuals die, but the groups they belong to typically continue to exist. In this way, the individual survives death symbolically through the continuation of the group. Thus, when meaning is needed because death is salient, one way in which people confer meaning is by defending their own group identities. If nostalgia provides meaning, it should reduce the need to defend one's meaning-providing group following mortality salience.

We (Juhl et al., 2010) hypothesized that people who regularly engage in nostalgia (high proneness individuals) would not respond to mortality salience with the typically observed ingroup identity defense. To test this prediction, we measured nostalgia proneness, manipulated mortality salience as described before, and then asked participants to evaluate an essay critical of their university (a group identity threat). Specifically, this essay, which participants were told was authored by a fellow student, asserted that the university is not as good as everyone thinks it is and that attending it was a big mistake. After reading the essay, participants responded to items evaluating the essay (e.g., "How much do you agree with this person's opinion?") and the author (e.g., "How much do you think you would like this person?"). As hypothesized and consistent with past research, mortality salience increased negative evaluations of the critical essay and essay author. However, also as predicted, this effect only occurred among individuals low on nostalgia proneness. People who frequently utilize nostalgia did not need to turn to other sources of meaning when death was salient. They did not feel compelled to defend their university identity.

We (Juhl et al., 2010) further tested nostalgia as a regulator of existential threat by assessing its potential to mitigate mortality salience-induced death-anxiety. We assessed nostalgia proneness, manipulated mortality salience, and assessed death anxiety with the eight-item Death of Self subscale from the Revised Collett-Lester Fear of Death Scale (Lester, 1990). For this scale, participants indicate how anxious they feel about different aspects of death, e.g., "the shortness of life"; "the total isolation of death". We proposed that having people reflect on their mortality would increase their anxiety about death but that nostalgia, to the extent it confers meaning, would mitigate this effect. The results supported this proposal. Mortality salience increased death anxiety, but only among individuals low in nostalgia proneness. These findings in particular help provide evidence for the notion that nostalgia prevents death thoughts from becoming death fears.

In a final experiment, we (Juhl et al., 2010) sought to provide a more rigorous test of the hypothesis that people high in nostalgia proneness are in fact using nostalgia as a meaning-providing resource when mortality is salient. That is, if nostalgia proneness buffers the effects of mortality salience because nostalgia-prone people utilize nostalgic memories to affirm meaning following reminders of mortality, then reminders of mortality should increase state nostalgia for those high in nostalgia proneness. To test this, we again measured nostalgia proneness, manipulated mortality salience, and subsequently assessed state nostalgia (by asking participants how much they missed various aspects of their past such as "someone I loved" and "holidays I went on" (Batcho, 1995). The findings demonstrated that high-prone nostalgia individuals do in fact turn to nostalgia to manage mortality concerns. For people high, but not low, in nostalgia proneness, mortality salience increased state nostalgia.

More recently, we (Routledge, Juhl, Abeyta, & Roylance, 2014) considered the potential for nostalgia to mitigate some of the more socially problematic outcomes associated with TMT. As previously noted, research identifies mortality concerns as a contributing factor to intergroup conflict (Greenberg et al., 2008). Building on this work, further studies sought to determine if mortality concerns can encourage more aggressive and even self-harming behaviors to the extent that such actions are associated with the defense of an enduring symbolic identity. In other words, because people realize that death is inevitable, they may be willing to sacrifice their transient physical self in the service of a more meaningful and symbolically immortal self that is derived from social and cultural structures. In support of this possibility, Pyszczynski et al. (2006) found that in response to mortality salience, relative to a control condition, Iranian college students indicated increased positivity towards fellow students who supported martyrdom attacks against the US as well as increased willingness to consider joining the cause. Similarly, we (Routledge & Arndt, 2008) found in a sample of British students that mortality salience, relative to a control condition, increased endorsement of items such as "I would die for England" and "My personal safety is not as important as the continuation of the British way of life". Importantly, in our study, this effect was only observed if participants were not oriented towards another group identification that promised enduring meaning via the continuation of the group. In other words, the effect of mortality salience on self-sacrifice appears to be motivated by the need to affirm enduring meaning. We (Routledge et al., 2014) thus proposed that nostalgia, because it provides meaning, may mitigate mortality salience provoked self-sacrifice. We tested this possibility in two studies.

In the first study, American university students completed a measure of nostalgia proneness (Routledge et al., 2008), were randomly assigned to think about their mortality or the experience of extreme pain, and then completed a measure of nationalistic self-sacrifice (Routledge & Arndt, 2008). Specifically, participants indicated the extent to which they agreed with items such as "I would die for my nation" and "My personal safety is not as important as the continuation of the American way of life". Consistent with past research that mortality salience inspires nationalist self-sacrifice, participants in the mortality salience condition scored significantly higher on self-sacrifice than participants in the control condition. However, in support of the proposal that nostalgia may mitigate this effect, this pattern of results was only observed among those scoring low in nostalgia proneness. People who regularly engage in nostalgia did not respond to the heightened awareness of death with an increased willingness to self-sacrifice for their nation.

In our second study, we (Routledge et al., 2014) sought to further this analysis by using an experimental manipulation of nostalgia, measuring death-related cognition, and focusing on a different domain relevant to terror management defenses. Specifically, we recruited a sample of adults from the Internet who indicated being religious and administered a measure of death thought accessibility (Greenberg et al., 1994). This was the same measure described previously. Specifically, participants completed word stems with either death or not death-related words. Though in our previous work we (Routledge et al., 2008) used this measure as a dependent variable, as is often done in terror management research, a number of studies have utilized it as predictor variable (e.g., Routledge et al., 2010; Vess et al., 2009). That is, at any given moment, people may vary in the extent to which death thoughts are accessible and naturally occurring high death thought accessibility should predict outcomes similar to when such thoughts are made accessible via a mortality salience experimental induction.

Following this measure, participants were randomly assigned to bring to mind and spend a few minutes writing about either an experience of nostalgia or a recent ordinary autobiographical experience (Wildschut et al., 2006). Finally, participants completed a measure of self-sacrifice similar to the one previously discussed. However, this time, instead of assessing nationalist self-sacrifice, we assessed religious self-sacrifice with items such as "I would die for my religion" and "My personal safety is not as important as the continuation of my religion". We thought focusing on religious self-sacrifice would provide a particularly strong test of nostalgia's potential to mitigate existential threat-induced self-sacrifice because religious identities provide a very potent sense of enduring meaning. That is, religious self-sacrifice may be an especially attractive terror management defense so nostalgia would have to be a powerful meaning-making resource to reduce the attraction to religious self-sacrifice. Demonstrating that nostalgia is a powerful source of meaning, the results indicated that death thought accessibility was a significant predictor of religious self-sacrifice, but only in the non-nostalgic control condition. Inducing nostalgia disrupted the relationship between accessible death thoughts and religious self-sacrifice. Nostalgia provides an attractive alternative means of managing existential concerns about mortality.

In sum, numerous studies provide clear evidence that nostalgia helps regulate the existential threat of death-awareness. Mortality salience decreased perceptions of meaning and increased death thought accessibility, existential anxiety, and meaning-related defenses, but only among non-nostalgic individuals. People who regularly engage in nostalgia or for whom nostalgia was experimentally induced appeared to be insulated from the cognitive, emotional, and attitudinal effects of heightened death-awareness. Further, research demonstrated that those who regularly engage in nostalgia (high nostalgia proneness) were in fact recruiting nostalgia in response to heightened death awareness. Though these studies provide strong evidence for nostalgia as a resource people can use to regulate existential threat, they all focused on one particularly type of threat – death awareness. This poses the question: does nostalgia similarly work to counter other threats relevant to meaning?

Studies do, in fact, demonstrate that nostalgia mitigates a wide range of threats to meaning. First, my colleagues and I (Routledge et al., 2011) demonstrated that nostalgia reduces defensive responses to arguments that life is objectively meaningless. In this study, participants were first randomly assigned to bring to mind and briefly write about a nostalgic or ordinary autobiographical experience (Wildschut et al., 2006). Next, participants were randomly assigned to read either the meaninglessness essay or limitations of computers essay previously described in Chapter 3. As a reminder, one essay argued that humans are cosmically insignificant and the other articulated the many things that computers can and cannot do. Finally, participants were asked to evaluate the essay and the author with items such as "The author is a reliable source" and "The essay is convincing in conveying its point". We proposed that participants should respond more negatively to the meaning threat essay than the limitations of computers control essay. That is, people should want to defend meaning by negatively evaluating the meaning threat essay and author. However, if nostalgia serves as a meaning resource, then participants who were first given the opportunity to engage in nostalgia should be less in need of defending meaning and thus less inclined to negatively evaluate the meaning threat essay and author. The results supported these predictions. In the non-nostalgic control condition, participants who read the meaning threat essay evaluated it and the author more negatively than participants who read the essay on the limitations of computers. In the nostalgia condition, participants evaluated these two essays similarly. Looked at differently, for those who read the life is meaningless essay, participants who engaged in nostalgia evaluated the essay more positively than participants who did not engage in nostalgia. Nostalgia reduced the need to defend against meaning threat.

In another study, we (Routledge et al., 2012) sought to further test nostalgia as a resource to regulate meaning threat by considering a distinct threat to meaning. Theory and research suggest that perceiving the world as structured and predictable contributes to perceptions of meaning (Juhl & Routledge, 2010; Landau et al., 2004; Proulx et al., 2010; Vess et al., 2009). An organized, predictable, and stable world (i.e., a meaningful world) provides the requisite foundation for establishing the sense that one's life has meaning (Arndt et al., 2013). In other words, it may be difficult to perceive one's own life as making sense if the broader world does not make sense. Consistent with this possibility, Proulx et al. (2010) proposed that stimuli that violate one's expectations about the world would threaten meaning. To test this proposal, in one study, Proulx and colleagues exposed participants to absurd or representational art and told them that they would later be asked to make sense of the art, i.e., to explain the meaning of it. In the absurd art condition, participants viewed Rene Magritte's 'The Son of Man'. This painting challenges expectations about the visual world, as it consists of an unexpected juxtaposition of objects – an apple hovering in front of a man's face. In the representational art condition, participants viewed John Constable's 'Landscape With a Double Rainbow'. This painting displays a rainbow on the beach. The researchers then assessed their desire to see the world in a clear, unambiguous, and orderly way, i.e. a need for structure (Thompson, Naccarato, Parker, & Moskowitz, 2001). Viewing absurd art (art that violates expectations about the world) increased participants' need for structure, which the authors interpreted as evidence for threatened meaning, i.e., structure seeking as meaning-making.

We (Routledge et al., 2012) employed the general paradigm utilized by Proulx et al. (2010) to determine if nostalgia mitigates an expectations violation meaning threat. Specifically, American university student participants were presented with a piece of art on a computer screen and were then told to spend a few minutes studying the piece of art because they would later be asked to explain the meaning of it. Participants viewed either the absurd or representational art used by Proulx et al. (2010). Next, participants were asked to bring to mind a nostalgic or recent positive experience. Finally, participants completed the presence of meaning subscale (Steger et al., 2006) previously described. In support of the proposal that nostalgia mitigates meaning threat, participants who were told that they were going to have to make sense of the absurd art reported significantly lower levels of perceived meaning in life than participants told that they were going to have to make sense of the representational art, but only in the non-nostalgic recent positive experience condition. Nostalgia eliminated the effect of trying to make sense of absurd art on meaning. Looked at differently, for participants who were instructed to try and make sense of absurd art, those who brought to mind a nostalgic experience reported significantly higher levels of meaning than those who brought to mind a positive recent past experience. These findings suggest that nostalgia can even mitigate threats that undermine meaning by violating people's expectations about the world.

In their research on nostalgia as an antidote to boredom, van Tilburg et al. (2013) also tested whether or not nostalgia restores meaning following experiences of boredom. Specifically, the induced boredom with the reference copying task previously described. They then instructed participants to bring to mind a memory from the past and assessed the extent to which that memory generated nostalgia. Subsequently, participants reported how much that memory gave them a sense of meaning and completed the presence of meaning subscale (Steger et al., 2006) previously described. Structural equation analysis was used to test the relation between variables. The results supported the proposal that nostalgia regulates meaning threat. Boredom increased nostalgic feelings in the memory task and nostalgia in turn predicted increased meaning in life. Nostalgia serves to restore meaning when people are experiencing the meaning threat of boredom.

We (Abeyta, Routledge, & Kramer, 2015c) sought to extend this area of research into the domain of health. A number of studies have evidenced an association between health and meaning (see Heintzelman & King, 2014). Much of this work has focused on how meaning influences health. For instance, studies indicate that perceptions of meaning in life are associated with healthy immune functioning (Bower, Kemeny, Taylor, & Fahey, 1998) and longevity in old age (Krause, 2009) and across adulthood (Hill & Turiano, 2014). However, health may also contribute to perceptions of meaning. Perceptions of meaning in life are influenced by variables such as emotion (positive emotions predict meaning; e.g., King, Hicks, Krull, & Del Gaiso, 2006), worldviews representing the notion that people ultimately get what they deserve (Pyszczynski, Greenberg, & Solomon, 1997), and general feelings that the world makes sense (Heine, Proulx, & Vohs, 2006; Park, 2010). Thus, to the extent that poor health undercuts positive emotions, is associated with self-blame (Shaver & Drown, 1986), and makes one feel like the world makes no sense (Janoff-Bulman 2010), it may also undermine perceptions of life as meaningful. And this compromised meaning may in turn lead to further health decline. Indeed, a study by Steger, Fitch-Martin, Donnelly, and Rickard (2014) evidenced that perceptions of meaning promote a positive health orientation which, in turn, is associated with health promoting behaviors. Thus, it is important to identify interventions that may counter the potential effect of poor health leading to decreased meaning.

We (Abeyta *et al.*, 2015c) tested the potential for nostalgia to serve as such an intervention. We recruited a sample of undergraduate students from an American university and administered a subjective health measure consisting of five items chosen from the 36-item RAND health survey v. 1.0 (Hays, Sherbourne, & Mazel, 1993). Specifically, participants responded to questions such as "Please rate your current health status" on a scale ranging from "very poor" to "very good". After completing the subjective health measure, participants were randomly assigned to a nostalgia or control condition. This study employed a music induction of nostalgia (Abeyta & Routledge, 2015a). Specifically, participants were instructed to conduct a Youtube search to find a song that made them nostalgic (nostalgia condition) or a song they enjoyed but only recently discovered (control condition). After finding the song, participants were instructed to listen to it. After listening to the song, participants completed the presence of meaning subscale (Steger *et al.*, 2006).

As predicted, subjective health was related to perceptions of meaning. People who reported being in poor health also reported lower meaning in life. Nostalgia, however, had the predicted effect of mitigating this relationship. In the nostalgia condition, the relationship between subjective health and meaning was nonsignificant. Looked at differently, at low levels of poor subjective health, participants in the nostalgia condition reported significantly higher levels of meaning in life than participants in the control condition. Nostalgia serves as a meaning-making resource for people in poor health.

In all, a number of studies focusing on different conditions of existential threat identify nostalgia as a resource that people can employ to protect or increase meaning when meaning is challenged. Contemplations of mortality, information highlighting the cosmic insignificance of human life, experiences that challenge expectations about the world, the state of boredom, and poor health all serve as attacks on meaning. And nostalgia provides a defense against each of these attacks.

When the meaningfulness of life is in question, people are able to revisit meaningful past experiences via nostalgic reflection and this activity serves to shore up perceptions of meaning in the present.

Nostalgia as a Resource for People Who Lack Meaning in Life

As noted early on in this chapter, meaning in life is a critical component of psychological and physical health. In other words, people who are dispositionally high in meaning are more likely to be well-adjusted and healthy. Likewise, those who are dispositionally low in meaning are more likely to suffer from chronic maladjustment. Indeed, much of the work on the psychologically of meaning has focused on the association between trait levels of perceived meaning and a wide range of indicators of psychological health and well-being (Hicks & Routledge, 2013). In the previous sections, I discussed the growing body of work demonstrating the effects of nostalgia on state levels of meaning and the moderating effects of nostalgia on situationally-threatened meaning. That is, I reviewed studies showing that nostalgia leads to higher state perceptions of meaning and, following an experience that serves to threaten in the moment perceptions of meaning, nostalgia restores meaning. A separate question relates to the widely observed association between low dispositional meaning and poor psychological health. Can induced nostalgia help those with low dispositional meaning? That is, will having people who tend to perceive life as meaningless and purposeless engage in nostalgic reflection help restore psychological health?

Studies have explored the possibility that a nostalgia induction might disrupt the association between low meaning and psychological maladjustment. In one study, we (Routledge et al., 2011) measured dispositional levels of meaning with the Purpose in Life scale, e.g., "My personal existence is purposeful and meaningful" (McGregor & Little, 1998). Subsequently, we randomly assigned participants to bring to mind and briefly write about either a nostalgic or ordinary event from their life (Wildschut et al., 2006). After this manipulation, participants completed the State Vitality Scale (Ryan & Frederick, 1997), which includes items such as "At this moment, I feel alive and vital" and "I am looking forward to each new day". Vitality was selected as the dependent variable because it is an indicator of eudaemonic well-being, a critical component of adaptive functioning. That is, vitality represents the extent to which a person feels energized and as if they are a fully functional person.

Based on previous research, people who lack meaning in life should report low vitality. That is, these people should not feel energized and fully functioning. The data supported this prediction: low purpose in life was significantly associated with low vitality. However, nostalgia successfully disrupted this association: the relationship between dispositional meaning and vitality became non-significant in the nostalgia condition. Looked at differently, for people who scored low on dispositional meaning, nostalgia increased vitality relative to the ordinary autobiographical memory condition. Nostalgia promotes psychological well-being for those who are vulnerable to the psychological maladjustment associated with a lack of perceived meaning in life.

People who perceive their lives as meaningless may be particularly vulnerable to experiencing stress in challenging situations (Park & Folkman, 1997). Might nostalgia serve a stress-buffering function for these individuals? We (Routledge et al., 2011) tested this possibility by utilizing a well-established stress experimental paradigm: the Trier Social Stress Test (TSST) (Kirschbaum, Pirke, & Hellhammer, 1993; Kudielka, Hellhammer, & Kirschbaum, 2007). First, we administered a brief, single item measure of dispositional meaning to British undergraduate student participants ("My life has meaning"). Then, we administered a baseline measure of subjective stress. In this measure, participants indicated the extent to which they currently feel "jittery", "fearful", and "ashamed". After this measure, participants were randomly assigned to bring to mind and briefly write about a nostalgic or ordinary autobiographical experience (Wildschut et al., 2006). Next, participants completed the TSST. The TSST consists of a public speaking and arithmetic task and has been shown to reliably increase psychological stress responses (Schlotz et al., 2008). Specifically, following the nostalgia or ordinary memory induction, two research assistants dressed in laboratory coats entered the room and were seated at a desk, facing the participant. The experimenter then told the participants that they would be playing the role of a job candidate for the vacant position of a tour guide and that they needed to prepare a five-minute introduction with the goal of trying to convince the panel of research assistants of their suitability for this position. The participants were provided with paper and pencil and given three minutes to prepare their presentations. After the preparation time expired, one of the panel members instructed the participants to make their presentations. If the participants finished before five minutes, a panel member instructed them to continue. After this task, a panel member instructed the participants to subtract serially the number 17 from 2,023 as fast and accurately as possible. Following each mistake, participants were instructed to start over. This task lasted for five minutes. Immediately following this task, the participants again responded to the stress items previously administered at baseline. They were then given a 30-minute rest period and then responded to the stress items one more time.

The results provided support that nostalgia helps people with meaning deficits to cope with stressful experiences. As would be predicted, in general, subjective stress increased immediately after the stressful job interview task and returned to baseline levels when assessed again 30 minutes later. However, trait levels of meaning and induced nostalgia determined just how stressed people felt right after the stressful task. Specifically, when nostalgia was not induced, subjective stress was higher for those low in trait meaning than those high in trait meaning. In other words, lacking meaning in life increases vulnerability to stress. This finding provides further evidence for the assertion that meaning serves critical functions for psychological health. People who do not perceive their lives as meaningful are at greater risk of experiencing stress during a challenging life experience. Critically, nostalgia mitigated this effect. That is, inducing nostalgia decreased subjective stress. In fact, nostalgia decreased subjective stress for low meaning participants to levels similar to high meaning participants. In other words, nostalgia eliminated the stress-vulnerability associated with deficits in meaning in life.

Though the research on nostalgia as a resource for people suffering from a lack of meaning in life is relatively limited at this point, the results that have been observed are encouraging. They suggest that nostalgia can mitigate some of the psychological and emotional challenges associated with low perceptions of meaning. Additional research is needed to consider the potential long-term benefits of nostalgia for people who perceive their lives as lacking meaning. In addition, future work should test the potential for repeated nostalgia exercises to lead to higher levels of meaning for people with meaning deficits. Will regularly revisiting meaningful past experiences through nostalgia inspire hope for finding new meaning among those who tend to see their present lives as meaningless and lacking purpose? In addition, might nostalgia have intervention potential for clinical disorders that are often associated with meaning deficits, e.g., depression?

Closing Thoughts

In all, the evidence paints a clear picture regarding the existential utility of nostalgia. Nostalgic memories involve the life experiences that people cherish. Nostalgic memories are meaningful memories. And when people revisit these memories they subsequently report a greater sense of meaning in life. Since nostalgia elevates meaning, not surprisingly, when meaning is under threat, people tend to become nostalgic. And this compensatory response is effective. Nostalgia restores meaning following experiences or states that undermine meaning. In addition, nostalgia reduces the need to turn to other forms of meaning defense. Considering that some forms of meaning defense involve ingroup bias, prejudice, and even potentially self-harming behaviors, nostalgia may offer a more pro-social means of maintaining existential security. Finally, nostalgia appears to serve a psychological function for those who have meaning deficits. A brief nostalgia exercise improves psychological health for those who lack meaning in life to levels that are comparable to those who perceive their lives as full of meaning. Thus, not only does nostalgia promote meaning, it also generates the states of well-being that are associated with perceptions of meaning. Nostalgia is a critical meaning-making resource.

8
INDIVIDUAL DIFFERENCES AND NOSTALGIA

Throughout this book I have answered many questions regarding the psychology of nostalgia such as: How do people conceptualize nostalgia? What characterizes the experience of nostalgia? How common is nostalgia? What triggers nostalgia? And what functions does nostalgia serve? I answered these questions from the vantage point of the "typical" person. In other words, in an effort to speak generally about how nostalgia works, I did not consider the potential for individual differences to influence the answers to these questions. And as the empirical psychological study of nostalgia is itself rather new, there has been relatively little attention paid to individual differences. The research that has been conducted in this area does, however, suggest that individual differences play an important role in the extent to which people are nostalgia prone, how people experience nostalgia, and the extent to which nostalgia serves specific functions. In the present chapter, I provide a review of the emerging literature on individual differences and nostalgia. First, I consider trait differences in people's propensity to be nostalgic and discuss recent work elucidating psychological characteristics that may contribute to these differences in nostalgia proneness. I then discuss recent research suggesting that individual differences can influence the content of nostalgia as well as its functionality. I close this chapter with suggestions for future research focused on better revealing the role that individual differences play in nostalgia.

Nostalgia Proneness as an Individual Difference

Are you a nostalgic person? That is, are you the type of person that enjoys regularly re-experiencing the past? Maybe you like to listen to music from your youth, watch movies that were released during your childhood, or look through old photo albums. Chances are you probably do enjoy some of these or related activities as many of us could describe ourselves as "nostalgic people". In fact, if you remember some of the data presented in Chapter 2, nostalgia is a common experience. In one study of young adults, the most common response to a nostalgia frequency question was three to four times a week (Wildschut et al., 2006). It is typical for people to engage in nostalgia many times per week. In that same study, nearly 80 percent of participants indicated experiencing nostalgia as least once per week. And less than 5 percent of participants indicated experiencing nostalgia less than once a month. Other studies paint a similar picture. For example, we (Hepper et al., 2015) reported that approximately 74 percent of participants aged 18–30 experience nostalgia at least once a week and only 15 percent of people in this age group experience nostalgia less than once a month. In general, people tend to be nostalgic.

However, there is also variability in nostalgia proneness. For example, in one of our studies (Wildschut et al., 2006), only 16 percent of participants indicated that they experience nostalgia at least once a day. Thus, not surprisingly, there are people on both ends of the continuum. Many of us frequently engage in nostalgia. However, there are some people for whom nostalgia is a daily activity and some for whom nostalgia is rare. To this end, nostalgia can be treated as an individual difference.

There are a few different scales that have been used to assess nostalgia proneness. The Time Perspective Inventory (TPI) (Zimbardo & Boyd, 1999) is a measure that assesses positive and negative attitudes toward the past, present, and future. Some of the past-focused items reflect nostalgia proneness. These include items such as "I get nostalgic about my childhood" and "It gives me pleasure to think about my past". Though the TPI was not developed for the explicit purpose of conducting nostalgia research, these nostalgic-relevant items have been utilized with success in nostalgia studies (e.g., Routledge et al., 2008). And, consistent with the notion that nostalgia promotes well-being, research has found that people who tend to perceive the past as positive report higher levels of psychological well-being and lower levels of anxiety and depression (Bryant, Smart, & King, 2005; Zimbardo & Boyd, 1999).

Batcho's (1995) Nostalgia Inventory (BNI) was specifically designed to assess nostalgia. In the BNI, participants indicate the extent to which they miss 20 items from their past, e.g., "my family", "my childhood toys", "my school", "not knowing sad or evil things". One advantage of the BNI is that it taps into a wide range of people, places, objects, experiences, and feelings from the past that people may be nostalgic about. However, a drawback of this measure is that people are instructed to indicate how much they miss these things as opposed to how nostalgic they are for them. However, in some instances, the wording of the scale has been changed to more explicitly assess nostalgia. A second drawback is that people may vary in the extent to which they are nostalgic for each of the 20 things listed and thus when the scale is summed and averaged, the overall score is influenced by how much they miss those particular things as opposed to a more general proclivity to engage in nostalgia. It is worth noting, however, that the BNI does typically form a highly reliable composite, thus suggesting that people tend to respond to the different items similarly. In addition, a number of studies have employed a state version of the BNI to test triggers of nostalgia and found theoretically-consistent results (e.g., Juhl et al., 2010; Wildschut et al., 2006).

In his analysis of nostalgia's relation to consumer preferences, Holbrook (1993) also proposed that nostalgia can be treated as a predisposition or individual difference and specifically asserted that it is "a potential facet of individual character – a psychographic variable, aspect of lifestyle, or general costumer characteristics – that may vary among costumers, independent of time – or age-related factors" (p. 246). To assess nostalgia as an individual difference, Holbrook (1993) created a 20-item nostalgia proneness inventory which included items such as "Things used to be better in the good old days" and "The truly great sports heroes are long dead and gone". The Holbrook nostalgia proneness scale has a number of drawbacks. First, since this scale was developed specifically in the context of studying consumer preferences, many of the items (e.g., "Compared to the classics, today's music is trash" and "Products are getting shoddier and shoddier") focused attention on consumer-related nostalgia. Furthermore, many of the items were worded to suggest that nostalgia reflects a dislike of the present or the view that the past was far superior to the present. In other words, Holbrook appeared to be defining nostalgia proneness more as a measure of preference for a particular time period and less as an indicator of the extent to which people like to revisit the past. Finally, for some of the items, it seems difficult to interpret what precisely is being assessed, e.g., "Sometimes, I wish I could return to the womb".

More recently, we (Routledge et al., 2008) developed a nostalgia proneness inventory (the Southampton Nostalgia Scale or SNS) with the goal of establishing a face valid measure that specifically assesses frequency and importance of nostalgia. We initially used this measure to test the potential for nostalgia proneness to buffer existential threat (see Chapter 7). The SNS consists of five items such as "How often do you experience nostalgia?" and "How important is it for you to bring to mind nostalgic experiences?" We (Routledge et al., 2008) found the SNS is significantly correlated with the nostalgia items from the TPI as well as the BNI. A more recent version of the SNS contains two additional items (Barrett et al., 2010).

Many studies have now demonstrated that high nostalgia proneness as measured with the SNS predicts outcomes similar to those caused by experimentally-induced nostalgia (Juhl et al., 2010; Routledge et al., 2008). People who regularly engage in nostalgia appear to gain some psychological benefits from this proclivity. And we (Routledge et al., 2008) demonstrated that the effects of nostalgia proneness are not the result of other relevant individual differences such as self-esteem and satisfaction with life as the effect of nostalgia proneness remained significant even when controlling for a number of other variables. An advantage of the SNS over other nostalgia measures it that is explicitly uses the term nostalgia. And when this instrument is used, researchers typically provide a dictionary definition of the word nostalgia prior to having participants respond to the scale. A limitation of the SNS is that it focuses broadly on how often people engage in and the extent to which they value nostalgia and thus does not assess specific domains of nostalgia.

In sum, a number of scholars have proposed that nostalgia can be treated as a trait and have developed different instruments to assess nostalgia proneness. Studies do indicate that most people engage in nostalgic reflection fairly regularly. Nostalgia is not a rare experience confined to specific age or cultural groups. However, research on the frequency of nostalgia establishes that there is variability in how often people employ nostalgia. For some, nostalgia is a sentiment experienced daily. For others, nostalgia is far less frequent.

What Variables Influence Individual Differences in Nostalgia?

If nostalgia has trait-like qualities, an important question is: what makes someone a nostalgia-prone person? Not surprisingly, nostalgia proneness (as measured by the SNS) is positively correlated with positive attitudes about the past (Routledge et al., 2008). The more pleasant, meaningful, and personally rewarding autobiographical memories people have to draw from, the more they will be motivated to nostalgically revisit the past. This idea is consistent with a resource model of nostalgia: people employ nostalgia to meet psychological needs and counter negative psychological states (see Routledge et al., 2013). Positive past experiences provide the meaningful memories (a psychological resource) that people can bring online via nostalgic reflection to meet psychological needs in the present. In other words, nostalgia prone individuals may have (or believe that they have) more meaningful memories to draw from. Indeed, as previously discussed, people high in nostalgia proneness were most able to maintain a strong sense of meaning in life following an existential threat (Routledge et al., 2008) and this appears to be the result of these individuals actually employing nostalgia as a resource in response to threat (Juhl et al., 2010). In short, people are more likely to be prone to nostalgia if they perceive the past positively. Of course, the other possibility is that nostalgia proneness influences perceptions of the past. That is, perhaps people who are high in trait nostalgia are more likely to have a positively biased view of the past than those low in trait nostalgia. Might nostalgia proneness alter our views of the past? This is a question for future research. For example, longitudinal data could prove informative in determining whether present perceptions of life experiences influence future nostalgic proclivities or whether present nostalgic proclivities influence future perceptions of past experiences.

In terms of personality, studies have found a positive relation between neuroticism and nostalgia proneness (Barrett et al., 2010). Considering the research just discussed suggesting that positive perceptions of the past relate to nostalgia proneness, it is interesting that neuroticism, a trait that reflects chronic negative affect, is also positively associated with nostalgia proneness. The nostalgia as threat regulation perspective could help explain this relation. If people high in neuroticism are more sensitive to psychological threat or simply more apt to experience negative affective states, they may also be more in need of using psychological resources (i.e., nostalgia) to regulate this threat. As previously discussed (Chapter 3), negative affective states trigger nostalgia. Thus, chronic negative affect may be positively associated with frequency of nostalgia.

My colleagues and I (Seehusen et al., 2013) considered another explanation of the link between neuroticism and nostalgia proneness. Specifically, we tested in two studies the possibility that neuroticism predicts nostalgia proneness because neuroticism is associated with a high need to belong (Leary, Kelly, Cottrell, & Schreindorfer, 2006) and that it may be the need to belong (not neuroticism) that influences trait nostalgia. These studies were partially described in Chapter 3 in which I discussed the effects of belongingness needs on nostalgia.

In the first study, a sample of Dutch nationals completed measures of nostalgia proneness (the SNS; Routledge et al., 2008), neuroticism (Denissen, Geenen, Selfhout, & van Aken, 2008), and the need to belong (the need to belong scale or NTBS; Leary et al., 2006). The NTBS specifically assesses the extent to which people are concerned about maintaining social acceptance and avoiding social rejection. It includes items such as "I try hard not to do things that will makes other people avoid or reject me". Consistent with previous work, we found a significant and positive relationship between neuroticism and nostalgia proneness: people high in neuroticism tend to be higher in trait nostalgia. In addition, the need to belong was significantly and positively correlated with both neuroticism and nostalgia proneness. Further, when controlling for the need to belong, the relationship between neuroticism and nostalgia proneness became non-significant. In contrast, the relationship between the need to belong and nostalgia proneness remained significant when controlling for neuroticism. Thus, the relationship between neuroticism and nostalgia proneness appears to be explained by the need to belong. People high in neuroticism are more concerned about belongingness, which, in turn, is associated with a greater tendency to be nostalgic.

A second study replicated and expanded on this finding. Participants completed the seven-item expanded version of the SNS (Barret et al., 2010), a measure of neuroticism (e.g., "I see myself as someone who gets nervous easily"; John, Donahue, & Kentle, 1991), the NTBS (Leary et al., 2006), and the Belongingness Orientation Scale (Lavigne et al., 2011) which, as described in Chapter 3, differentiates between growth and deficit-reduction orientations. As a reminder, the deficit reduction dimension of the scale consists of items such as "My relationships are important to me because they fill a void in my life" and the growth dimension consists of items such as "My relationships are important to me because they allow me to learn about myself".

As before, neuroticism was significantly and positively correlated with nostalgia proneness and the need to belong. In addition, neuroticism was significantly and positively correlated with deficit-reduction orientation but negatively correlated with growth orientation. Also replicating Study 1, the relationship between neuroticism and nostalgia proneness became non-significant when controlling for the need to belong. Expanding on this finding, though the relationship between neuroticism and nostalgia proneness similarly became non-significant when controlling for deficit-reduction orientation, this relationship remained significant when controlling for growth orientation. In other words, it appears to be the deficit-reduction dimension of a belongingness motivation that accounts for the relationship between neuroticism and nostalgia proneness. People high in neuroticism are concerned about their belongingness needs and these concerns are, in turn, associated with a greater tendency to be nostalgic. This explanation of how neuroticism relates to nostalgia proneness is consistent with the findings on the triggers of nostalgia discussed in Chapter 3. That is, research indicates that trait loneliness is associated with higher nostalgia proneness (Zhou et al., 2008) and belongingness threats increase state nostalgia (Seehusen et al., 2013; Wildschut et al., 2006).

Based on this, it might be that other individual differences that are associated with known triggers of nostalgia may predispose people to be nostalgia prone. If nostalgia serves to help regulate psychological threat, than people that are particularly vulnerable to negative psychological states may be inclined to frequently engage in nostalgia, to the extent that nostalgia offers these people psychological security. Much work is needed in this area.

Future research should also more comprehensively consider demographic variables that may be associated with trait nostalgia. For example, as discussed in Chapter 2, nostalgia appears to be commonly experienced across all age groups. We (Hepper et al., 2015), for instance, found little evidence of a strong age effect on nostalgia proneness. We did find some evidence that young adults (aged 18–30) and older adults (aged 76–91) tend to be more nostalgia prone than middle aged adults and proposed that this may result from life transitions that tend to be associated with these age cohorts. However, this was a single study and much more work is needed to test the potential for age to relate to frequency and importance of nostalgia. Another potential demographic variable that could influence nostalgia is gender. However, most research on nostalgia has tended to not find gender differences, though when gender differences are observed the result is that females score higher on nostalgia than males (see Sedikides et al., 2015b). Much work is needed to fully reveal what makes someone a nostalgic person.

Individual Difference and the Content of Nostalgia

Though the research linking individual differences to the content of nostalgic experience is rather sparse at this point, the studies that do exist suggest that traits can significantly impact what people focus on when reflecting on nostalgic experiences. Consider, for example, research concerning how the trait of narcissism influences the content of nostalgic narratives.

Narcissism is a personality trait that reflects an extreme focus on oneself, often at the expense of others. People high in narcissism tend to be self-centered, self-aggrandizing, vain, dominant, entitled, and manipulative. Narcissists are driven by individual success rather than interpersonal harmony. In other words, they are high on agency and low on communion (Back, Schmukle, & Egloff, 2010; Campbell & Foster, 2007; Horton & Sedikides, 2009; Morf, Horvath, & Torchetti, 2011).

As previously discussed, nostalgic memories focus both on agency and communion (Abeyta et al., 2015d; Wildschut et al., 2006). These memories prominently feature the self but are also highly focused on social connections. Since people high in narcissism focus more on agency than communion, we (Hart et al., 2011) proposed that for these individuals, nostalgic memories would be particularly high in agentic themes and low in communion themes. We tested this hypothesis in two studies. In the first study, American undergraduate participants completed the Narcissistic Personality Inventory (NPI) (Raskin & Terry, 1988) which includes items such as "If I ruled the world it would be a much better place". They were then instructed to write about a nostalgic event (Wildschut et al., 2006). We then examined the narrative content of the nostalgia writing task with the Linguistic Inquiry and Word Count (LIWC) (Pennebaker, Francis, & Booth, 2001) which assigns each word of the text to one or more linguistic categories. For this study, we created an agency-communion dictionary which consisted of a total of 190 agency words such as achieve, competitive, competent, dominant, and leader and a total of 188 communal words such as thoughtful, understanding, cooperate, listen, and charitable. After subjecting all of the narratives to this coding process, we examined how trait differences in narcissism related to agency and communion word usage. As predicted, there was a significant and positive relationship between narcissism and the use of agentic words. However, there was no significant relationship between narcissism and use of communal words. The nostalgic narratives of narcissists are more likely to contain agentic themes, but not less likely to contain communal themes than the nostalgic narratives of people low in the trait of narcissism.

In a second study, we (Hart et al., 2011) tested the relation between narcissism and the content of nostalgia using a slightly different approach. Specifically, again, participants completed the NPI (Raskin & Terry, 1988). They then completed a measure assessing the extent to which they were nostalgic about agentic and communal objects and experiences. Agentic objects and experiences included things such as "past successes/achievements" and "being able to focus on what I want". Communal objects and experiences included things such as "my family" and "being part of a group or community". Replicating the findings of Study 1, narcissism was significantly and positively correlated with nostalgia for agentic objects and experiences, but unrelated to nostalgia for communal objects and experiences.

In all, these studies suggest that personality traits associated with self-focus such as narcissism influence the extent to which nostalgia is self-focused or agentic as well as the extent to which people are nostalgic for past experiences that highlight personal success and agency. As previously discussed, nostalgia bolsters both feelings of connectedness and self-esteem. For narcissists, nostalgia may be a particularly potent self-affirming resource. Narcissism does not appear to influence the sociality of nostalgia. However, it does influence the role of the self.

These findings pave the way for future research to consider how traits associated with conceptions of self might influence nostalgia. For example, theory and research indicate that there are individual and cultural differences in the extent to which people define themselves in terms of individual characteristics or social roles and affiliations (Cross, Hardin, & Gercek-Swing, 2011; Markus & Kitayama, 1991). Such differences may have important implications for people's nostalgic memories. People who tend to define themselves in terms of individual pursuits may have more agency-related nostalgic memories. Likewise, those who tend to define themselves in terms of their social connections may have more communion-related nostalgic memories. In addition, though research generally does not find large differences in the frequency or importance of nostalgia as a function of gender and culture, might variables such as these, to the extent that they are related to differences in conceptions of self, influence the nostalgic experience? For example, might cultural differences in variables such as individualism and collectivism predict cultural differences in the content of nostalgic memories?

The only other research to date that has considered the role that individual differences may play in the content of nostalgic narratives focused on attachment style. As previously discussed, nostalgic memories are highly social in nature (Wildschut et al., 2006). When people nostalgically reflect on the past, they tend to think about interpersonal relationships. We (Abeyta et al., 2015d) thus proposed that attachment style may influence the interpersonal details that people focus on when engaging in nostalgic reflection. According to attachment theory, attachment styles represent the extent to which individuals rely on close relationships as stable and available sources of psychological security (Ainsworth & Bell, 1970; Bowlby, 1969). Attachment styles are conceptualized along dimensions of attachment-related avoidance and attachment-related anxiety. Attachment-related avoidance reflects the extent to which people view interpersonal relationships as unavailable sources of psychological security, whereas attachment-related anxiety reflects the extent to which people view themselves as worthy of loving relationships (Brennan, Clark, & Shaver, 1998; Hazan & Shaver, 1987).

Based on other recent research (Wildschut et al., 2010; Juhl, Sand, & Routledge, 2012), by demonstrating that attachment-related avoidance but not anxiety has implications for the social function of nostalgia (a topic I discuss in the next section), we (Abeyta et al., 2015d) reasoned that the avoidance dimension would influence the social content of nostalgic memories. Since nostalgic memories tend to be social in nature, we did not believe that attachment style would influence the general sociality of these memories. Instead, we believed attachment style would affect the particular nature of the social themes. We specifically proposed that in nostalgic narratives there would be a negative relationship between attachment-related avoidance and the extent to which these narratives made reference to feeling loved, protected, and trusted by others – concepts that are key to attachment security.

We tested this proposal in a sample of American undergraduate students. Participants completed the 36-item Experiences in Close Relationships scale (ECR) (Brennan et al., 1998), which measures individual difference in attachment-related avoidance and anxiety. Participants then were randomly assigned to write about a nostalgic or ordinary experience from their past (Wildschut et al., 2006). Subsequently, trained coders independently rated the narratives on a number of content dimensions. One coding category assessed the degree of social interaction referenced in the narrative (i.e., general social content), one category assessed the degree to which the narrative referenced a strong sense of feeling loved, protected, and trusted by others (i.e., attachment-related social content), one category assessed the degree of personal competence, success, and power referenced (i.e., agency content), and another category assessed the emotionality expressed (i.e., positive and negative affect).

Consistent with past research (Wildschut et al., 2006), nostalgic narratives contained more references to social relationships, more agentic themes, and stronger positive (but not negative) emotions than ordinary narratives. Further, though neither attachment dimension influenced the general social content of nostalgic narratives, the avoidance dimension interacted with condition (nostalgia versus ordinary) on attachment-related social content and agency content. Specifically, at low, but not high, levels of attachment-related avoidance, people who wrote nostalgic narratives made more references to feeling loved, protected, and trusted by others than those who wrote non-nostalgic narratives. Looked at differently, within the nostalgia writing condition, but not the ordinary memory condition, lower levels of attachment-related avoidance were associated with a greater amount of attachment-relevant social themes. In addition, at high levels of attachment-related avoidance, people in the nostalgia condition made more references to agentic themes than those in the control condition. Looked at differently, within the nostalgia condition, but not the ordinary memory condition, high levels of attachment-related avoidance were associated with high frequency of agency content.

It is important to reiterate that attachment style did not influence the general sociality of nostalgic narratives. Regardless of differences in attachment style, nostalgic memories are more social than non-nostalgic memories. However, attachment style does influence the nature of these memories. The nostalgic memories of people low in avoidance are more likely to reflect a sense of being loved, trusted, and comforted by others than the nostalgic memories of those high in avoidance. However, the nostalgic memories of people high in avoidance are more likely to reflect a sense of confidence, success, and power than the nostalgic memories of those low in avoidance. Even though nostalgic memories by and large feature close relationships, attachment-related avoidance may have important implications for shaping the specifics of these memories.

In sum, thus far there have only been two published papers considering the role individual differences play in shaping the content of nostalgic memories. This work indicates that psychological traits are important to consider when exploring the particulars of people's nostalgic reflections. Clearly, there is some consensus in what people are nostalgic for and how they reflect on these experiences. However, when getting down to the details, personality matters. And researchers interested in further demarcating the content of nostalgic memories would be wise to consider the critical role that individual differences may play.

Individual Differences and the Functions of Nostalgia

In the previous section, I described research indicating that individual differences can play a role in the nature of the nostalgic experience, the types of themes that are the focus of nostalgic feelings. If individual differences can influence the content of nostalgic memories, might they also impact the functions that nostalgia serves? There are now a number of published studies demonstrating that individual differences sometimes do moderate the functions of nostalgia.

First let us return to the trait of narcissism. In our research on narcissism and nostalgia (Hart *et al.*, 2011), in addition to considering how narcissism influences the content of nostalgia, we examined how narcissism relates to the self and social-related functions of nostalgia. In Study 2 of this series of studies, after participants completed the NPI and before they completed the measure of nostalgic proclivity towards agentic and communal objects and experiences, they were instructed to bring to mind a nostalgic event and list four keywords relevant to this experience (Wildschut *et al.*, 2006). They then responded to items assessing the extent to which thinking about this event made them experience self-positivity (e.g., "makes me feel good about myself" and "makes me feel I have many positive qualities") and social connectedness (e.g., "makes me feel loved and "makes me feel connected to loved ones"). Echoing the findings on agentic and communal content of nostalgia, we found that narcissism was significantly and positively associated with self-positivity but was unrelated to social connectedness.

In our third and final study, we further explored the effects of narcissism on the functions of nostalgia using a sample of Dutch nationals. We assessed narcissism with a shortened version of the NPI (Ames, Rose, & Anderson, 2006). Next, we instructed participants to bring to mind a nostalgic song and to report the name of the song and recording artist. Finally, participants rated how much the song made them feel "good about myself" and "connected with the people I care about". Replicating the results of Study 2, we observed that narcissism was significantly and positively correlated with self-positivity and not significantly related to social connectedness. These findings indicate that people high in the trait of narcissism derive more self-esteem from nostalgia that those low in narcissism. However, despite the fact that narcissists tend to be low in communal orientation (Morf et al., 2011; Sedikides, Campbell, Reeder, Elliot, & Gregg, 2002), these findings suggest that nostalgia may still serve a social function for narcissists. Considering that nostalgic memories tend to involve social themes regardless of individual differences, perhaps revisiting these social memories still serves to boost feelings of connectedness among narcissists even though they do not prioritize communal goals.

Researchers have also explored how attachment style relates to nostalgia's functions. In a series of studies, we (Wildschut et al., 2010) provided the first test of whether attachment style moderates the effects of nostalgia. Attachment style influences how people regulate distress. Specifically, people low in attachment-related avoidance, rely on social bonds to regulate distress (Feeney 2006; Mikulincer & Shaver, 2008). Based on this, we proposed that people low in attachment-related avoidance might be more inclined to use nostalgia as a means to bolster feelings of social connectedness than people high in attachment-related avoidance. Nostalgic memories tend to be highly social in nature (Abeyta et al., 2015d, Wildschut et al., 2006) and when social bonds are threatened (e.g., feeling of loneliness) people often become more nostalgic (e.g., Wildschut et al., 2006). Thus, an individual difference such as attachment-related avoidance that predicts who is most likely to utilize social bonds for psychological security should predict the extent to which people reap social connectedness benefits from nostalgia.

In our (Wildschut et al., 2010) first study, we sought to determine if attachment style, and attachment-related avoidance in particular, predicted the extent to which people use nostalgia as a defense against loneliness. A sample of British undergraduates completed a revised version of the Experience in Close Relationship Scale (ECR-R) (Fraley, Walker, & Brennan, 2000) which, like the original ECR Scale, assesses both attachment-related avoidance and anxiety. Next, participants were asked to describe in writing the circumstances under which they became nostalgic. We then coded participant responses on whether or not loneliness was described as a trigger of nostalgia. In support of our prediction, attachment-related avoidance, but not anxiety, predicted whether or not loneliness was indicated as a nostalgia trigger: people low in attachment-related avoidance, were more likely to list loneliness as a trigger than people high in attachment-related avoidance. This study provides initial evidence for the assertion that attachment style influences the social functionality of nostalgia. People low in avoidance, appear to regulate social distress by turning to nostalgia.

In a second study, utilizing a student and adult British sample, we administered the ECR-R and a measure of loneliness (UCLA Loneliness Scale, v. 3; Russell, 1996). The loneliness measure consists of three subscales which include Isolation (e.g., "How often do you feel isolated from others?"), Relational Connectedness (e.g., "How often do you feel that there are people who really understand you?") and Collective Connectedness (e.g., "How often do you feel like you have a lot in common with people around you?"). We then assessed frequency of nostalgia with two items (e.g., "Generally speaking, how often do you bring to mind nostalgic experiences?"). Providing further support for the notion that attachment style influences the social functionality of nostalgia, we found an interaction between attachment-related avoidance, but not anxiety, and loneliness. Specifically, loneliness was associated with increased nostalgia, but only among those low in attachment-related avoidance. We then examined more specifically each subscale of loneliness. For Isolation and Relational Connectedness, the same pattern of results emerged. For people low, but not high, in attachment-related avoidance, higher Isolation and Deficits in Relational Connectedness were associated with increased nostalgia. No significant interaction between attachment-related avoidance and Collective Connectedness was observed. For people low in attachment-related avoidance, feelings of isolation and a lack of connectedness to others inspire the use of nostalgia.

In the third study of this package we sought to provide experimental evidence for the idea that people low in attachment-related avoidance use nostalgia to regulate social threat. Thus, after assessing attachment dimensions with the ECR-R among a sample of British undergraduates, we manipulated social threat by providing participants with personality feedback suggesting that they were likely to end up alone later in life (social threat) or end up having rewarding relationships (social affirmation; Twenge, Baumeister, Tice, & Stucke, 2001). Participants then received a dictionary definition of nostalgia and responded to three items assessing state nostalgia, e.g., "Right now, I am feeling nostalgic" (Wildschut et al., 2006). Paralleling the findings of the previous two studies, social threat increased state nostalgia, but only among those low in attachment-related avoidance.

In our final two studies of this package, we sought to provide more direct evidence that the social function of nostalgia is influenced by attachment-related avoidance. In Study 4, British undergraduates completed the ECR-R and were then randomly assigned to bring to mind and briefly write about a nostalgic or ordinary experience (Wildschut et al., 2006). Subsequently, participants completed measures of social connectedness (e.g., "Thinking about this event makes me feel loved"), self-esteem (e.g., "Thinking about this event makes me value myself more"), positive affect (e.g., "Thinking about this event makes me feel happy") and negative affect (e.g., "Thinking about this event makes me feel sad").

First, results replicated previous research on the functions of nostalgia. Main effects of nostalgia were observed on social connectedness, self-esteem, and positive affect but not on negative affect. That is, nostalgia increased feelings of connectedness, self-esteem, and positive mood. However, an interaction between attachment-related avoidance and nostalgia was also observed on the social connectedness function. Specifically, the effect of nostalgia increasing feelings of connectedness was only observed among participants low in attachment-related avoidance. In addition, attachment style did not influence the other functions of nostalgia. In other words, the effects of attachment-related avoidance are specific to the social function of nostalgia.

In our final study, we sought to expand upon the findings of Study 4 by testing whether or not attachment-related avoidance might similarly serve to influence the extent to which nostalgia positively influences people's confidence in their ability to provide emotional support to close ones. In a sample of US undergraduates, we administered a brief six-item measure of attachment-related avoidance and anxiety drawn from the Relationship Scales Questionnaire (RSQ) (Griffin & Bartholomew, 1994) and randomly assigned participants to the same nostalgia or control condition used in Study 4. Finally, participants completed the Emotional Support Scale from the Interpersonal Competence Questionnaire (Buhrmester et al., 1988) which assesses perceived competence to provide emotional support to others, e.g., "Helping a close companion get to the heart of a problem he or she is experiencing" and "Being a good and sensitive listener for a companion who is upset". Replicating the findings of the previous study, nostalgia increased the extent to which people perceived themselves to be competent at providing emotional support to close ones. However, this effect was only observed among those low in attachment-related avoidance.

In two studies, we (Juhl, Sand, & Routledge, 2012) built upon our (Wildschut et al., 2010) previous findings by considering the potential for attachment style to influence the extent to which nostalgia influences attitudes and feelings regarding romantic relationships. Research shows that low levels of attachment-related avoidance are associated with successful romantic relationships and positive attitudes about romantic relationships. High levels of attachment-related avoidance are associated with lower levels of intimacy, less relationship satisfaction, and more relationship problems (Collins & Feeney, 2000; Feeney, Noller, & Callan, 1994; Hazen & Shaver, 1987; Levy & Davis, 1988; Mikulincer, 1998). Therefore, we (Juhl et al., 2012) proposed that attachment-related avoidance would moderate the effect of nostalgia on the extent to which people in romantic relationships are satisfied with their relationships as well as the extent to which single people are motivated to pursue romantic relationships.

In our first study we focused on people currently in a romantic relationship. Specifically, American undergraduates who had indicated that they were currently in a romantic relationship completed a measure of attachment-related avoidance and anxiety (ECR-R; Fraley et al., 2000) and were then randomly assigned to a nostalgia or ordinary writing condition (Wildschut et al., 2006). Subsequently, all participants responded to items assessing relationship satisfaction, e.g., "Right now, how satisfied are you with your current relationship?" and "Right now, how successful is your current relationship?". As predicted, results identified a significant interaction between attachment-related avoidance, but not anxiety, and nostalgia. Consistent with past research, in general, low attachment-related avoidance was associated with high levels of relationship satisfaction. However, this relationship was made stronger by nostalgia. For those low in attachment-related avoidance, nostalgia increased relationship satisfaction. For those high in attachment-related avoidance, nostalgia decreased relationship satisfaction.

In our second study we focused on single people. Specifically, American undergraduates who had indicated that they were currently not in a romantic relationship completed a measure of attachment-related avoidance and anxiety (ECR-R; Fraley et al., 2000) and were then randomly assigned to a nostalgia or ordinary writing condition (Wildschut et al., 2006). Subsequently, all participants responded to items assessing their desire to start a romantic relationship, e.g., "Right now, how much do you desire to start a romantic relationship?" and "Right now, how open are you to starting a serious relationship?". The results were nearly identical to those of the previous study. Lower levels of attachment-related avoidance were associated with a greater desire to start a relationship. However, there was also a significant interaction between attachment-related avoidance, but not anxiety, and nostalgia such that nostalgia strengthened the relationship between avoidance and relationship desire. Nostalgia made people low in attachment-related avoidance more interested in pursuing a romantic relationship and people high in attachment-related avoidance less interested in pursuing a romantic relationship.

These findings echo those of our previous work (Wildschut et al., 2010). In all, individual differences in attachment style, and attachment-related avoidance in particular, have clear implications for the social function of nostalgia. For those low in attachment-related avoidance, nostalgia serves a social distress-regulation function: loneliness and social threat increased feelings of nostalgia for people low but not high in attachment-related avoidance. Furthermore, for these low avoidance people, nostalgia strengthens feelings of connectedness to others and contributes to positive attitudes about romantic relationships.

It is worth noting that though the vast majority of the contemporary research indicates that nostalgia's effects are positive, our results suggest that nostalgia may sometimes be problematic and that individual differences may prove critical to understanding when this is the case (Juhl et al., 2012). Specifically, we observed that at high levels of attachment-related avoidance, nostalgia decreases relationship satisfaction among coupled people and the desire to seek out a relationship among single people. This is not to say that nostalgia does not have benefits for people high in attachment-related avoidance. Nostalgia serves multiple functions (Routledge et al., 2013) and people high in avoidance may still gain self-related and existential benefits from engaging in nostalgia. Indeed, as previously discussed, high avoidance is associated with higher frequency of agentic content in nostalgia narratives (Abeyta et al., 2015d) and attachment-related avoidance does not influence the extent to which nostalgia increases positive mood and self-esteem (Wildschut et al., 2010). However, nostalgia may prove problematic for these individuals in the social domain. Additional work is needed to better understand why nostalgia appears to push people high in attachment-related avoidance away from intimate relationships. Since attachment-related avoidance predicts the extent to which nostalgic memories involve intimate feelings of trust (Abeyta et al., 2015d), perhaps the nature of the social content of these memories influences attitudes about current and potential future relationships. Clearly, we have a lot to learn about how attachment style affects nostalgia and relevant social outcomes.

One other study also suggests that nostalgia may have negative consequences for some individuals. In an online experiment with US and UK participants, Verplanken (2012) examined how nostalgia affects individuals who are habitual worriers. Participants completed a measure of mood (PANAS; Watson et al., 1988). Next, habitual worrying was assessed in two steps based on a methods developed by Verplanken et al. (2007). First, participants were instructed to write down three thoughts they occasionally had and that they found most worrying. They then responded to a series of items assessing the extent to which they habitually worried about those thoughts, e.g. "Having these worrying thoughts is something I find hard not to do". Participants were then instructed to bring to mind and visualize in detail a nostalgic or everyday experience. After this manipulation, mood was reassessed with the PANAS and anxiety and depression were assessed with the Hospital Anxiety and Depression Scale (Zigmond & Snaith, 1983) that contains seven items related to anxiety (e.g., "I feel tense or wound up") and seven items related to depression (e.g., "I feel cheerful"). Controlling for baseline affect, results replicated past research indicating that nostalgia increases positive mood. And scores on the habitual worrying measure did not moderate this effect. Even among chronic worriers, nostalgia appears to enhance positive mood. However, there was a significant interaction between habitual worry scores and nostalgia on the anxiety and depression measure such that nostalgia appeared to increase anxiety and depression among those with high (+ 1 SD above the mean) habitual worry scores. This finding suggests that nostalgia may have affectively mixed effects on individuals who tend to worry as it increased positive affect and also anxiety and depression scores for these individuals. However, it is important to note that this was a single study. Future research is needed. Based on these findings, a potentially fruitful direction of future research would be to consider more broadly how individual differences in trait negative affect (e.g., neuroticism) may influence the affective content and functions of nostalgia.

Closing Thoughts

Over the last ten years, social psychologists have conducted dozens of studies considering the content, triggers, and functions of nostalgia. As a result, we have learned quite a bit. In fact, one could argue that we have learned more about nostalgia in the last ten years than we had in the previous centuries. And yet, there is so much more to learn. As discussed in this chapter, a more complete consideration of individual differences will be critical for future efforts to better describe the many ways that people do nostalgia. Individual differences may also prove vital for understanding who is prone to nostalgia and the circumstances that trigger nostalgia. Finally, many of the functions that nostalgia serves may depend on individual differences. Thus far, the only psychological traits that have received significant attention with regards to the functionality of nostalgia are narcissism and attachment style. If we want to form a more detailed and complete picture of the psychology of nostalgia, we will need to more fully consider the many personal characteristics that distinguish us as these traits may be reflected in our nostalgic memories and have consequences for how we engage these memories as well as how they impact our current psychological functioning.

9
THE FUTURE OF THE PAST
Emerging Research on Nostalgia

The concept of nostalgia has been around for centuries. However, the bulk of the scientific work on nostalgia has been done within the last ten years. As noted in the last chapter, though we have learned quite a bit about the experience of nostalgia, the situations and characteristics that instigate nostalgia, and the psychological functions that nostalgia serves, there is still much we do not know. And though I never assumed that in writing this book I would be able to provide a complete analysis of the psychology of nostalgia, I did endeavor to present a current and representative review of the psychological research on this topic. In this final chapter, knowing that empirical interest in nostalgia continues to grow, I discuss some, though certainly not all, of the emerging research that is taking this area of scholarship into new and exciting directions.

A Motivational Approach to the Study of Nostalgia

Future research on the psychology of nostalgia may benefit from the development of a broad regulatory model of nostalgia. Psychologists have argued that behavior is driven by avoidance and approach action tendencies (Carver, 2001; Higgins, 1997). That is, people are motivated to avoid unpleasant states and approach pleasant ones. Approach and avoidance motivations have been argued to occur in parallel (Cacioppo, Gardner, & Bernston, 1999) and the coordination of these motivations may prove vital for adaptive functioning (Carver, 2006; Elliot, 2008; Tamir & Diener, 2008). As discussed throughout this book, negative psychological states trigger nostalgia and nostalgia promotes positive psychological states (see Routledge et al., 2013). In other words, nostalgia serves a restorative function and may thus, more broadly, serve an approach/avoidance regulatory function. Across five studies, we (Stephan et al., 2014) tested this possibility. We specifically hypothesized that nostalgia is a psychological mechanism that serves a motivational regulatory function by counteracting avoidance motivation and facilitating approach motivation.

In our first study we explored that natural relationship between nostalgia and approach and avoidance motivation. In a large sample of Dutch nationals, we assessed trait nostalgia (Routledge et al., 2008) as well as approach and avoidance motivation using a measure of the behavioral inhibition and behavioral approach systems (BIS/BAS) (Carver & White, 1994). The BIS (avoidance motivation) contains items such as "I worry about making mistakes" and the BAS (approach motivation) consists of three sub-factors related to fun seeking (e.g., "I will often do things for no other reason than that they might be fun"), drive or goal-pursuit (e.g., "I go out of my way to get things I want"), and reward responsiveness (e.g., "It would excite me to win a contest").

In support of an approach/avoidance regulatory model, we found that avoidance motivation (BIS) was positively associated with trait nostalgia and, in turn, trait nostalgia was positively associated with approach motivation (all three BAS sub-factors). In addition, avoidance motivation (BIS) was negatively, though not significantly, associated with the fun seeking and drive components of BAS and positively correlated with the reward responsiveness dimension. Further supporting the regulatory hypothesis, the negative relationships between avoidance motivation and dimensions of approach motivation (fun seeking and drive) became stronger and significant after controlling for nostalgia. Further analyses established an indirect effect of avoidance motivation on approach motivation via nostalgia.

Building on the correlation effects of Study 1, in Study 2, we sought to experimentally test the link from avoidance motivation to nostalgia. To manipulate avoidance motivation, American community participants were instructed to think about the future and list five instances or situations that they were worried about and would like to avoid. Participants in a control condition listed five ordinary instances or situations that could happen in the future. A manipulation check confirmed the effectiveness of the avoidance induction. Participants then completed a measure of nostalgia (Batcho, 1995). Finally, participants completed the BAS measure of approach motivation. Supporting the proposal that avoidance motivation triggers nostalgia, participants who brought to mind experiences they wanted to avoid reported greater nostalgia than participants who brought to mind normal (non-threatening) experiences. Further, avoidance-induced nostalgia was associated with higher levels of fun seeking and drive dimensions of approach motivation. Also, when controlling for nostalgia, manipulated avoidance significantly decreased approach motivation on the dimensions of fun seeking and drive. Once again, there was an indirect effect of avoidance motivation on approach motivation via nostalgia.

Since Study 2 involved manipulating avoidance and measuring nostalgia, we designed Study 3 to test the effect of manipulated nostalgia on approach motivation.

American and European participants were randomly assigned to bring to mind and write down keywords relevant to a nostalgic or ordinary experience (Wildschut et al., 2006) and then completed the BAS scale. Consistent with the findings of Studies 1 and 2, participants in the nostalgia condition reported higher levels of fun seeking and drive (but not reward responsiveness) dimensions of approach motivation.

Having established each link of the regulatory model experimentally, we then sought to consider behavioral indicators of nostalgia-induced approach motivation. In Study 4, after receiving a nostalgia or control induction (Wildschut et al., 2006), Chinese undergraduate participants were asked to set up two chairs for what they believed was going to be a social encounter with another participant. If nostalgia increases approach motivation, will it lead participants to place two chairs closer together (social approach)? Study 5 offered a similar behavioral test but instead of a chair placement task, we assessed helping behavior. Specifically, after a nostalgia induction, Chinese undergraduate participants were provided with an opportunity to spontaneously help the experimenter. Specifically, the experimenter walked into the room and spilled a box of pencils. Will nostalgia increase people's willingness to offer help? The results of both studies provided behavioral evidence for the assertion that nostalgia increases approach motivation. Participants in the nostalgia condition placed the chairs for the social interaction closer together (Study 4) and picked up a greater number of pencils (Study 5) than participants in the control condition.

In all, this research offers support for a broad regulatory model of nostalgia. Avoidance motivation inspires nostalgia. And nostalgia, in turn, increases approach motivation. This regulatory analysis has important implications for the study of nostalgia. To the extent that the specific instances of psychological threat (e.g., loneliness, meaninglessness, negative affect, boredom) that trigger nostalgia could be similarly characterized as avoidance-related, having a more generalized regulatory conceptual model of nostalgia may prove helpful for future work seeking to probe nostalgia's ability to counter a wide range of psychological threats.

Nostalgia and Health

Another important area for future research relates to how nostalgia may influence health. There is now clear evidence that nostalgia has psychological utility. When people engage in nostalgic reflection they experience a boost to positive mood, feelings of connectedness to others, self-esteem, and meaning in life. In addition, nostalgia promotes psychological growth and approach motivation. Thus, one important future research direction will be to determine if the benefits of nostalgia extend beyond the psychological. If nostalgia is good for mental health and well-being, might it also benefit physical health? Though little research has been conducted on this topic, early findings are encouraging. Below, I review this emerging work and discuss theoretically guided possibilities for future research testing how nostalgia may benefit health.

A recent series of studies we (Abeyta & Routledge, 2015a) conducted suggests that one way nostalgia may prove beneficial to health is by restoring feelings of youthfulness. History is full of stories about the quest for youth. In American culture we often think of the desire for youth as being a reflection of the goal of wanting to look young. However, the quest for youth can be focused on feeling young and not just looking young. And recapturing feelings of youthfulness may be a worthy endeavor because youth is associated with health and vitality. Indeed, research suggests feeling young is beneficial for successful aging as it predicts a reduced risk of mortality (Kotter-Grühn, Kleinspehn-Ammerlahn, Gerstorf, & Smith, 2009), and is related to psychological well-being and positive health appraisals (e.g., Hubley & Russell, 2009). Building on this idea, we (Abeyta & Routledge, 2015a) proposed that nostalgia may prove beneficial for health and that this may result, in part, from nostalgia's capacity to increase feelings of youthfulness.

The first question then is whether or not nostalgia increases perceived youthfulness. We (Abeyta & Routeldge, 2015a) proposed that it would, based on previous findings in the literature. Consider, for example, research I previously discussed in Chapter 2 on the prototypical features of nostalgia. This research indicates that revisiting the events and feelings of one's youth is a central feature of nostalgia (Hepper *et al.*, 2012). Nostalgic memories tend to feature childhood or adolescent experiences. Other research further indicates that nostalgia offers a way for people to connect with their younger selves. For instance, as previously discussed in Chapter 2, Stephan *et al.* (2012) found that, compared to positive and ordinary memories, nostalgic memories contained more concrete connections between the past and present. This link between past and present facilitated by nostalgia promotes self-continuity by making people feel concretely connected to who they were in the past. Indeed, as previously discussed, recent research indicates that recalling a nostalgic memory, relative to recalling and ordinary memory, increases continuity between past and present selves (Sedikides *et al.*, 2015a). In sum, nostalgia makes people feel connected with their younger selves. Thus, nostalgia should inspire a sense of youthfulness.

To test this, across three studies involving samples of American adults, we (Abeyta & Routledge, 2015a) experimentally manipulated nostalgia and assessed either how old people currently felt in years and/or self-reported feelings of youthfulness. Specifically, in the first study, participants ranging in age from 18 to 62 conducted a Youtube search for a song that made them feel nostalgic or a song they enjoyed but only recently discovered. After listening to and briefly writing about the song, participants responded to the item "At times, people feel older or younger than they actually are. At this moment, what age do you feel?" They provided their answer on a scale ranging from much younger to much older than their current age. Participants then reported their actual age.

The results provided evidence for nostalgia-induced youthfulness. Specifically, there was a significant interaction between actual age and nostalgia on subjective age. Nostalgia did not inspire feelings of youthfulness for young adults. This is consistent with past work on subjective age indicating that how old people feel does not dramatically deviate from actual age until middle-adulthood (e.g., Montepare & Lachman, 1989). However, nostalgia did increase youthful feelings for adults in their 40s and beyond. More precisely, the effect of nostalgia on subjective age became statistically significant at age 42. Beginning in middle age, nostalgia makes people feel younger than their actual age.

In a second study, we sought to replicate and expand upon this finding. Specifically, in this study, participants were randomly assigned to write about either a nostalgic or ordinary past experience (Wildschut et al., 2006). Subsequently, participants rated on a scale how youthful they currently felt and also indicated, in years, the age they currently felt. Participants then reported their actual age. Results were consistent with the findings of Study 1. Nostalgia interacted with actual age to influence youthfulness. This time, nostalgia significantly increased feelings of youthfulness and decreased subjective age for participants 38 years of age or older.

One drawback of the first two studies is that participants in the nostalgia condition may have been mentally travelling back further in time than participants in the control condition. In the control condition of Study 1, by using pleasant music, we controlled for the possibility that the effect of nostalgia may merely be the result of induced positive mood. In fact, in that study we also measured affect and observed no significant differences between conditions on positive or negative affect. However, because the song in this condition was supposed to be a piece that participants had only recently discovered, it did not control for a possible temporal effect. Maybe any exercise of mental time travel to the past, nostalgic or not, would make people feel younger. Study 2 also did not rule out this possibility as participants in the ordinary autobiographical experience condition may have also not travelled mentally back in time as far as participants in the nostalgia condition. To rule out this possible alternative explanation, in Study 3, we instructed all participants to specifically bring to mind an experience from high school.

Specifically, since the first two studies indicated that the effect of nostalgia on subjective age and youthfulness emerges around age 40, we recruited participants age 40 and over. Participants in the nostalgic condition were instructed to "bring to mind a nostalgic memory from high school. That is, think of a fond memory from high school that stands out in your mind as truly nostalgic". Participants in the control condition were instructed to "bring to mind an ordinary memory from high school. That is, think about a mundane occurrence, an experience that you would describe as normal or typical". Participants in both conditions then wrote about this experience. Next, participants responded to items assessing perceived youthfulness. Results were consistent with the previous studies. Nostalgia increased feelings of youthfulness. Since both conditions involved reflecting on an experience from high school, these results indicate that it is nostalgia in particular and not merely mentally travelling back in time that generates feelings of youthfulness.

Importantly, in this study, we also considered the potential for nostalgia-induced youthfulness to have an impact on health. After the measure of youthfulness, participants completed measures of subjective health, confidence about physical fitness, and health-related optimism. We chose subjective health items that reflect an individual's appraisal of their general health. For example, on a scale ranging from very poor to very good, participants were asked to "Please rate your current health status". They also responded to items such as, "I seem to get sick a little easier than other people" (Hays, Shelbourne, & Mazel, 1993). We created confidence in physical fitness items to reflect the perception that people can maintain the same level of physical activity as younger adults. For example, participants responded to items such as "How confident are you that you could do as much physical activity as a 20 year old can without getting overly fatigued or sore?" and "How confident are you that you can keep up with an average 20 year old of your sex?" Finally, we measured health-related optimism with items such as "How do you estimate the likelihood that your health status will worsen in the near future?" and "If you compare yourself with an average person of your sex and age, how likely is it for you that your health will worsen in the near future?" (Warner et al., 2012). Results supported a model linking nostalgia-induced youthfulness to positive health outcomes. Nostalgia increased perceptions of youthfulness, which in turn predicted greater subjective health, more confidence about physical abilities, and increased health-related optimism.

In all, these studies provide promising preliminary research indicating that nostalgia may have benefits that extend beyond psychological states. Specifically, these findings suggest that as people get older, nostalgia may help them remain feeling youthful and physically agentic. And as a result of these feelings of youthfulness, people feel healthier and more optimistic about their future health. This work contributes to research indicating that feeling younger is associated with successful aging (e.g., Hubley & Russell, 2009; Kotter-Grühn, et al., 2009). However, future research is needed to determine if these perceptions of youthfulness and related physical health and agency translate to actual physical health and activity. If nostalgia can, in fact, motivate "youthful" behavior, it may serve as an attractive intervention for increasing health-promotional behaviors such as physical exercise. Building on the regulatory model previously discussed, by activating an approach-orientation, nostalgia may lead to a wide range of positive health behaviors. Clearly, much work is needed in this area.

Beyond the Individual: Personal vs. Collective Nostalgia

Throughout this book I have discussed nostalgia at the personal level. That is, when considering the effects of nostalgia, I have focused on the individual. My discussion focused on the individual because, for the most part, that is what the research has focused on. How does nostalgia influence one's psychological states and attitudes? However, nostalgia may influence outcomes that have consequences beyond the individual. Nostalgia is, after all, a highly social emotional experience. Nostalgic memories tend to be about experiences shared with others. Thus, nostalgia may have implications for groups to the extent that nostalgic memories involve experiences shared with groups (collective nostalgia).

A recent series of studies by Wildschut et al. (2014) explored this possibility. Though a number of scholar have offered qualitative considerations of collective or group-related nostalgia (Brown & Humphreys, 2002; Milligan, 2003; Velikonja, 2009; Volkan, 1999), Wildschut and colleagues sought to empirically assess the impact that nostalgia may have on group-related attitudes, emotions, and motivation.

In their first study, Wildschut et al. (2014) tested the proposal that reflecting on a collective nostalgic experience (i.e., a an experience shared with ingroup members) would increase positive attitudes toward the ingroup as well as motivation to spend more time with the ingroup. Specifically, British undergraduate participants were randomly assigned to one of four conditions: collective nostalgia, personal nostalgia, collective positive event, no reflective task. Participants in the collective nostalgia condition were instructed to bring to mind a nostalgic event from their student life that they had experienced together with other students at their university. Participants in the personal nostalgic condition were instructed to bring to mind a nostalgic event from their personal life as a unique individual. Participants in the collective positive event condition were instructed to bring to mind a lucky event from their student life that they had experienced with other students at their university. In the no-event condition, participants completed the dependent variable without engaging in any kind of reflective task. To assess evaluation of the ingroup, participants rated the extent to which students at their university were presently: "humorous", "warm", "flexible", "fun to be with", "dependable", and "trustworthy". To assess ingroup motivation, participants responded to items indicating the extent to which they wanted to be involved with other students as a group at the university, e.g., "I want to talk to them" and "I want to spend time with them". Supporting the proposition that collective nostalgia has unique implications for the group, results indicated that participants in the collective nostalgia condition rated the ingroup significantly more positively than the participants in all other conditions. Similarly, collective nostalgia, relative to all other conditions, increased motivation to get more involved with the ingroup. When people reflect nostalgically on an experienced shared with a group, they subsequently feel more positive about that group and experience a greater motivation to engage the group.

In the second study of their package, Wildschut and colleagues furthered their analysis by considering the potential for collective self-esteem to mediate the effect of collective nostalgia on ingroup attitudes. Using a sample of British undergraduates, the researchers had participants bring to mind and briefly write about a collective nostalgia experience, individual nostalgia experience, or an ordinary experience. Subsequently, participants completed a measure of collective self-esteem, e.g., "I am a worthy member of the University of Southampton community" and "Being a member of the social group of students at the University of Southampton is an important reflection of who I am" (Luhtanen &

Crocker, 1992). Finally, participants responded to a measure related to investment in the ingroup. Specifically, participants read about a publicity campaign that the university was planning to implement that would involve asking current students to volunteer time. They were then asked to indicate how many hours (0–10) they would be willing to volunteer. Results indicated that collective nostalgia, relative to ordinary and non-nostalgia recall conditions, increased collective self-esteem as well as the number of hours participants were willing to volunteer for the ingroup. Finally, the effect of collective nostalgia on ingroup volunteering was mediated by collective self-esteem.

Wildschut *et al.* (2014) further sought to explore potential moderators of the effects of collective nostalgia. They proposed that collective nostalgia would be most impactful on those who highly identify with their social group. To test this, in a study involving Irish undergraduate students, participants first completed a measure of social identification focused on nationality (Tarrant, North, & Hargreaves, 2004). Specifically, they responded to items such as "I identify with this group" and "I think this group is important". Participants then recalled a nostalgic event they experienced with other Irish people (collective nostalgia) or an ordinary event that they had experienced with other Irish people (collective ordinary event). Participants then were led to believe that they were playing a resource distribution computer game online with other players and that they would be randomly assigned to a particular role in the game. In actuality, all participants were assigned to the role of observer, which involved monitoring the other players. In this role, the participant was essentially able to punish another participant if they did not reasonably distribute tokens (money) to the third player. The researchers created names for the other players that would indicate to the participant whether they were also part of the ingroup (Irish) or were part of an outgroup (from another nation; Van Tilburg & Igou, 2011). They procedure was designed such that the outgroup member did not distribute very much money to the ingroup member. The dependent measure was the extent to which the participant wanted to spend her or his own allocated tokens to punish the outgroup player. The researchers found that collective nostalgia significantly increased the number of tokens participants sacrificed in order to punish the outgroup player who transgressed against the ingroup player. However, this effect was only significant for participants who scored high on ingroup identification. In other words, among people who highly identified with being Irish, collective nostalgia motivated a willingness to make a personal sacrifice for a fellow Irish individual who had been treated unfairly.

In sum, the effects of nostalgia appear to extend beyond the individual. When people reflect upon nostalgic experiences shared with a group, they are more inclined to support that group and more interested in engaging that group. And the effect of collective nostalgia on ingroup attitudes appears to be driven by elevated collective self-esteem. Also, for those who highly identify with the group, collective nostalgia drives defense of the group, even if such behavior involves personal sacrifice. The findings of Wildschut et al. (2014) have important implications for the study of group-related processes. For one, collective nostalgia may be one psychological resource that promotes the preservation of groups and harmony in groups. That is, nostalgia for times spent with ingroup members may serve as a social glue that helps keep a group connected and motivates efforts to maintain a group identity as groups are challenged by the diverse goals and ambitions of individual members.

In addition, future research should also consider the potential dangers associated with collective nostalgia. Depending on the group and the social context, collective nostalgia could contribute to negative social outcomes. For example, collective nostalgia for past experiences that marginalize outgroup members could contribute to continued prejudice and social conflict. When the television program Mad Men first aired and immediately gained popularity, I remember reading stories about people's (particularly white men) nostalgia for the work environment of decades past. Of course, the work environment portrayed in Mad Men is likely to not be an accurate portrayal of the average white-collar business day during the 1950s and 1960s. I am assuming most professionals were not permitted to drink alcohol and take periodic naps on their office couches throughout the workday. Importantly, as is highlighted in the show over subsequent seasons, women and ethnic minorities were often subject to discriminatory practices that prevented them from fully participating in the workforce or being fairly financially compensated. Thus, collective nostalgia, to the extent that it reinforces discriminatory practices against other groups either directly or indirectly may have negative social consequences. Much work is needed to fully explore the potential social benefits and consequences of collective nostalgia.

Nostalgia in the Internet Age

I regularly get calls from reporters about my research on nostalgia and I am frequently asked questions related to nostalgia's prevalence on the Internet. Do people use the Internet as a tool to nostalgically revisit their pasts? Critically, do people reap benefits from this type of nostalgic experience? Of course, the Internet offers many ways to experience nostalgia. The question then is: does website-induced nostalgia serve psychological functions? My colleagues and I (Cox, Kersten, Routledge, Brown, & Van Enkevort, 2015) conducted three studies to address this question.

In the first study, we (Cox et al., 2015) exposed participants to one of two websites we created to look very similar to actual websites. The nostalgia website was based on the Dear Old Love website which contains short love notes that readers have posted. Participants in this condition read ten one-sentence love notes. The control condition website (eChat) was designed to also be social but to focus on ordinary daily activities. In other words, some participants were looking at old love notes and some participants were looking at people's comments on everyday life. Our goal with these websites was to create stimuli that closely resembled actual websites. After participants were exposed to the websites, we measured state nostalgia (e.g., "Right now I am having nostalgic feelings"). We subsequently measured affect with the PANAS (Watson et al., 1988) and satisfaction with life (Diener et al., 1985).

First, we determined whether or not our nostalgia website successfully induced nostalgia. It did. Participants in the Dear Old Love condition reported significantly higher levels of nostalgia than participants in the eChat condition. We then tested the effects of website exposure on affect and satisfaction with life. Participants in the Dear Old Love condition reported significantly higher levels of both positive affect and satisfaction with life than participants in the eChat condition. There was no significant effect on negative affect. Finally, we sought to determine if nostalgia was responsible for these effects on affect and well-being. We conducted mediation analyses in which felt nostalgia was entered as a mediator. These mediation tests revealed that website-induced nostalgia mediated the observed effects. Visiting websites that increase nostalgic feelings, benefits mood and well-being.

In the second study, we (Cox et al., 2015) wanted to further this analysis of website-induced nostalgia by using a different nostalgia-related website and considering a different psychological function. In the nostalgia condition, we had participants view pictures from the website Dear Photograph. This website consists of photographs in which people are reproducing scenes from their past. Specifically, the pictures are of people holding up old photographs at the same location where that old photo was taken. The website thus serves as a communal photo album connecting past to present. In the control condition, we had participants view pictures taken from the website Flickr. This website also consists of people's photos, but does not explicitly reference the past.

Again, we measured state nostalgia. Subsequently, to test a social connectedness function of website-induced nostalgia, we assessed perceptions of connectedness to others with items such as "I feel close and connected with other people who are important to me" and "I feel a strong sense of intimacy with the people I spend time with" (Sheldon, Abad, & Hinsch, 2011).

Participants who looked at Dear Photograph reported significantly higher levels of nostalgia and social connectedness than participants who looked at Flickr. Further, felt nostalgia mediated the effect of website on social connectedness. Website-induced nostalgia also benefits social well-being.

In our final study, we again assigned participants to look at images from Dear Photograph or Flickr. However, we used two different Flickr control conditions. One Flickr condition was the same as before. The second Flickr condition featured pictures specifically involving close relationships, e.g., romantic couples, families. We included this additional condition to help control for the high level of sociality that may be present in many nostalgia-based images. Participants again completed a measure of felt nostalgia and the PANAS.

ticipants in the Dear Photograph condition reported significantly higher levels of felt nostalgia than participants in either Flickr condition. A similar effect was observed on positive affect. That is, participants in the Dear Photograph condition reported significantly higher levels of positive affect than participants in either Flickr condition. Once again, there was no significant effect on negative affect. Finally, as in the previous studies, the effect of website was mediated by felt nostalgia.

In all, these three studies take the work that has been discussed in this book on the functions of nostalgia in a more applied direction. Website-induced nostalgia positively contributes to psychological and social well-being. These studies are the first to test whether social media websites increase nostalgia and well-being. Therefore, much more work is needed to understand how people use the Internet as a nostalgia resource. For instance, what individual differences and situations might motivate people to seek out nostalgia on the Internet? Considering previous research indicating that a number of psychological threats trigger nostalgia (see Routledge *et al.*, 2013), might people visit nostalgia-related websites or engage in nostalgia-related activities such as posting old photos on social media sites when the feel distressed or vulnerable? And does web-based nostalgia counter these negative feelings and restore psychological well-being?

REFERENCES

Abeyta, A., & Routledge, C. (2015a). *The fountain of youth: The effects of nostalgia on subjective age and implications for health*. Unpublished manuscript, North Dakota State University.

Abeyta, A., Routledge, C., & Juhl, J. (2015b). *Looking back to move forward: Nostalgia as a psychological resource for promoting relationship goals and overcoming relationship challenges*. Unpublished manuscript, North Dakota State University.

Abeyta, A., Routledge, C., & Kramer, M. (2015c). *Nostalgia mitigates the relationship between poor subjective health and low meaning in life*. Unpublished manuscript, North Dakota State University.

Abeyta, A., Routledge, C., Sedikides, C., & Wildschut, R. T. (2015d). Attachment-related avoidance and the social content of nostalgic memories. *Journal of Social and Personal Relationships, 32*, 406–413. doi: 10.1177/0265407514533770

Ainsworth, M. D. S., & Bell, S. M. (1970). Attachment, exploration, and separation: Illustrated by the behavior of one-year-olds in a strange situation. *Child Development, 41*, 49–67.

Alicke, M. D., & Sedikides, C. (2009). Self-enhancement and self-protection: What they are and what they do. *European Review of Social Psychology, 20*, 1–48. doi: 10.1080/10463280802613866

Allen, N. (2012, December 28). Hollywood makes 2013 the year of the sequel. *The Telegraph*. Retrieved from http://www.telegraph.co.uk/culture/film/film-news/9770154/Hollywood-makes-2013-the-year-of-the-sequel.html.

Ames, D. R., Rose, P., & Anderson, C. P. (2006). The NPI-16 as a short measure of narcissism. *Journal of Research in Personality, 40*(4), 440–450.

Anderson, N. H. (1968). Likableness ratings of 555 personality-trait words. *Journal of Personality and Social Psychology, 9*, 272–279.

Anderzén, I., & Arnetz, B. B. (1999). Psychophysiological reactions to international adjustment: Results from a controlled, longitudinal study. *Psychotherapy and Psychosomatics, 68*, 67–75.

Arndt, J., Cox, C. R., Goldenberg, J. L., Vess, M., Routledge, C., Cooper, D. P., & Cohen, F. (2009). Blowing in the (social) wind: Implications of extrinsic esteem contingencies for terror management and health. *Journal of Personality and Social Psychology, 96*, 1191–1205. doi: 10.1037/a0015182

Arndt, J., Landau, M. J., Vail, K., & Vess, M. (2013). An edifice for enduring personal value: A terror management perspective on the human quest for multi-level meaning. In K. Markman, K. T. Proulx, & M. Lindberg, (Eds.), *The psychology of meaning* (pp 49–69). Washington, DC: American Psychological Association.

Aron, A., Aron, E. N., & Smollan, D. (1992). Inclusion of other in the self scale and the structure of interpersonal closeness. *Journal of Personality and Social Psychology, 63*(4), 596.

Back, M. D., Schmukle, S. C., & Egloff, B. (2010). Why are narcissists so charming at first sight? Decoding the narcissism–popularity link at zero acquaintance. *Journal of Personality and Social Psychology, 98*(1), 132.

Baldwin, M., Biernat, M., & Landau, M. J. (2015). Remembering the real me: Nostalgia offers a window to the intrinsic self. *Journal of Personality and Social Psychology, 108*(1), 128–147.

Baldwin, M., & Landau, M. J. (2014). Exploring nostalgia's influence on psychological growth. *Self and Identity, 13*, 162–177. doi: 10.1080/15298868.2013.772320

Bargh, J. A., & T. L. Chartrand (2000). Studying the mind in the middle: A practical guide to priming and automaticity research. In H. Reis & C. Judd (Eds.), *Handbook of research methods in social psychology* (pp. 253–285). New York: Cambridge University Press.

Barrett, F. S., Grimm, K. J., Robins, R. W., Wildschut, T., Sedikides, C., & Janata, P. (2010). Music-evoked nostalgia: Affect, memory, and personality. *Emotion, 10*, 390–403. doi: 10.1037/a0019006

Barrett, L. F., & Russell, J. A. (1998). Independence and bipolarity in the structure of current affect. *Journal of Personality and Social Psychology, 74*, 967–984. doi: 10.1037/0022-3514.74.4.967

Batcho, K. I. (1995). Nostalgia: A psychological perspective. *Perceptual and Motor Skills, 80*, 131–143. doi: 10.2466/pms.1995.80.1.131

Batcho, K. I. (1998). Personal nostalgia, world view, memory, and emotionality. *Perceptual and Motor Skills, 87*, 411–432. doi: 10.2466/pms.1998.87.2.411

Batson, C. D. (1991). *The altruism question: Toward a social-psychological answer*. Hillsdale, NJ: Erlbaum.

Batson, C. D., Fultz, J., & Shoenrade, P. A. (1987). Distress and empathy: Two qualitative distinct vicarious emotions with different motivational consequences. *Journal of Personality, 55*, 10–38.

Baumeister, R. (1991). *Meanings of life*. New York: Guilford Press.

Baumeister, R. F., DeWall, C. N., Ciarocco, N. J., & Twenge, J. M. (2005). Social exclusion impairs self-regulation. *Journal of Personality and Social Psychology, 88*(4), 589–604. doi: 10.1037/0022-3514.88.4.589

Baumeister, R. F., & Leary, M. R. (1995). The need to belong: Desire for interpersonal attachments as a fundamental human motivation. *Psychological Bulletin, 117*, 497–529. doi: 10.1037/0033-2909.117.3.497

Baumeister, R. F., Smart, L., & Boden, J. M. (1996). Relation of threatened egotism to violence and aggression: The dark side of high self-esteem. *Psychological Review, 103*(1), 5.

Becker, E. (1971). *The birth and death of meaning*. New York: Free Press.

Becker, E. (1973). *The denial of death*. New York: Free Press.

Bellow, S. (2013). *Mr Sammler's planet*. London: Penguin.

Berglas, S., & Jones, E. E. (1978). Control of attributions about the self through self-handicapping strategies: The appeal of alcohol and the role of underachievement. *Personality and Social Psychology Bulletin, 4*(2), 200–206.

References

Best, J., & Nelson, E. E. (1985). Nostalgia and discontinuity: A test of the Davis hypothesis. *Sociology and Social Research, 69,* 221–233.

Bower, J. E., Kemeny, M. E., Taylor, S. E., & Fahey J. L. (1998). Cognitive processing, discovery of meaning, CD4 decline, and AIDS-related mortality among bereaved HIV-seropositive men. *Journal of Consulting and Clinical Psychology, 66,* 979–986.

Bowlby, J. (1969). *Attachment and loss, Volume I: Attachment.* New York: Basic Books.

Boym, S. (2001). *The future of nostalgia.* New York: Basic Books.

Brennan, K. A., Clark, C. L., & Shaver, P. R. (1998). Self-report measurement of adult attachment. In J. A. Simpson & W. S. Rholes (Eds.), *Attachment theory and close relationships* (pp. 46–76). New York: Guilford Press.

Brown, A. D., & Humphreys, M. (2002). Nostalgia and the narrativization of identity: A Turkish case study. *British Journal of Management, 13*(2), 141.

Brown, S., Kozinets, R. V., & Sherry, J. F. (2003). Teaching old brands new tricks: Retro branding and the revival of brand meaning. *Journal of Marketing, 67,* 19–33.

Bryant, F. B., Smart, C.M., & King S.P. (2005). Using the past to enhance the present: Boosting happiness through positive reminiscence. *Journal of Happiness Studies, 6,* 227–260.

Buhrmester, D., Furman, W., Wittenberg, M. T., & Reis, H. T. (1988). Five domains of interpersonal competence in peer relationships. *Journal of Personality and Social Psychology, 55*(6), 991.

Burke, B., Martens, A., & Faucher, E. (2010). Two decades of terror management theory: A meta-analysis of mortality salience research. *Personality and Social Psychology Review, 14*(2), 155–195. doi: 10.1177/1088868309352321

Cacioppo, J. T., Gardner, W. L., & Berntson, G. G. (1999). The affect system has parallel and integrative processing components: Form follows function. *Journal of Personality and Social Psychology, 76,* 839–855. doi: 10.1037/0022-3514.76.5.839

Cacioppo, J. T., & Hawkley, L. C. (2003). Social isolation and health, with an emphasis on underlying mechanisms. *Perspectives in Biology and Medicine, 46*(3), S39–S52.

Cacioppo, J. T., Hawkley, L. C., & Thisted, R. A. (2010). Perceived social isolation makes me sad: 5-year cross-lagged analyses of loneliness and depressive symptomatology in the Chicago Health, Aging, and Social Relations Study. *Psychology and Aging, 25*(2), 453.

Cacioppo, J. T., Hughes, M. E., Waite, L. J., Hawkley, L. C., & Thisted, R. A. (2006). Loneliness as a specific risk factor for depressive symptoms: cross-sectional and longitudinal analyses. *Psychology and Aging, 21*(1), 140.

Campbell, W. K., & Foster, J. D. (2007). The narcissistic self: Background, an extended agency model, and ongoing controversies. In C. Sedikides & S. Spencer (Eds.), *Frontiers in social psychology: The self* (pp. 115–138). Philadelphia: Psychology Press.

Campbell, W. K., & Sedikides, C. (1999). Self-threat magnifies the self-serving bias: A meta-analytic integration. *Review of General Psychology, 3,* 23–43. doi: 10.1037/1089-2680.3.1.23

Carnelley, K. B., & Janoff-Bulman, R. (1992). Optimism about love relationships: General vs specific lessons from one's personal experiences. *Journal of Social and Personal Relationships, 9,* 5–20. doi: 10.1177/0265407592091001

Carver, C. S. (2001). Affect and the functional bases of behavior: On the dimensional structure of affective experience. *Personality and Social Psychology Review, 5,* 345–356. doi: 10.1207/S15327957PSPR0504_4

Carver, C. S. (2006). Approach, avoidance, and the self-regulation of affect and action. *Motivation and Emotion, 30,* 105–110. doi: 10.1007/s11031-006-9044-7

Carver, C. S., & White, T. L. (1994). Behavioral inhibition, behavioral activation and affective responses to impending reward and punishment: The BIS/BAS scales. *Journal of Personality and Social Psychology, 67*, 319–333. doi: 10.1037/0022-3514.67.2.319

Castelnuovo-Tedesco, P. (1980). Reminiscence and nostalgia: The pleasure and pain of remembering. In S. I. Greenspan & G. H. Pollack (Eds.), *The course of life: Psychoanalytic contributions toward understanding personality development: Vol. III: Adulthood and the aging process* (pp. 104–118). Washington: US Government Printing Office.

Chandler, M. J., Lalonde, C. E., Sokol, B. W., Hallett, D., & Marcia, J. E. (2003). Personal persistence, identity development, and suicide: A study of native and non-native North American adolescents. *Monographs of the Society for Research in Child Development*, i–138.

Chandler, M. J., & Proulx, T. (2008). Cultures in collision: Commentary on O'Sullivan-Lago, de Abreu, and Burgess. *Human Development, 51*(5–6), 374–381. doi: 10.1159/000170899

Cheung, W. Y., Wildschut, T., Sedikides, C., Hepper, E. G., Arndt, J., & Vingerhoets, A. J. J. M. (2013). Back to the future: Nostalgia increases optimism. *Personality and Social Psychology Bulletin, 39*, 1484–1496.

Cohen, S. (2004). Social relationships and health. *American Psychologist, 59*(8), 676–684. doi: 10.1037/0003-066X.59.8.676

Collins, N. L., & Feeney, B. C. (2000). A safe haven: An attachment theory perspective on support seeking and caregiving in intimate relationships. *Journal of Personality And Social Psychology, 78*(6), 1053–1073. doi: 10.1037/0022-3514.78.6.1053

Cox, C. R., Kersten, M., Routledge, C., Brown, E. M., & Van Enkevort, E. A. (2015). When past meets present: The relationship between website-induced nostalgia and well-being. *Journal of Applied Social Psychology, 45*(5), 282–299.

Crocker, J., & Wolfe, C.T. (2001). Contingencies of self-worth. *Psychological Review, 108*, 593–623.

Cross, S. E., Hardin, E. E. & Gercek-Swing, B. (2011). The what, how, and why of self-construal. *Personality and Social Psychology Review, 15*, 142–179.

Cutrona, C. E., & Russell, D. W. (1987). The provisions of social relationships and adaptation to stress. *Advances in Personal Relationships, 1*(1), 37–67.

Dalebroux, A., Goldstein, T. R., & Winner, E. (2008). Short-term mood repair through art-making: Positive emotion is more effective than venting. *Motivation and Emotion, 32*(4), 288–295.

Darwin, C. (1896). *The expression of the emotions in man and animals.* New York: D. Appleton and Company. (Original work published 1872)

Davis, F. (1977). Nostalgia, identity and the current nostalgia wave. *The Journal of Popular Culture, 11*(2), 414–424.

Davis, F. (1979). *Yearning for yesterday: A sociology of nostalgia.* New York: The Free Press.

Deci, E. L., & Ryan, R. M. (2000). The "what" and "why" of goal pursuits: human needs and the self-determination of behavior. *Psychological Inquiry, 11*, 227–268.

Denissen, J. J., Geenen, R., Selfhout, M., & Van Aken, M. A. (2008). Single-item big five ratings in a social network design. *European Journal of Personality, 22*(1), 37–54.

DeWall, C. N., & Baumeister, R. F. (2006). Alone but feeling no pain: Effects of social exclusion on physical pain tolerance and pain threshold, affective forecasting, and interpersonal empathy. *Journal of Personality and Social Psychology, 91*(1), 1.

DeWall, C. N., Baumeister, R. F., & Vohs, K. D. (2008). Satiated with belongingness? Effects of acceptance, rejection, and task framing on self-regulatory performance. *Journal of Personality and Social Psychology, 95*(6), 1367.

Diener, E., & Diener, C. (1996). Most people are happy. *Psychological Science, 7*, 181–185. doi: 10.1111/j.1467-9280.1996.tb00354.x

Diener, E., Horwitz, J., & Emmons, R. A. (1985). Happiness of the very wealthy. *Social Indicators Research, 16*, 263–274.
Elliot, A. J. (Ed.) (2008). *Handbook of approach and avoidance motivation*. Mahwah, NJ: Erlbaum.
Elliot, A. J., Gable, S. L., & Mapes, R. R. (2006). Approach and avoidance motivation in the social domain. *Personality and Social Psychology Bulletin, 32*, 378–391.
Eysenck, H. J., & Eysenck, S. B. G. (1975). *Eysenck personality questionnaire*. Kent: Hodder and Stroughton.
Feeney, J. A. (2006). Parental attachment and conflict behavior: Implications for offspring's attachment, loneliness, and relationship satisfaction. *Personal Relationships, 13*(1), 19–36.
Feeney, J. A., Noller, P., & Callan, V. J. (1994). Attachment style, communication and satisfaction in the early years of marriage. In K. Bartholomew, D. Perlman, K. Bartholomew, & D. Perlman (Eds.), *Attachment processes in adulthood* (pp. 269–308). London: Jessica Kingsley Publishers.
Fein, S., & Spencer, S. J. (1997). Prejudice as self-image maintenance: Affirming the self through derogating others. *Journal of Personality and Social Psychology, 73*(1), 31.
Florian, V., & Kravetz, S. (1983). Fear of personal death: Attribution, structure, and relation to religious belief. *Journal of Personality and Social Psychology, 44*(3), 600–607. doi: 10.1037/0022-3514.44.3.600
Fodor, N. (1950). Varieties of nostalgia. *Psychoanalytic Review, 37*, 25–38.
Fraley, R. C., Waller, N. G., & Brennan, K. A. (2000). An item response theory analysis of self-report measures of adult attachment. *Journal of Personality and Social Psychology, 78*(2), 350.
Frankl, V. E. (1997). *Man's search for ultimate meaning*. New York: Plenum.
Gable, S. L. (2006). Approach and avoidance social motives and goals. *Journal of Personality, 74*(1), 175–222.
Gardner, W. L., Pickett, C. L., & Knowles, M. L. (2005). Social snacking and shielding: Using social symbols, selves, and surrogates in the service of belongingness needs. In K. D. Williams, J. P. Forgas, & von Hippel, W (Eds.), *The social outcast: Ostracism, social exclusion, rejection, and bullying* (pp. 227–241). New York: Psychology Press.
Goodson, I., Moore, S., & Hargreaves, A. (2006). Teacher nostalgia and the sustainability of reform: The generation and degeneration of teachers' missions, memory, and meaning. *Educational Administration Quarterly, 42*(1), 42–61. doi: 10.1177/0013161X05278180
Green, J. D., & Campbell, W. K. (2000). Attachment and exploration in adults: Chronic and contextual accessibility. *Personality and Social Psychology Bulletin, 26*(4), 452–461. doi: 10.1177/0146167200266004
Greenberg, J., Pyszczynski, T., & Solomon, S. (1986). The causes and consequences of a need for self-esteem: A terror management theory. In R. F. Baumeister (Ed.), *Public self and private self* (pp.189–212). New York: Springer-Verlag.
Greenberg, J., Pyszczynski, T., Solomon, S., Simon, L., & Breus, M. (1994). Role of consciousness and accessibility of death-related thoughts in mortality salience effects. *Journal of Personality and Social Psychology, 67*(4), 627.
Greenberg, J., Solomon, S., & Arndt, J. (2008). A basic but uniquely human motivation. In J. Y. Shah & W. L. Gardner, *Handbook of motivation science* (pp. 114–134). New York: Guilford Press.
Greenwald, A. G., & Farnham, S. D. (2000). Using the implicit association test to measure self-esteem and self-concept. *Journal of Personality and Social Psychology, 79*(6), 1022.
Griffin, D. W., & Bartholomew, K. (1994). Models of the self and other: Fundamental dimensions underlying measures of adult attachment. *Journal of Personality and Social Psychology, 67*(3), 430.

Gross, J. J. (1998). The emerging field of emotion regulation: An integrative review. *Review of General Psychology, 2*(3), 271–299. doi: 10.1037/1089-2680.2.3.271

Grossman, P., Niemann, L., Schmidt, S., & Walach, H. (2004). Mindfulness-based stress reduction and health benefits: A meta-analysis. *Journal of Psychosomatic Research, 57*(1), 35–43.

Haddock, G., Zanna, M. P., & Esses, V. M. (1993). Assessing the structure of prejudicial attitudes: The case of attitudes toward homosexuals. *Journal of Personality and Social Psychology, 65*(6), 1105.

Harlowe, L., Newcomb, M., & Bentler, P. (1986). Depression, self-derogation, substance abuse, and suicide ideation: Lack of purpose in life as a mediational factor. *Journal of Clinical Psychology, 42*, 5–21.

Hart, C. M., Sedikides, C., Wildschut, T., Arndt, J., Routledge, C., & Vingerhoets, A. J. (2011). Nostalgic recollections of high and low narcissists. *Journal of Research in Personality, 45*(2), 238–242.

Havlena, W. J., & Holak, S. L. (1991a). "The good old days": Observations on nostalgia and its role in consumer behavior. *Advances in Consumer Research, 18*, 323–329.

Havlena, W. J., & Holak, S. L. (1991b). A time-allocation analysis of nostalgia-evoking events. In J. C. Chabat & M. V. Venkatesan (Eds.), *Proceedings of the VIIth John-Labatt Marketing Research Seminar, Time and Consumer Behavior*. Montreal: UQAM.

Hawkley, L. C., & Cacioppo, J. T. (2010). Loneliness matters: A theoretical and empirical review of consequences and mechanisms. *Annals of Behavioral Medicine, 40*(2), 218–227.

Hays, R. D., Sherbourne, C. D., & Mazel, R. M. (1993). The rand 36-item health survey 1.0. *Health Economics, 2*(3), 217–227.

Hazan, C., & Shaver, P. (1987). Romantic love conceptualized as an attachment process. *Journal of Personality and Social Psychology, 52*(3), 511.

Heine, S. J., Proulx, T., & Vohs, K. D. (2006). The meaning maintenance model: On the coherence of social motivations. *Personality and Social Psychology Review, 10*(2), 88–110.

Heintzelman, S. J., & King, L. A. (2014). Life is pretty meaningful. *American Psychologist, 69*(6), 561–574.

Hendrickson, B., Rosen, D., & Aune, R. K., (2010). An analysis of friendship networks, social connectedness, homesickness and satisfaction levels of international students. *International Journal of Intercultural Relations, 35*, 281–295. doi: 10.1016/j.ijintrel.2010.08.001

Hepper, E. G., Ritchie, T. D., Sedikides, C., & Wildschut, T. (2012). Odyssey's end: Lay conceptions of nostalgia reflect its original Homeric meaning. *Emotion, 12*, 102–119. doi: 10.1037/a0025167

Hepper, E. G., Robertson, S., Wildschut, T., Sedikides, C., & Routledge, C. (2015). *The socioemotional time capsule: Nostalgia shields wellbeing from limited time horizons*. Unpublished manuscript, University of Surrey.

Hepper, E. G., Wildschut, T., Sedikides, C., Ritchie, T. D., Yung, Y.-F., Hansen, N., & Zhou, X. (2014). Pancultural nostalgia: Prototypical conceptions across cultures. *Emotion, 14*, 733–747. doi: 10.1037/a0036790

Hertz, D. G. (1990). Trauma and nostalgia: New aspects of the coping of aging holocaust survivors. *Israeli Journal of Psychiatry and Related Sciences, 27*, 189–198.

Hicks, J., & Routledge, C. (Eds.) (2013). *The experience of meaning in life: Classical perspectives, emerging themes, and controversies*. New York: Springer Press.

Hicks, J. A., Schlegel, R. J., & King, L. A. (2010). Social threats, happiness, and the dynamics of meaning in life judgments. *Personality and Social Psychology Bulletin, 36*, 1305–1317.

Higgins, E. T. (1997). Beyond pleasure and pain. *American Psychologist, 52*, 1280–300. doi: 10.1037/0003-066X.52.12.1280

Hill, P. L., & Turiano, N. A. (2014). Purpose in life as a predictor of mortality across adulthood. *Psychological Science*, Online advance copy. Doi 10.1177/0956797614531799

Hirsch, Alan R. (1992). Nostalgia: A neuropsychiatric understanding. *Advances in Consumer Research, 19*, 390–395.

Hofer, J. (1934). Medical dissertation on nostalgia. (C. K. Anspach, Trans.). *Bulletin of the History of Medicine, 2*, 376–391. (Original work published 1688)

Holak, S. L., & Havlena, W. J. (1992). Nostalgia: An exploratory study of themes and emotions in the nostalgic experience. *Advances in Consumer Research, 19*, 380–386.

Holbrook, M. B. (1993). Nostalgia and consumption preferences: Some emerging patterns of consumer tastes. *Journal of Consumer Research, 20*(9), 245–256.

Holbrook, M. B., & Schindler, R. M. (1989). Some exploratory findings on the development of musical tastes. *Journal of Consumer Research, 16*, 119–124. doi: 10.1086/209200

Holbrook, M. B., & Schindler, R. M. (1994). Age, sex, and attitude toward the past as predictors of consumers' aesthetic tastes for cultural products. *Journal of Marketing Research, 31*, 412–422.

Holbrook, M. B., & Schindler, R. (1996). Market segmentation based on age and attitude toward the past: Concepts, methods, and findings concerning nostalgic influences on customer tastes. *Journal of Business Research, 37*, 27–39. doi: 10.1016/0148-2963(96)00023-9

Holmes, T., & Rahe, R. (1967). The social readjustment rating scale. *Journal of Psychosomatic Research, 11*(2), 213–218. doi: 10.1016/0022-3999(67)90010-4

Horton, R. S., & Sedikides, C. (2009). Narcissistic responding to ego threat: When the status of the evaluator matters. *Journal of Personality, 77*(5), 1493–1526.

House, J. S., Landis, K. R., & Umberson, D. (1988). Social relationships and health. *Science, 24*, 540–545.

Hubley, A. M., & Russell, L. B. (2009). Prediction of subjective age, desired age, and age satisfaction in older adults: Do some health dimensions contribute more than others? *International Journal of Behavioral Development, 33*(1), 12–21. doi: 10.1177/0165025408099486

Jackson, S. W. (1986). *Melancholia and depression: From Hippocratic times to modern times.* New Haven, CT: Yale University Press.

Janoff-Bulman, R. (2010). *Shattered assumptions.* New York: Simon and Schuster.

John, O. P., Donahue, E. M., & Kentle, R. L. (1991). The big five inventory—versions 4a and 54. Berkeley: University of California, Berkeley, Institute of Personality and Social Research.

Jones, W. H., Freemon, J. E., & Goswick, R. A. (1981). The persistence of loneliness: Self and other determinants1. *Journal of Personality, 49*(1), 27–48.

Josephson, B. R. (1996). Mood regulation and memory: Repairing sad moods with happy memories. *Cognition & Emotion, 10*(4), 437–444.

Juhl, J., & Routledge, C. (2012). The effects of individual differences in trait self-esteem and mortality salience on search for meaning. *Journal of Personality and Social Psychology, 99*(6), 897–916.

Juhl, J., Routledge, C., Arndt, J., Sedikides, C., & Wildschut, T. (2010). Fighting the future with the past: Nostalgia buffers existential threat. *Journal of Research in Personality, 44*, 309–314. doi: 10.1016/j.jrp.2010.02.006

Juhl, J., Sand, E. C., & Routledge, C. (2012). The effects of nostalgia and avoidant attachment on relationship satisfaction and romantic motives. *Journal of Social and Personal Relationships, 29*(5), 661–670. doi: 10.1177/0265407512443433

Juslin, P. N., Liljestrom, S., Vastfjall, D., Barradas, G., & Silva, A. (2008). An experience sampling study of emotional reactions to music: Listener, music, and situation. *Emotion, 8*, 668–683.

Kaplan, H. A. (1987). The psychopathology of nostalgia. *Psychoanalytic Review, 74*, 465–486.
Kashdan, T. B., Gallagher, M. W., Silvia, P. J., Winterstein, B. P., Breen, W. E., Terhar, D., & Steger, M. F. (2009). The curiosity and exploration inventory – II: Development, factor structure, and initial psychometrics. *Journal of Research in Personality, 43*, 987–998. doi: 10.1016/j.jrp
Kasser, T., & Ryan, R. M. (1996). Further examining the American dream: Differential correlates of intrinsic and extrinsic goals. *Personality and Social Psychology Bulletin, 22*, 80–87.
Kernis, M. H., & Goldman, B. M. (2006). A multicomponent conceptualization of authenticity: Research and theory. *Advances in Experimental Social Psychology, 38*, 284–357.
Kerns, K. A., Brumariu, L. E., & Abraham, M. M., (2008). Homesickness at summer camp: associations with the mother-child relationship, social self-concept, and peer relationships in middle childhood. *Journal of Developmental Psychology, 54*, 473–498.
King, L. A., Hicks, J. A., Krull, J. L., & Del Gaiso, A. K. (2006). Positive affect and the experience of meaning in life. *Journal of Personality and Social Psychology, 90*, 179–196.
King, L. A., Scollon, C. K., Ramsey, C., & Williams, T. (2000). Stories of life transition: Subjective well-being and ego development in parents of children with Down syndrome. *Journal of Research in Personality, 34*(4), 509–536.
Kirschbaum, C., Pirke, K. M., & Hellhammer, D. H. (1993). The "Trier Social Stress Test"–a tool for investigating psychobiological stress responses in a laboratory setting. *Neuropsychobiology, 28*(1–2), 76–81.
Kline, L. W. (1898). The migratory impulse vs. love of home. *The American Journal of Psychology, 10*, 1–81. doi: 10.2307/1412678
Koole, S. L. (2009). The psychology of emotion regulation: An integrative review. *Cognition and Emotion, 23*, 4–41.
Kotter-Grühn, D., Kleinspehn-Ammerlahn, A., Gerstorf, D., & Smith, J. (2009). Self-perceptions of aging predict mortality and change with approaching death: 16-year longitudinal results from the Berlin Aging Study. *Psychology and Aging, 24*(3), 654–667. doi: 10.1037/a0016510
Kudielka, B. M., Hellhammer, D. H., Kirschbaum, C., Harmon-Jones, E., & Winkielman, P. (2007). Ten years of research with the Trier Social Stress Test—revisited. In E. Harmon-Jones & P. Winkielman (Eds.), *Social neuroscience: Integrating biological and psychological explanations of social behavior* (pp. 56–83). New York: Guildford Press.
Kunzendorf, R. G., & Maguire, D. (1995). *Depression: the reality of "no meaning" versus the delusion of negative meaning.* Unpublished manuscript. Lowell, MA: University of Massachusetts.
Kyung, E. J., Menon, G., & Trope, Y. (2010). Reconstruction of things past: Why do some memories feel so close and others so far away? *Journal of Experimental Social Psychology, 46*(1), 217–220. doi: 10.1016/j.jesp.2009.09.003
Lambert, N. M., Stillman, T. F., Hicks, J. A., Kamble, S., Baumeister, R. F., & Fincham, F. D. (2013). To belong is to matter: Sense of belonging enhances meaning in life. *Personality and Social Psychology Bulletin, 39*(11), 1418–1427. doi: 10.1177/0146167213499186
Landau, M. J., Greenberg, J., & Solomon, S. (2008). The never-ending story: A terror management perspective on the psychological function of self continuity. In F. Sani, *Self continuity: Individual and collective perspectives.* New York: Psychology Press.
Landau, M. J., Johns, M., Greenberg, J., Pyszczynski, T., Solomon, S., & Martens, A. (2004). A function of form: Terror management and structuring of the social world. *Journal of Personality and Social Psychology, 87*, 190–210.
Larsen, R. J. (2000). Toward a science of mood regulation. *Psychological Inquiry, 11*(3), 130.

Lasaleta, J. D., Sedikides, C., & Vohs, K. D. (2014). Nostalgia weakens the desire for money. *Journal of Consumer Research, 41*, 713–729. doi: 10.1086/677227

Lavigne, G. L., Vallerand, R. J., & Crevier-Braud, L. (2011). The fundamental need to belong: On the distinction between growth and deficit-reduction orientations. *Personality and Social Psychology Bulletin, 37*, 1185–1201. doi: 10.1177/0146167211405995

Leary, M. R., Kelly, K. M., Cottrell, C. A., & Schreindorfer, L. S. (2006). *Individual differences in the need to belong: Mapping the nomological network*. Unpublished manuscript. Wake Forest University.

Lenton, A. P., Bruder, M., Slabu, L., & Sedikides, C. (2013). How does "being real" feel? The experience of state authenticity. *Journal of Personality, 81*(3), 276–289.

Lester, D. 1990. The Collett-Lester Fear of Death Scale. *Death Studies, 14*, 451–468.

Levy, M. B., & Davis, K. E. (1988). Lovestyles and attachment styles compared: Their relations to each other and to various relationship characteristics. *Journal of Social and Personal Relationships, 5*(4), 439–471.

Liberman, N., Trope, Y., & Stephan, E. (2007). Psychological distance. In A. W. Kruglanski & E. T. Higgins (Eds.), *Social psychology: Handbook of basic principles*. New York: Guilford Press.

Lifton, R. J. (1979). *The broken connection*. New York: Simon & Schuster.

Luhtanen, R., & Crocker, J. (1992). A collective self-esteem scale: Self-evaluation of one's social identity. *Personality and Social Psychology Bulletin, 18*, 302–318. doi: 10.1177/0146167292183006

Mackie, D. M., Devos, T., & Smith, E. R. (2000). Intergroup emotions: Explaining offensive action tendencies in an intergroup context. *Journal of Personality and Social Psychology, 79*, 602–616. doi: 10.1037/0022-3514.79.4.602

Maner, J. K., DeWall, C. N., Baumeister, R. F., & Schaller, M. (2007). Does social exclusion motivate interpersonal reconnection? Resolving the "porcupine problem". *Journal of Personality and Social Psychology, 92*(1), 42.

Markus, H. (1977). Self-schemata and processing of information about the self. *Journal of Personality and Social Psychology, 35*, 63–78.

Markus, H. R., & Kitayama, S. (1991). Culture and the self: Implications for cognition, emotion, and motivation. *Psychological Review, 98*(2), 224.

Marsh, A., Smith, L., Piek, J., & Saunders, B. (2003). The purpose in life scale: Psychometric properties for social drinkers and drinkers in alcohol treatment. *Educational and Psychological Measurement, 63*, 859–871.

Maslow, A. H. (1954), *Motivation and personality*. New York: Harper.

Maslow, A. H., Frager, R., & Cox, R. (1970). Motivation and personality (Vol. 2). In J. Fadiman & C. McReynolds (Eds.), *Motivation and personality*. New York: Harper & Row.

Matt, S. J. (2007). You can't go home again: Homesickness and nostalgia in U.S. history. *Journal of American History, 94*, 469–497. doi: 10.2307/25094961

McAdams, D. P., Reynolds, J., Lewis, M., Patten, A. H., & Bowman, P. J. (2001). When bad things turn good and good things turn bad: Sequences of redemption and contamination in life narrative and their relation to psychosocial adaptation in midlife adults and in students. *Personality and Social Psychology Bulletin, 27*(4), 474–485.

McCann, W. H. (1941). Nostalgia: A review of the literature. *Psychological Bulletin, 38*, 165–182. doi: 10.1037/h0057354

McFarlin, D. B., & Blascovich, J. (1984). On the Remote Associates Test (RAT) as an alternative to illusory performance feedback: A methodological note. *Basic and Applied Social Psychology, 5*, 223–228.

McGregor, I., & Little, B. R. (1998). Personal projects, happiness, and meaning: On doing well and being yourself. *Journal of Personality and Social Psychology*, 74, 494–512.

Mednick, S. (1962). The associative basis of the creative process. *Psychological Review*, 69(3), 220.

Mikulincer, M. (1997). Adult attachment style and information processing: Individual differences in curiosity and cognitive closure. *Journal of Personality and Social Psychology*, 72, 1217–1230.

Mikulincer, M. (1998). Adult attachment style and affect regulation: Strategic variations in self-appraisals. *Journal of Personality and Social Psychology*, 75, 420–435.

Mikulincer, M., & Shaver, P. R. (2001). Attachment theory and intergroup bias: Evidence that priming the secure base schema attenuates negative reactions to out-groups. *Journal of Personality and Social Psychology*, 81(1), 97.

Mikulincer, M., & Shaver, P. R. (2008). Adult attachment and affect regulation. In J. Cassidy & P. R. Shaver (Eds.), *Handbook of attachment: Theory, research and clinical applications* (pp. 503–531). New York: Guilford Press.

Milligan, M. J. (2003). Displacement and identity discontinuity: The role of nostalgia in establishing new identity categories. *Symbolic Interaction*, 26(3), 381–403. doi: 10.1525/si.2003.26.3.381

Mills, M. A., & Coleman, P. G. (1994). Nostalgic memories in dementia: A case study. *International Journal of Aging and Human Development*, 38, 203–219. doi: 10.2190/NCAJ-0G0L-VTQ4-V1L8

Montepare, J. M., & Lachman, M. E. (1989). "You're only as old as you feel": Self-perceptions of age, fears of aging, and life satisfaction from adolescence to old age. *Psychology and Aging*, 4(1), 73–78. doi: 10.1037/0882-7974.4.1.73

Morf, C. C., Horvath, S., & Torchetti, L (2011). Narcissistic self-enhancement. In M. D. Alicke and C. Sedikides (Eds.), *Handbook of self-enhancement and self-protection* (pp. 399–424). New York: Guildford Press.

Muehling, D. D., & Pascal, V. J. (2012). An involvement explanation for nostalgia Advertising effects. *Journal of Promotion Management*, 18(1), 100–118.

Muehling, D. D., Sprott, D. E., & Sultan, A. J. (2014). Exploring the boundaries of nostalgic advertising effects: A consideration of childhood brand exposure and attachment on consumers' responses to nostalgia-themed advertisements. *Journal of Advertising*, 43(1), 73–84. doi: 10.1080/00913367.2013.815110

Neumann, E. (1971). *The origins and history of consciousness* (R. F. C. Hull, Trans.). Princeton, NJ: Princeton University Press. (Original work published 1949)

Orcutt, J. (1984). Contrasting effects of two kinds of boredom on alcohol use. *Journal of Drug Issues*, 14, 161–173.

O'Sullivan, L. (2012). The time and place of nostalgia: Re-situating a French disease. *Journal of the History of Medicine and Allied Sciences*, 67, 626–649. doi: 10.1093/jhmas/jrr058

Padelford, B. (1974). Relationship between drug involvement and purpose in life. *Journal of Clinical Psychology*, 30, 303–305.

Parfit, D. (1971). Personal identity. *The Philosophical Review*, 80, 3–27.

Park, C. L. (2010). Making sense of the meaning literature: An integrative review of meaning making and its effects on adjustment to stressful life events. *Psychological Bulletin*, 136, 257–301.

Park, C. L., & Folkman, S. (1997). Meaning in the context of stress and coping. *Review of General Psychology*, 1(2), 115.

Pascal, V. J., Sprott, D. E., & Muehling, D. D. (2002). The influence of evoked nostalgia on consumers' responses to advertising: An exploratory study. *Journal of Current Issues and Research in Advertising*, *24*(1), 39–49.

Pavey, L., Greitemeyer, T., & Sparks, P. (2011). Highlighting relatedness promotes prosocial motives and behavior. *Personality and Social Psychology Bulletin*, *37*(7), 905–917.

Pennebaker, J. W., Booth, R. J., & Francis, M. E. (2007). *Linguistic inquiry and word count: LIWC2007: Operator's manual*. Austin, TX: LIWC.net.

Pennebaker, J. W., Francis, M. E., & Booth, R. J. (2001). *Linguistic inquiry and word count: LIWC 2001*. Mahway: Lawrence Erlbaum Associates.

Peters, R. (1985). Reflections on the origin and aim of nostalgia. *Journal of Analytical Psychology*, *30*, 135–148. doi: 10.1111/j.1465-5922.1985.00135.x

Proulx, T., Heine, S. J. and Vohs, K. D. (2010). When is the unfamiliar the uncanny? Meaning affirmative after exposure to absurdist literature, humor, and art. *Personality and Social Psychology Bulletin*, *36*, 817–829.

Pyszczynski, T., Abdollahi, A., Solomon, S., Greenberg, J., Cohen, F., & Weise, D. (2006). Mortality salience, martyrdom, and military might: The great Satan versus the axis of evil. *Personality and Social Psychology Bulletin*, *32*(4), 525–537.

Pyszczynski, T., Greenberg, J., & Solomon, S. (1997). Why do we need what we need? A terror management perspective on the roots of human social motivation. *Psychological Inquiry*, *8*, 1–21.

Pyszczynski, T., Greenberg, J., Solomon, S., Arndt, J., & Schimel, J. (2004). Why do people need self-esteem? A theoretical and empirical review. *Psychological Bulletin*, *130*, 435–468. doi: 10.1037/0033-2909.130.3.435

Raskin, R., & Terry, H. (1988). A principal-components analysis of the Narcissistic Personality Inventory and further evidence of its construct validity. *Journal of Personality and Social Psychology*, *54*(5), 890.

Reid, C. A., Green, J. D., Wildschut, T., & Sedikides, C. (2014). Scent-evoked nostalgia. *Memory*, *23*(2), 157–166.

Rosenberg, M. (1965). *Society and the adolescent self-image*. Princeton, NJ: Princeton University Press.

Rosenblatt, A., Greenberg, J., Solomon, S., Pyszczynski, T., & Lyon, D. (1989). Evidence for terror management theory I: The effects of mortality salience on reactions to those who violate or uphold cultural values. *Journal of Personality and Social Psychology*, *57*, 681–690. doi: 10.1037/0022-3514.57.4.681

Routledge, C., & Arndt, J. (2005). Time and terror: Managing temporal consciousness and the awareness of mortality. In A. Strathman & J. Joireman (Eds.), *Understanding behavior in the context of time: Theory, research, and applications* (pp. 59–84). Mahwah, NJ: Erlbaum.

Routledge, C., & Arndt, J. (2008). Self-sacrifice as self-defence: Mortality salience increases efforts to affirm a symbolic immortal self at the expense of the physical self. *European Journal of Social Psychology*, *38*(3), 531–541.

Routledge, C., Arndt, J., & Goldenberg, J. L. (2004). A time to tan: Proximal and distal effects of mortality salience on sun exposure intentions. *Personality and Social Psychology Bulletin*, *30*(10), 1347–1358.

Routledge, C., Arndt, J., Sedikides, C., & Wildschut, T. (2008). A blast from the past: The terror management function of nostalgia. *Journal of Experimental Social Psychology*, *44*, 132–140. doi: 10.1016/j.jesp.2006.11.001

Routledge, C., Arndt, J., Vess, M., & Sheldon, K. M. (2008). The life and death of creativity: The effects of mortality salience on self versus social-directed creative expression. *Motivation and Emotion*, *32*(4), 331–338.

Routledge, C., Arndt, J., Wildschut, T., Sedikides, C., Hart, C., Juhl, J., Vingerhoets, A. J., & Scholtz, W. (2011). The past makes the present meaningful: Nostalgia as an existential resource. *Journal of Personality and Social Psychology, 101,* 638–652. doi: 10.1037/a0024292

Routledge, C., & Juhl, J. (2010). When death thoughts lead to death fears: Mortality salience increases death anxiety for individuals who lack meaning in life. *Cognition and Emotion, 24*(5), 848–854.

Routledge, C., Juhl, J., Abeyta, A., & Roylance, C. (2014). Using the past to promote a peaceful future: Nostalgia proneness mitigates existential threat induced nationalistic and religious self-sacrifice. *Social Psychology, 45,* 339–346.

Routledge, C., Ostafin, B., Juhl, J., Sedikides, C., Cathey, C., & Liao, J. (2010). Adjusting to death: The effects of mortality salience and self-esteem on psychological well-being, growth motivation, and maladaptive behavior. *Journal of Personality and Social Psychology, 99,* 897–916. doi: 10.1037/a0021431

Routledge, C., Wildschut, T., Sedikides, C., Juhl, J., & Arndt, J. (2012). The power of the past: Nostalgia as a meaning-making resource. *Memory, 20,* 452–460.

Routledge, C., Wildschut, T., Sedikides, C., & Juhl, J. (2013). Nostalgia as a resource for psychological health and well-being. *Social and Personality Psychology Compass, 7*(11), 808–818. doi: 10.1111/spc3.12070

Rubia, K. (2009). The neurobiology of meditation and its clinical effectiveness in psychiatric disorders. *Biological Psychology, 82*(1), 1–11. doi: 10.1016/j.biopsycho.2009.04.003

Rukeyser, M. (1968). *The speed of darkness.* New York: Random House.

Russell, D., Peplau, L. A., & Cutrona, C. E. (1980). The revised UCLA Loneliness Scale: Concurrent and discriminant validity evidence. *Journal of Personality and Social Psychology, 39,* 472–480. doi: 10.1037/0022-3514.39.3.472

Russell, D. W. (1996). UCLA Loneliness Scale (Version 3): Reliability, validity, and factor structure. *Journal of Personality Assessment, 66,* 20–40. doi: 10.1207/s15327752jpa6601_2

Rutledge, R. H. (1977). An old Yankee surgeon entertains a new idea. *Surgery, 121,* 575–580. doi:10.1016/S0039-6060(97)90114-8

Ryan, R. M., & Deci, E. L. (2000). Self-determination theory and the facilitation of intrinsic motivation, social development, and well-being. *American Psychologist, 55*(1), 68.

Ryan, R. M., & Deci, E. L. (2001). On happiness and human potentials: A review of research on hedonic and eudaimonic well-being. *Annual Review of Psychology, 52*(1), 141–166.

Ryan, R. M., & Frederick, C. M. (1997). On energy, personality and health: Subjective vitality as a dynamic reflection of well-being. *Journal of Personality, 65,* 529–565.

Sadeh, N., & Karniol, R. (2012). The sense of self-continuity as a resource in adaptive coping with job loss. *Journal of Vocational Behavior, 80*(1), 93–99. doi: 10.1016/j.jvb.2011.04.009

Scharfe, E., & Bartholomew, K. I. M. (1994). Reliability and stability of adult attachment patterns. *Personal Relationships, 1*(1), 23–43.

Scheier, M. F., Carver, C. S., & Bridges, M. W. (1994). Distinguishing optimism from neuroticism (and trait anxiety, self-mastery, and self-esteem): A reevaluation of the Life Orientation Test. *Journal of Personality and Social Psychology, 67*(6), 1063.

Schindler, R. M., & Holbrook, M. B. (2003). Nostalgia for early experience as a determinant of consumer preferences. *Psychology and Marketing, 20,* 275–302.

Schlegel, R. J., Hicks, J. A., Arndt, J., & King, L. A. (2009). Thine own self: True self-concept accessibility and meaning in life. *Journal of Personality and Social Psychology, 96*(2), 473.

Schlotz, W., Kumsta, R., Layes, I., Entringer, S., Jones, A., & Wüst, S. (2008). Covariance between psychological and endocrine responses to pharmacological challenge and psychosocial stress: A question of timing. *Psychosomatic Medicine, 70*(7), 787–796.

Sedikides, C. (1993). Assessment, enhancement, and verification determinants of the self-evaluation process. *Journal of Personality and Social Psychology, 65,* 317–338.

Sedikides, C., Campbell, W. K., Reeder, G., Elliot, A. J., & Gregg, A. P. (2002). Do others bring out the worst in narcissists? The "others exist for me" illusion. In Y. Kashima, M. Foddy, & M. Platow (Eds.), *Self and identity: Personal, social, and symbolic* (pp. 103–123). Mahwah, NJ: Lawrence Erlbaum Associates.

Sedikides, C., Gaertner, L., & Toguchi, Y. (2003). Pancultural self-enhancement. *Journal of Personality and Social Psychology, 84,* 60–79.

Sedikides, C., & Gregg, A. P. (2003). Portraits of the self. In M.A. Hogg & J. Cooper (Eds.), *Sage handbook of social psychology* (pp. 110–138). London: Sage Publications.

Sedikides, C., & Gregg, A. P. (2008). Self-enhancement: Food for thought. *Perspectives on Psychological Science, 3,* 102–116. doi: 10.1111/j.1745-6916.2008.00068.x

Sedikides, C., & Strube, M. J. (1997). Self-evaluation: To thine own self be good, to thine own self be sure, to thine own self be true, and to thine own self be better. In M. P. Zanna (Ed.), *Advances in experimental social psychology* (Vol. 29, pp. 209–269). New York: Academic Press.

Sedikides, C., Wildschut, T., & Baden, D. (2004). Nostalgia: Conceptual issues and existential functions. In J. Greenberg, S. Koole, & T. Pyszczynski (Eds.), *Handbook of experimental existential psychology* (pp. 200–214). New York: Guilford Press.

Sedikides, C., Wildschut, T., Cheung, W., Routledge, C., Hepper, E., Arndt, J., Vail, K., Zhou, X., Brackstone, K., & Vingerhoets, A. (2015). *Nostalgia fosters self-continuity by augmenting social connectedness: Implications for eudaimonic well-being.* Manuscript in preparation.

Sedikides, C., Wildschut, T., Routledge, C., & Arndt, J. (2015a). Nostalgia counteracts self-discontinuity and restores self-continuity. *European Journal of Social Psychology, 45*(1), 42–61.

Sedikides, C., Wildschut, T., Routledge, C., Arndt, J., Hepper, E. G., & Zhou, X. (2015b). To nostalgize: Mixing memory with affect and desire. *Advances in Experimental Social Psychology,* 51, 189–273. doi: 10.1016/bs.aesp.2014.10.001

Seehusen, J., Cordaro, F., Wildschut, T., Sedikides. C., Routledge, C., Blackhart, G. C., Epstude, K., & Vingerhoets, A. J. J. M. (2013). Individual differences in nostalgia proneness: The integrating role of the need to belong. *Personality and Individual Differences, 55,* 904–908

Shank, R. C., & Abelson, R. P. (1995). Knowledge and memory: The real story. In R. S. Wyer, Jr. (Ed.), *Knowledge and memory: The real story* (pp.1–85). Hillsdale, NJ: Lawrence Erlbaum Associates, Inc.

Shaver, K. G., & Drown, D. (1986). On causality, responsibility, and self-blame: A theoretical note. *Journal of Personality and Social Psychology, 50*(4), 697.

Sheldon, K. M., Abad, N., & Hinsch, C. (2011). A two-process view of Facebook use and relatedness need-satisfaction: Disconnection drives use, and connection rewards it. *Psychology of Popular Media Culture, 1*(S), 2–15. doi: 10.1037/2160-4134.1.S.2

Simpson, J. A. (2007). Psychological foundations of trust. *Current directions in psychological science, 16*(5), 264–268.

Solomon, S., Greenberg, J., Schimel, J., Arndt, J, & Pyszczynski, T. (2004). Human awareness of mortality and the evolution of culture. In M. Schaller & C. Crandall (Eds.), *The psychological foundations of culture* (pp. 15–40). New York: Erlbaum.

Stathopoulou, G., Powers, M. B., Berry, A. C., Smits, J. A., & Otto, M. W. (2006). Exercise interventions for mental health: a quantitative and qualitative review. *Clinical Psychology: Science and Practice, 13*(2), 179–193.

Steger, M. F., Fitch-Martin, A., Donnelly, J., & Rickard, K. M. (2014). Meaning in life and health: Proactive health orientation links meaning in life to health variables among American undergraduates. *Journal of Happiness Studies, 15*(2), 1–15.

Steger, M. F., Frazier, P., Oishi, S., & Kaler, M. (2006). The Meaning in Life Questionnaire: Assessing the presence of and search for meaning in life. *Journal of Counseling Psychology, 53*, 80–93. doi:10.1037/0022-0167.53.1.80

Steger, M. F., Kashdan, T. B., Sullivan, B. A., & Lorentz, D. (2008). Understanding the search for meaning in life: Personality, cognitive style, and the dynamic between seeking and experiencing meaning. *Journal of Personality, 76*, 199–228.

Stephan, E., Sedikides, C., & Wildschut, T. (2012). Mental travel into the past: Differentiating recollections of nostalgic, ordinary, and positive events. *European Journal of Social Psychology, 42*, 290–298. doi: 10.1002/ejsp.1865

Stephan, W. G., & Stephan, C. W. (1985). Intergroup anxiety. *Journal of Social Issues, 41*(3), 157–175.

Stephan, E., Wildschut, T., Sedikides, C., Zhou, X., He, W., Routledge, C., Cheung, W. Y., & Vingerhoets, A. J. J. M. (2014). The mnemonic mover: Nostalgia regulates avoidance and approach motivation. *Emotion, 14*, 545–561. doi: 10.1037/a0035673

Steptoe, A., Shankar, A., Demakakos, P., & Wardle, J. (2013). Social isolation, loneliness, and all-cause mortality in older men and women. *Proceedings of the National Academy of Sciences, 110*(15), 5797–5801.

Stillman, T. F., Baumeister, R. F., Lambert, N. M., Crescioni, A. W., DeWall, C. N., & Fincham, F. D. (2009). Alone and without purpose: Life loses meaning following social exclusion. *Journal of Experimental Social Psychology, 45*, 686–694.

Tam, T., Hewstone, M., Kenworthy, J., & Cairns, E. (2009). Intergroup trust in Northern Ireland. *Personality and Social Psychology Bulletin, 35*(1), 45–59.

Tamir, M., & Diener, E. (2008). Approach-avoidance goals and well-being: One size does not fit all. In A. J. Elliot (Ed.), *Handbook of approach and avoidance motivation* (pp. 415–430). Mahwah, NJ: Erlbaum.

Tarrant, M., North, A. C., & Hargreaves, D. J. (2004). Adolescents' intergroup attributions: A comparison of two social identities. *Journal of Youth and Adolescence, 33*(3), 177–185. doi: 10.1023/b:joyo.0000025317.96224.75

Thayer, R. E. (1997). *The origin of everyday moods: Managing energy, tension, and stress.* Oxford: University Press.

Thayer, R. E., Newman, J. R., & McClain, T. M. (1994). Self-regulation of mood: Strategies for changing a bad mood, raising energy, and reducing tension. *Journal of Personality and Social Psychology, 67*(5), 910.

Thoits, P. (1995). Stress, coping, and social support processes: Where are we? What next? *Journal of Health and Social Behavior, 35*, 53–79.

Thompson, M. M., Naccarato, M. E., Parker, K. C., & Moskowitz, G. B. (2001). The personal need for structure and personal fear of invalidity measures: Historical perspectives, current applications, and future directions. In G. B. Moskowitz (Ed.), *Cognitive social psychology: The Princeton symposium on the legacy and future of social cognition* (pp. 19–39). Hillsdale, NJ: Erlbaum.

Thurber, C. A. & Walton, E. A. (2007). Preventing and treating homesickness. *Pediatrics, 119*, 843–858. doi: 10.1542/peds.2006-2781

Trope, Y., & Liberman, N. (2010). Construal-level theory of psychological distance. *Psychological Review, 117*(2), 440–463. doi: 10.1037/a0018963

Turner, R. N., Wildschut, T., & Sedikides, C. (2012). Dropping the weight stigma: Nostalgia improves attitudes toward persons who are overweight. *Journal of Experimental Social Psychology, 48*, 130–137. doi: 10.1016/j.jesp.2011.09.007

Turner, R. N., Wildschut, T., Sedikides, C., & Gheorghiu, M. (2013). Combating the mental health stigma with nostalgia. *European Journal of Social Psychology, 43*(5), 413–422. doi: 10.1002/ejsp.1952

Twenge, J. M., Baumeister, R. F., DeWall, C. N., Ciarocco, N. J., & Bartels, J. M. (2007). Social exclusion decreases prosocial behavior. *Journal of Personality and Social Psychology, 92*(1), 56.

Twenge, J. M., Baumeister, R. F., Tice, D. M., & Stucke, T. S. (2001). If you can't join them, beat them: Effects of social exclusion on aggressive behavior. *Journal of Personality and Social Psychology, 81*, 1058–1069. doi: getuid.cfm?uid=2001-05428-007

Twenge, J. M., Catanese, K. R., & Baumeister, R. F. (2002). Social exclusion causes self-defeating behavior. *Journal of Personality and Social Psychology, 83*(3), 606.

Twenge, J. M., Catanese, K. R., Baumeister, R. F. (2003). Social exclusion and the deconstructed state: Time perception, meaninglessness, lethargy, lack of emotion, and self-awareness. *Journal of Personality and Social Psychology, 85*(3), 409–423. doi: 10.1037/0022-3514.85.3.409

Updegraff, J. A., Silver, R., & Holman, E. (2008). Searching for and finding meaning in collective trauma: Results from a national longitudinal study of the 9/11 terrorist attacks. *Journal of Personality and Social Psychology, 95*, 709–722.

Van Tilburg, W. A. P., & Igou, E. R. (2011). On boredom and social identity: A pragmatic meaning-regulation approach. *Personality and Social Psychology Bulletin, 37*(12), 1679–1691. doi: 10.1177/0146167211418530

Van Tilburg, W. A. P., & Igou, E. R. (2012). On the meaningfulness of behavior: An expectancy x value approach. *Motivation and Emotion, 37*, 373–388. doi: 10.1007/s11031-012-9316-3

Van Tilburg, W. A. P., Igou, E. R., & Sedikides, C. (2013). In search of meaningfulness: Nostalgia as an antidote to boredom. *Emotion, 13*, 450–461. doi: 10.1037/a0030442

Velikonja, M. (2009). Lost in transition: Nostalgia for socialism in post-socialist countries. *East European Politics and Societies, 23*, 535–551. doi: 10.1177/0888325409345140

Verplanken, B. (2012). When bittersweet turns sour: Adverse effects of nostalgia on habitual worriers. *European Journal of Social Psychology, 42*, 285–289. doi: 10.1002/ejsp.1852

Verplanken, B., Friborg, O., Wang, C. E., Trafimow, D., & Woolf, K. (2007). Mental habits: Metacognitive reflection on negative self-thinking. *Journal of Personality and Social Psychology, 92*, 526–541.

Vess, M., Arndt, J., Routledge, C., Sedikides, C., & Wildschut, T. (2012). Nostalgia as a resource for the self. *Self and Identity, 3*, 273–284. doi: 10.1080/15298868.2010.521452

Vess, M., Routledge, C., Landau, M. J., & Arndt, J. (2009). The dynamics of death and meaning: The effects of death-relevant cognitions and personal need for structure on perceptions of meaning in life. *Journal of Personality and Social Psychology, 97*, 728–744.

Vignoles, V. L. (2011). Identity motives. In S. J. Schwartz, K. Luyckx, & V. L. Vignoles, (Eds.), *Handbook of identity theory and research* (pp. 403–432). New York: Springer.

Vignoles, V. L., Regalia, C., Manzi, C., Golledge, J., & Scabini, E. (2006). Beyond self-esteem: Influence of multiple motives on identity construction. *Journal of Personality and Social Psychology, 90*, 308–333.

Volkan, V. D. (1999). Nostalgia as a linking phenomenon. *Journal of Applied Psychoanalytic Studies, 1*, 169–179. doi: 10.1023/A:1023037222314

Waisberg, J., & Porter, J. (1994). Purpose in life and outcome of treatment for alcohol dependence. *British Journal of Clinical Psychology, 33*, 49–63.

Wallach, M. A., & Kogan, N. (1965). *Modes of thinking in young children: A study of the creativity–intelligence distinction*. New York: Holt, Rinehart, & Winston.

Warner, L. M., Schwarzer, R., Schüz, B., Wurm, S., & Tesch-Römer, C. (2012). Health-specific optimism mediates between objective and perceived physical functioning in older adults. *Journal of Behavioral Medicine, 35*(4), 400–406. doi: 10.1007/s10865-011-9368-y

Watson, D., Clark, L. A., & Tellegen, A. (1988). Development and validation of brief measures of positive and negative affect: The PANAS scales. *Journal of Personality and Social Psychology, 55*, 1063–1070.

Weiss, R. S. (1973). *Loneliness: The experience of emotional and social isolation*. Cambridge, MA: MIT Press.

Werman, D. S. (1977). Normal and pathological nostalgia. *Journal of the American Psychoanalytic Association, 25*, 387–398.

Wildschut, T., Bruder, M., Robertson, S., Van Tilburg, W. P., & Sedikides, C. (2014). Collective nostalgia: A group-level emotion that confers unique benefits on the group. *Journal of Personality and Social Psychology, 107*(5), 844–863. doi: 10.1037/a0037760

Wildschut, T., Sedikides, C., Arndt, J., & Routledge, C. (2006). Nostalgia: Content, triggers, functions. *Journal of Personality and Social Psychology, 91*, 975–993.

Wildschut, T., Sedikides, C., Routledge, C., Arndt, J., & Cordaro, F. (2010). Nostalgia as a repository of social connectedness: The role of attachment-related avoidance. *Journal of Personality and Social Psychology, 98*, 573–586. doi: 10.1037/a0017597

Williams, T., Schimel, J., Hayes, J., & Martens, A. (2009). The moderating role of extrinsic contingency focus on reactions to threat. *European Journal of Social Psychology, 40*, 300–320.

Wong, P. T. P. (1998). Implicit theories of meaningful life and the development of the personal meaning profile. In P. T. P. Wong & P. S. Fry (Eds.), *The human quest for meaning. A handbook of psychological research and clinical applications* (pp. 111–140). Mahwah, NJ: Erlbaum.

Wong, P. T. P., & Fry, P. S. (1998). *The human quest for meaning: A handbook of psychological research and clinical applications*. Mahwah, NJ: Lawrence Erlbaum Associates Publishers.

Wright, S. C., Aron, A., McLaughlin-Volpe, T., & Ropp, S. A. (1997). The extended contact effect: Knowledge of cross-group friendships and prejudice. *Journal of Personality and Social Psychology, 73*(1), 73.

Yalom, I. D. (1980). *Existential psychotherapy*. New York: Basic Books.

Ye, S., Ngan, R. Y. L., & Hui, A. N. (2013). The state, not the trait, of nostalgia increases creativity. *Creativity Research Journal, 25*(3), 317–323.

Zentner, M., Grandjean, D., & Scherer, K. R. (2008). Emotions evoked by the sound of music: Characterization, classification, and measurement. *Emotion, 8*, 494–521.

Zhou, X, Sedikides, C., Wildschut, C., & Gao, D. G. (2008). Counteracting loneliness: On the restorative function of nostalgia. *Psychological Science, 19*, 1023–1029.

Zhou, X., Wildschut, T., Sedikides, C., Chen, X., & Vingerhoets, A. J. J. M. (2012). Heartwarming memories: Nostalgia maintains physiological comfort. *Emotion, 12*, 678–684. doi: 10.1037/a0028236

Zhou, X., Wildschut, T., Sedikides, C., Shi, K., & Feng, C. (2012). Nostalgia: The gift that keeps on giving. *Journal of Consumer Research, 39*(1), 39–50.

Zigmond, A. S., & Snaith, R. P. (1983). The hospital anxiety and depression scale. *Acta Psychiatrica Scandinavica, 67*(6), 361–370.

Zimbardo, P. G., & Boyd, J. N. (1999). Putting time in perspective: a valid, reliable individual difference metric. *Journal of Personality and Social Psychology, 77,* 1271–1288.

Zimet, G. D., Dahlem, N. W., Zimet, S. G., & Farley, G. K. (1988). The multidimensional scale of perceived social support. *Journal of Personality Assessment, 52*(1), 30–41.

INDEX

Abad, N. 125
Abeyta, A. 20–1, 58–62, 92, 95–6, 107–8, 119–20
abstraction: significance for experiences of nostalgia 22
action, social: influence of nostalgia on 56–68
advertisements and advertising: impact of nostalgia inducing 6–7; significance as trigger of nostalgia 39
affect: impact of nostalgia on negative 44–7; impact of nostalgia on positive 47–9
Alternative Uses task 82
anxiety, death: nostalgia as meaning-provider for salience of 91–3; nostalgia as protector of thoughts and awareness of 90–1; perceptions of and implications for nostalgia 31–2; *see also* health
Arndt, J. 13, 16–20, 20–1, 23, 35, 89, 92
aspirations, human: influence of nostalgia on 57–63
attachment, interpersonal: influence of nostalgia on 53–4
attitudes, human: influence of nostalgia on intergroup 65–8; *see also* attachment, interpersonal; behaviours, human; motivation, social
authenticity, self-: potential of nostalgia to enhance maintenance of 79–81
Authenticity Inventory 80

Baldwin, M. 79–80, 81, 82
Barradas, G. 40
Barrett, F. 40
Batcho Nostalgia Inventory (BNI) 27, 36, 59, 60, 101–2
Batcho, K. 36
Baumeister, R. 30
behaviours, human: influence of nostalgia on 56–68; *see also* attachment, interpersonal; attitudes, human; goals, social; *see also influences and aspects e.g.* belongingness, sense of; relationships, interpersonal
Bellow, S. 89
belongingness, sense of: impact of nostalgia on perceived and real 52–6; *see also challenges to e.g.* loneliness; pessimism, relational
Belongingness Orientation Scale 30, 104
Best, J. 34
bias, attributional: influence of nostalgia on likelihood of 74–5
Biernat, M. 79–80, 81
boredom: impact as generator of nostalgia 32–4; significance of nostalgia as restoring meaning after 95
Brown, E. 124–6
Bruder, M. 79

campaigns, marketing: impact of nostalgia inducing 6–7
case studies: nostalgic experiences 18–20

Index

ceremonies, religious: centrality of as theme of nostalgia experiences 16
Cheung, W. 47–8, 55, 71, 73–4
cognition, self-relevant: influence of nostalgia related on self-esteem 71–2
Coleman, P. 6
Collett-Lester Fear of Death Scale (Revised) 91
connectedness, social: impact of nostalgia on perceived and real 52–6; influence of nostalgia on feelings of 77–8; role in relationship between nostalgia and life meaning 88; *see also challenges to e.g.* loneliness; pessimism, relational
Constable, J. 94–5
consumption, media: influence of nostalgia on 7
continuity, self-: characteristics of and ways nostalgia enhances 76–8; *see also* discontinuity, self-
Cox, C. 124–6
creativity: potential of nostalgia to enhance human 82–3
Crocker, J. 122–3
culture: impact on conceptualisation of nostalgia 14–15
Curiosity and Exploration Inventory 81

Darwin, C. 5
Davis, F. 6, 34, 35, 36, 37, 72–3, 76, 89
death: nostalgia as meaning-provider for salience of 91–3; nostalgia as protector of thoughts and awareness of 90–1; perceptions of and implications for nostalgia 31–2; *see also* health
Death of Self subscale 91
defence, self-: influence of nostalgia on need for mechanisms of 74–5
difference, individual: and content of nostalgia 105–9; and functions of nostalgia 109–14; and proneness to nostalgia 100–3; variables influencing in nostalgia 103–5
discontinuity, self-: influence of nostalgia on negating 76–8; significance as trigger for nostalgia 34–7; *see also* continuity, self-
disease, neurological: origins of nostalgia as symptom of 3–5
distance, psychological: significance for experiences of nostalgia 21
distress, human: debates over nostalgia as cause of 25–6; *see also types and triggers e.g.* boredom; discontinuity, self-;
loneliness; meaninglessness, human; moods, negative
Donnolly, J. 96

Elliot, A. 59
emotions: impact of nostalgia on negative 44–7; impact of nostalgia on positive 47–9; significance in experiences of nostalgia 20–1; understanding of nostalgia as a bittersweet 6
esteem, self-: characteristics of and ways nostalgia enhances 70–6
events, life: centrality of as theme of nostalgia experiences 17; influence of nostalgia on positive or negative interpretations of 77; *see also states of mind affecting e.g.* boredom; discontinuity, self-; meaninglessness, human
Experiences in Close Relationships (Revised) (ECR-R) Scale 53, 108, 110–11, 112–13
exploration: potential of nostalgia to enhance human 81–2
Exploration Inventory 81–2
expression, creative: potential of nostalgia to enhance human 82–3
Extrinsic Contingency Focus Scale 80

feelings, human: impact of nostalgia on negative 44–7; impact of nostalgia on positive 47–9; *see also particular e.g.* distress, human
Feng, C. 45
films: significance as trigger of nostalgia 39–40
Fitch-Martin, A. 96
Fraley, R. 112–13

Gable, S. 58
Gao, D. 23–4, 29
Gheorghui, 66–8
giving, philanthropic: influence of nostalgia on likelihood of 63–5
goals, social: influence of nostalgia on achievement of 56–68
Goodson, I. 35
Green, J. 39
growth, self-: characteristics of and ways nostalgia enhances 79–83

Hargreaves, A. 35
Hart, C. 106–7, 109

Havlena, W. 15–16, 17
Hays, R. 121
health: association between decreased life meaning and 95–6; emerging research on nostalgia and 118–21; *see also* mortality; stress; vitality, human
Hepper, E. 9–13, 14–15, 23, 48, 55, 70, 87, 101, 105
Hertz, D. 6
Hinsch, C. 125
Hirsch, A. 39
Hofer, J. 3, 25–6
Holak, S. 15–16, 17
Holbrook, M. 39–40, 102
Holbrook Nostalgia Proneness Scale 102
holidays and trips: centrality of as theme of nostalgia experiences 16
Holmes, T. 35
homesickness: relationship with understanding of nostalgia 5–6
Hospital Anxiety and Depression Survey 114
Hui, A. 82
humans: centrality of as theme of nostalgia experiences 17; *see also* attachment, interpersonal; behaviours, human; feelings, human; motivation, social; *see also factors impacting e.g.* aspirations, human; attitudes, human; health; meaninglessness, human; stress; vitality, human

Igou, E. 32, 33
illness: influence of nostalgia on attitudes towards mental 66–8; origins of nostalgia as symptom of 3–5; *see also* health; mortality
individuals, difference in: and content of nostalgia 105–9; and functions of nostalgia 109–14; proneness to nostalgia as an 101–3; variables influencing in nostalgia 103–5
inputs, sensory: significance as trigger of nostalgia 38–41
interactions, social: significance as trigger of nostalgia 38
internet: emerging research on nostalgia and 124–6
Interpersonal Competence Questionnaire 54, 112

Juhl, J. 90–1, 92, 112
Justin, P. 40

Kersten, M. 124–6
Kline, L. 3–4
Kramer, M. 95–6

Landau, M. 79–80, 81, 82
'Landscape with a Double Rainbow' (Constable) 94–5
Lasaletta, J. 46
Lenton, A. 79
Life Orientation Test (Revised) (LOT-R) 62
Lilkestrom, S. 40
Linguistic Inquiry and Word Count (LWIC) 106
loneliness: as potential trigger of nostalgia 28–31; significance as human challenge or support 52–3, 55–6, 57–8, 62–3
Loneliness Scale (UCLA) 28, 29, 56
Luhtanan, R. 122–3

McCann, W. 5
Magritte, R. 94
make-up, construal: significance for experiences of nostalgia 22
Mapes, R. 58
marketing: interpretation of nostalgia in age of 6–7; significance as trigger of nostalgia 39
Mazel, R. 121
Me/Not Me task 72
media: influence of nostalgia on consumption of 7
meaning, life: nostalgia as resource helping persons devoid of 97–9; significance of nostalgia for countering threats to 89–97; significance of nostalgia for promoting 85–9
meaninglessness, human: impact of belief of as generator of nostalgia 31–2
memories, social: role in relationship between nostalgia and life meaning 87–8; significance in experiences of nostalgia 21
Milligan, M. 34–5
Mills, M. 6
moods, negative: as cause of nostalgia 26–8; impact of nostalgia on feelings of 44–7
Moore, S. 35
mortality *see* death
motivation, social: emerging research on nostalgia and 118–21; influence of nostalgia on 57–63

movies: significance as trigger of nostalgia 39–40
Mr Sammler's Planet (Bellow) 89
Muehling, D. 7
Multidimensional Scale of Perceived Social Support 54, 56
music: impact on feelings of connectedness 55; influence of nostalgia related on self-esteem 71, 73–4; significance as trigger of nostalgia 40–1

Narcissistic Personality Inventory (NPI) 106, 109
Need to Belong Scale (NTBS) 104
negativity: as cause of nostalgia 26–8; impact of nostalgia on feelings of 44–7
Nelson, E. 34
Ngan, R. 82
nostalgia: and positive affect 47–9; as resource for those lacking meaning in life 97–9; boredom and meaninglessness as generator of 31–4; conceptualisations of humans of 9–15; debates over symptoms of vs. cause 25–6; definition and origin as medical disease 3–5; distinctiveness compared with other past-oriented reflection 20–22; emerging research on health and 118–21; emerging research on internet and 124–6; emerging research on personal and collective 121–4; emerging research on psychology of 116–18; experiences of humans of 15–20; frequency with which experienced 22–3; impact of negative mood on 26–8; impact on negative affect 44–7; individual difference and content of 105–9; individual differences and functions of 109–14; influence on human goals and action 56–68; influence on intergroup attitudes 65–8; influence on motivation and aspiration 57–63; influence on pro-social behaviours 63–5; influence on social connectedness 52–6; interpretation of in age of marketing 6–7; loneliness as trigger 28–31; proneness to as an individual difference 100–3; rise of interest of psychology in 5–6; self-discontinuity as trigger for 34–7; significance in countering threats to life meaning 89–97; significance in promoting life meaning 85–9; social and sensory triggers 37–41; variables influencing differences in 103–5; ways in which self-continuity enhanced by 76–8; ways in which self-esteem enhanced by 70–6; ways in which self-growth enhanced by 79–83
Nostalgia (journal) 17
Nostalgia Inventory (BNI) 27, 36, 59, 60, 101–2

obesity: influence of nostalgia on attitudes towards 65–6
optimism: influence of nostalgia on human 72–3
orientations, deficit reduction and growth 30

Pascal, V. 7
people: centrality of as theme of nostalgia experiences 17
pessimism, relational: significance as trigger for or restorer of nostalgia 62
philanthropy: influence of nostalgia on likelihood of 63–5
Positive and Negative Affect Schedule (PANAS) 45, 47, 49, 114, 125, 126
positivity: impact of nostalgia on feelings of 47–9
preferences, aesthetic: influence of nostalgia on 7
Presence of Meaning in Life Subscale 86, 87
protection and regulation: nostalgia as existential threat 89–90
Proulx, T. 94, 95
psychology: emerging research on nostalgia and 116–18: rise of interest in nostalgia 5–6
Purpose in Life Scale 85–6, 97
pursuits, social: influence of nostalgia on achievement of 56–68
Pyszczynski, T. 92

Rahe, R. 35
RAND Health Survey 96
regard, self: characteristics of and ways nostalgia enhances 70–6
regulation and protection: nostalgia as existential threat 89–90
Reid, C. 39, 54–5, 71, 86
Relationship Scale Questionnaire (RSQ) 112
relationships, interpersonal: centrality of as theme of nostalgia experiences 15–16;

importance for adaptive functioning 52; influence of nostalgia on 53–4; *see also* behaviours, human; connectedness, social; *see also challenges to e.g.* loneliness; pessimism, relational
religion: centrality of as theme of nostalgia experiences 16
Remote Associates Test (RAT0 74–5
research, emerging: on health and nostalgia 118–21; on nostalgia in age of internet 124–6; on personal and collective nostalgia 121–4; psychology of nostalgia 116–18
reunions, class: centrality of as theme of nostalgia experiences 16
Rickard, K. 96
Ritchie, T. 9–13, 14–15
Routledge, C. 13–14, 16–20, 20–1, 23, 32, 35, 55, 86–7, 89–90, 92–4, 95–6, 98, 102, 112, 117–18, 119–20, 124–6
Roylance, C. 92
Rukeyser, M. 12

Sand, E. 112
scales, measurement: belongingness 30, 104; death of self 91; experience in close relationships 53, 108, 110–11, 112–13; extrinsic contingency 80; fear of death 91; life purpose 85–6, 97; loneliness 28, 29, 56; meaning in life 86, 87; nostalgia and nostalgia proneness 27, 29, 30, 33, 36, 59, 101–3, 104; perceived social support 54, 56; relationships 112; self-esteem 70; social readjustment 35; vitality 97
Scheuchzer, J. 3
Schindler, R. 39–40
Sedikides, C. 9–13, 13–14, 16–20, 20–1, 23–4, 29, 32, 33, 35, 39, 45–6, 53, 65–8, 76–8, 79
Seehusen, J. 29–30, 103, 104
self (social self): centrality of as theme of nostalgia experiences 17–18; influence of nostalgia on 57–63
Self-Esteem Scale (Rosenberg) 70
senses, human: significance as trigger of nostalgia 38–41
Shi, K. 45
Shelbourne, C. 121
Shelden, K. 125
Silva, A. 40
Slabu, L. 79
smells: influence of nostalgia related on self-esteem 71; significance as trigger of nostalgia 39

Social Readjustment Rating Scale (SRRS) 35
Sonneveld, W. 71
'Son of Man, The' (Magritte) 94
Southampton Nostalgia Scale (SNS) 29, 30, 33, 102–3, 104
Sprott, C. 7
State Vitality Scale 97
Steger, M. 33, 96
Stephan, E. 22, 45–6, 48, 49, 63, 65, 79, 116–17, 119
stigmatisation: influence of nostalgia on intergroup 65–8
strategies, compensatory: supporting need for belongingness and connectedness 53
stress: association between decreased life meaning and 98–9
structure, life: nostalgia as reinforcing need for 94–5
Stucke, T. 30

terror management theory (TMT): role in regulation and protection of life meaning 89–90
thoughts and aware, death: nostalgia as meaning-provider for salience of 91–3; nostalgia as protector of 90–1; perceptions of and implications for nostalgia 31–2; *see also* health
Tice, D. 30
time: significance for experiences of nostalgia 21–2
Time Perspective Inventory (TPI) 101
Trier Social Stress Test (TSST) 98
'true self': potential of nostalgia to enhance maintenance of 79–81
Turner, R. 65–8
Twenge, J. 30

Van Enkevort, E. 124–6
Van Tilburg, W. 32, 33, 95
Vastfjall, D. 40
Verplanken, B. 114
Vess, M. 71–2, 74, 75
vitality, human: association between decreased life meaning and 97–8; *see also* health; stress
Vohs, K. 46

Warner, 121
weddings: centrality of as theme of nostalgia experiences 16

well-being, psychological: influence of nostalgia on possibility of beneficial 78

Wildschut, T. 9–13, 13–15, 16–20, 20–1, 23–4, 26–7, 28, 35, 38–9, 44–6, 47, 53–4, 65–8, 70–2, 80–1, 101, 110, 111–12, 117–18, 120, 121–3, 124

worth, self-: characteristics of and ways nostalgia enhances 70–6

Ye, S. 82

Zhou, X. 23–4, 29, 41, 45, 49, 54, 55–6, 63–5

eBooks
from Taylor & Francis
Helping you to choose the right eBooks for your Library

Add to your library's digital collection today with Taylor & Francis eBooks. We have over 50,000 eBooks in the Humanities, Social Sciences, Behavioural Sciences, Built Environment and Law, from leading imprints, including Routledge, Focal Press and Psychology Press.

Choose from a range of subject packages or create your own!

Benefits for you
- Free MARC records
- COUNTER-compliant usage statistics
- Flexible purchase and pricing options
- All titles DRM-free.

Benefits for your user
- Off-site, anytime access via Athens or referring URL
- Print or copy pages or chapters
- Full content search
- Bookmark, highlight and annotate text
- Access to thousands of pages of quality research at the click of a button.

Free Trials Available
We offer free trials to qualifying academic, corporate and government customers.

eCollections
Choose from over 30 subject eCollections, including:

Archaeology	Language Learning
Architecture	Law
Asian Studies	Literature
Business & Management	Media & Communication
Classical Studies	Middle East Studies
Construction	Music
Creative & Media Arts	Philosophy
Criminology & Criminal Justice	Planning
Economics	Politics
Education	Psychology & Mental Health
Energy	Religion
Engineering	Security
English Language & Linguistics	Social Work
Environment & Sustainability	Sociology
Geography	Sport
Health Studies	Theatre & Performance
History	Tourism, Hospitality & Events

For more information, pricing enquiries or to order a free trial, please contact your local sales team: www.tandfebooks.com/page/sales

www.tandfebooks.com

Made in the USA
Monee, IL
21 December 2023